Fellowshi

Making Sense of Twelve-Step Recovery

Michael Angelo

Table of Contents

This book is dedicated to all those seeking recovery from addiction and to the many millions already in twelve-step fellowship around the world.

With thanks to the following teachers who have each shared perennial wisdom and influenced my writing:

John David
Nassim Haramein
John Lennox
Sri Mooji
Richard Rohr
Rupert Spira
Bill Wilson

Other publications by Michael Angelo:

Far More Than We Think – Making Sense of Spirituality - 2013

1. Experience, Strength & Hope

"The world breaks everyone and afterward many are stronger in the broken places. But those that will not break it kills."
~ Ernest Hemingway, *A Farewell to Arms*

Since writing '*Far More Than We Think*' in 2013 my spiritual journey has continued apace. There have been several times when I have wanted to sit down and write this new book, but on each occasion there has been an intuitive hesitation that more would be revealed. This has indeed proved to be the case, and I have no doubt that yet more will be revealed. There is however a feeling now that I have reached a stage where I can usefully share my experience and understanding.

This book penetrates to the heart of spirituality, and the nature of addiction, and it would be reasonable to question whether or not I am suitably qualified to undertake such a task. In this regard I would like to briefly set out my particular experience over the last eight years in order to hopefully add some credibility to the chapters that follow.

I have been attending twelve-step recovery meetings since July 2010 and have been in recovery and abstinent from alcohol since May 2011. During this time I have attended over 1,000 meetings and listened to well over 10,000 individual shares. I have been guided through the twelve-step recovery program by a sponsor and have subsequently had the privilege of sponsoring 18 others partly or fully through the steps, all of which have provided valuable learning opportunities. In terms of participation in fellowship, I have held 19 different service positions within Alcoholics Anonymous and have been invited to share my experience over 100 times at a wide variety of meetings. I also have some limited experience of Co-Dependents Anonymous and Al-Anon.

Although I have an ongoing commitment to twelve-step recovery, the bulk of my experience and understanding has come from in-depth study and participation in a broad range of spiritual traditions and disciplines. This covers a number of the major religions as well as a good variety of other sources, both traditional and new age. I have read countless books, watched many hundreds of hours of video, taken on-line courses and attended numerous retreats, both in the UK and overseas. My travels have taken me to Israel, Palestine, India, Spain, Portugal and Italy. I have met and spoken with several spiritual 'masters' and talked with numerous people from a wide variety of spiritual and cultural backgrounds.

Such research can obviously never be complete. What has emerged so far is a clear, underlying model of reality that makes sense not only of spiritual teaching, which dates back thousands of years, but also the very latest scientific understanding. This model also explains why twelve-step recovery can work so effectively.

There is inevitably an element of arrogance in even trying to write this book, yet I believe that my motives are grounded in humility. I am happy to embrace my brokenness, and my ongoing recovery, and I also accept that I do not have all of the answers. Many others have travelled this path before me and there are many more to come. My experience is not unusual but it is nevertheless unique. The recovery landscape can be very confusing and my hope is that my particular way of trying to explain spiritual matters will be beneficial. Each recovery is individual, yet we can learn a great deal from each other by sharing our experience, strength and hope.

2. Preamble

Twelve-step recovery works simply because it is a spiritual solution to a spiritual problem. A spiritual solution requires action. As my understanding has grown, I increasingly see the necessity for persistent, consistent spiritual practice. There can be little recovery without it.

There are millions of people around the world engaged in twelve-step recovery, many of whom will undoubtedly have their own views and beliefs as to how and why the program has worked for them. There are many others too who are deeply skeptical for any number of reasons and believe that numerous alternative recovery strategies render the twelve-step solution unnecessary or out of date.

Given the potential for disagreement, and a multitude of differing viewpoints, it is perhaps understandable that I am a little hesitant to share my own particular understanding. Recovery is an individual journey, yet I am increasingly finding that my experience is helpful to others. If I can explain in broad terms why it is that recovery based on spiritual principles works, not only as a solution to addiction in general but also as a much-improved basis for living, then it seems to me that the effort needed to write and publish a book on this subject is very worthwhile.

Since completing my first book, my own spiritual journey has taken me in many different directions in pursuit of deeper knowledge and understanding. At the same time I have remained active in twelve-step fellowship and spend significant time sharing my experiences and trying to be of service as best I can. The combination of spiritual practice, continuing research and working with others has inevitably led to a deeper understanding, albeit an individual one. As I understand more, I marvel at the depth and profound wisdom of twelve-step literature. This wisdom is not new, nor do I claim any ownership of it. We all absorb new information in varying ways and at different speeds, and we often initially fail to grasp the significance of new concepts if they do not fit in with our pre-conceived ideas. The underlying principles of twelve-step recovery are radically transformative, yet we are prone to resistance because we do not really want to be transformed. We may want improvements in our lives, or relief from particular addictions, or perhaps just to feel better about ourselves, but the idea of complete transformation is often not attractive. The need for fundamental change implies that our current approach to life is not working for us. Such humility does not come easily. We are prone to justify our own behavior and blame others rather than fully admit that we ourselves are the problem.

One of the insidious features of any addiction is that the consequences of such behavior tend to get worse over a period of time. This can, and often does, lead to a point of desperation and, ironically, it is only then that we become fully willing to embrace a radical solution.

There are many treatment options available, and much has been written both for and against the efficacy of twelve-step recovery. Recovery rates are difficult to establish, due to problems of definition and data gathering, but peer reviewed studies indicate a success rate for Alcoholics Anonymous of only 5% to 10% (reference The Sober Truth by Lance and Zachery Dodes), with the likely rate towards to lower end of this range. This measurement relates to those who are sober after twelve months and still actively engaged in recovery. A recovery rate of only 5% coincides with an estimated spontaneous remission rate, indicating that those who do recover would probably have done so with or without a twelve-step recovery program. On the other hand, it is interesting to note that the same twelve-step program is used by numerous fellowships covering a range of addiction issues including substance misuse, behavioral issues and emotional health problems. The appendix at the end of this book lists 48 such fellowships and I have probably missed a few. It seems that there is something in this approach that works across a broad range of human conditions and from which a great many people have benefited, despite apparently disappointing success rates.

I do not consider myself qualified to conclude that twelve-step programs are the only way to fully recover from addiction related issues. What I can say, based upon my own recovery and the experiences of the many hundreds of people that I have met along the way, is that twelve-step recovery does work in a powerfully transformative way. The extent of such transformations varies greatly, which is understandable given that each case is unique despite the many similarities. If the program works so well for a minority of people, then perhaps a better understanding of why it works may increase the chances of success for others who still suffer.

Rather than claim that twelve-step recovery is a miracle solution for everyone, my assertion would be that such programs are a gateway to a life based on spiritual principles. My observation is that the personal ego mind of human beings is by nature fearful and selfish, and that such selfishness generally increases when perceived basic needs are threatened. A certain amount of selfishness is needed for simple survival and hence it is a necessary and key part of the human psyche. However this selfishness tends to extend beyond basic needs and impacts all aspects of our lives, both individually and collectively. A great deal of suffering arises from self-centered behavior, of which addiction is but one example.

Spiritual principles are fundamentally based on unconditional love for everyone and everything. The suggested antidote for fear based selfishness is therefore a movement towards selflessness based on unconditional love. This is the basis of twelve-step recovery – a program of action targeted specifically at moving the basis of identity and behavior away from the ego-self in favor of the underlying spiritual-self. This provides the power to overcome addiction and also tends to blossom into all aspects of life. A destructive, selfish, negative basis for existence gradually transforms into a productive, selfless and positive experience. Other treatment options may well lead to a cessation of specific addictions, but they risk missing the opportunity for such an enlightening metamorphosis. This is a shame, not only for the individual, who may well continue to suffer from negative emotional experiences, but also for all those with whom the individual interacts. An addict in recovery based on spiritual principles not only benefits personally and ceases to be a burden on society, but is also likely to lead a more useful and harmonious life. There are always exceptions of course, but my experience has been that the people I meet in recovery are generally of a level of self-honesty and humility, the like of which I have rarely met elsewhere.

In order to begin to understand why a program of action based on spiritual principles can work so powerfully, I believe that it is first necessary to explore in depth what spirituality actual means to each of us. This is a contentious area where there are innumerable viewpoints and beliefs. My own approach has been to remain open-minded and to investigate many avenues of spirituality, including the major religions, ancient and modern spiritual wisdom, wide-ranging spiritual practices and modern scientific theories. Much of this is outlined in detail in my first book 'Far More Than We Think – Making Sense of Spiritualty' but my continuing journey has deepened my experience and understanding, as I imagine it will always do. My knowledge is far from complete, and in many respects the more I learn and know, the more I realise that I will never fully know. What has emerged though is a broad concept of spirituality that encompasses all that I have discovered and experienced. The words and cultural settings may differ with apparent significance from one belief system to another, but the principles that underpin all of them are fundamentally the same.

It is tempting to think that the underlying nature of reality is too complex to begin to understand, yet the picture that emerges from spiritual wisdom is surprisingly simple. Just as the enormous complexity of the entire global computing landscape ultimately boils down to simple binary code, so the spiritual wisdom of the ages points to an almost unbelievable simplicity. It is so simple that most of us never think to consider it, yet once understood it suddenly explains a great many things which previously made no sense.

My intention therefore is to explain these simple spiritual principles, as best I can, and then use this understanding to analyse the nature of addiction, how and why twelve-step programs can work so powerfully, and also reflect on the benefits of fellowship and shared recovery. In addition I will consider why perhaps this solution does not seem to work for the vast majority.

My writing is not intended to be an academic exercise. I have drawn from numerous sources, all of which are available online and easily verifiable. If you find that you doubt what I am saying, then it would make sense to validate it for yourself. I have no reason to mislead. The chapters that follow are the truth, the whole truth and nothing but the truth, as best as I can tell. The writing deliberately makes extensive use of repetition and summary. It has been my experience that it often takes repeated exposure to new ideas before the wisdom begins to penetrate our pre-existing thoughts and beliefs.

My hope is that this book will be useful on several levels and eventually lead to improved success rates. To those already benefitting from the spiritual way of life, I offer these thoughts as an interesting perspective. For those in twelve-step recovery, but stalled at any particular level of understanding and practice, I hope that these words will encourage you to look deeper within yourselves. To the many who feel that twelve-step recovery is not for them, my hope is that these explanations will encourage you to give it a try. For those who have a loved one who is suffering from addiction, it is my wish that these words will give renewed hope that recovery is possible. Finally for those who are skeptical or antagonistic towards twelve-step fellowship, my hope is that this book will shed some light on the perceived murky undertones. The anonymity held so preciously by such fellowships is intended to safeguard the humility of those in recovery rather than hide any dark motives.

There will always be a minority who miss the point and use the fellowships for their own selfish ends, but the majority stand as testament to the tremendous positive benefits that spiritual action can bring.

3. Binary

Those of us who have grown up with the evolution of computing will be familiar with the understanding that the entire world of digital applications is ultimately based on binary. The base-2 numeral system, or binary numeral system, uses only two symbols, typically zero and one. Although the idea of binary existed in ancient cultures such as Egypt, China and India, it was not studied in Europe until the 16th and 17th centuries. It was only in 1937 that Claude Shannon produced his thesis at MIT that combined Boolean algebra with binary arithmetic using electronic relays and switches. This formed the basis of the extraordinary growth in computing power and complexity that we have subsequently witnessed and benefited from.

In simple terms, a switch can either be off or on, representing zero or one. The original or natural state is 'off', or zero, and the created or existential state is 'on', hence one. Each zero or one is called a 'bit' and eight bits comprise a 'byte', giving rise to 256 possible combinations. These individual combinations can then be assigned numeric, alphabetic or other meanings and hence we have the basis for computer logic.

In computer languages, this level of bits and bytes is known as machine code, which is created by a complier layer of software such as Assembler. Higher level languages such as Cobol, Fortran, Pascal, Basic, C, C ++, Visual Basic and Java can then be used to write programs in what is called source code, which are then converted through a compiler into machine code. Operating system software such as Unix, DOS, Linux, macOS and Windows also convert into machine code in order to manage hardware and software resources. We also have operating systems for smartphones and tablets such as Android and IOS that also work on the same basis. Then we have HTML, CSS and JavaScript that provide the building blocks for the World Wide Web. All of these languages and operating systems translate down through the various layers to produce binary.

Combinations of bytes also produce the possibility for data storage and retrieval. Familiar terms arise as one thousand bytes combine to produce a kilobyte; one thousand kilobytes produce a megabyte; one thousand megabytes become a gigabyte and one thousand gigabytes equal a terabyte. Again all of this is based on binary.

Data transmission is also based on binary; with Internet speeds and data transfer rates being measured in Megabits per second, where a Megabit is equal to one million bits. The transmission of data is simply the flow of binary between devices.

So the entire digital world that we live in, and depend upon, is based entirely on binary. Indeed the word 'digital' in this context refers to data or signals expressed as a series of the digits zero and one. It seems incredible that diverse and sophisticated applications such as Google, Facebook, Amazon and Netflix, as well as equipment such as desktops, laptops, servers, smartphones, tablets and digital cameras, all owe their functionality to unimaginable quantities of zeros and ones. All of this complexity is based on such simplicity.

Imagine if we were to give a smartphone to a group of scientists who were unfamiliar with digital technology, and ask them to produce a thesis on how it all operates. Separate groups would look at how the applications work, how the information is stored and retrieved, how the underlying logic fits together, how the calculations are processed, how the device is managed and how the data is transmitted. These discoveries would then lead to studies of the Internet, server farms, GPS, satellites and goodness knows what else. Theories would be developed and experiments undertaken to test their validity. After an inordinate amount of time and effort, all of this research would ultimately distill down to the remarkable discovery that the incredibly complex and multi-layered digital world originates from, and is entirely based upon, the simplicity of binary.

This hypothetical study is, for me, a good representation of the world of scientific research. The fields of physics, chemistry, biology, and many others, have made tremendous progress and produced countless wonderful applications to make our lives longer and easier. All they are doing ultimately however is trying to understand what is already here. The research continues of course, and will never end, but science has come far enough now to realise that the mind-blowing complexity of the apparently real world that we experience must ultimately be based on utter simplicity.

It is worth reflecting that the digital world that we inhabit has been invented, designed and implemented by human intellect, and that it continues to evolve. The understanding that, in reality, it is all a multilayered expression of the underlying binary is difficult to believe; yet it is nevertheless true. The advantage of the binary metaphor is that we already know in advance that zeros and ones are the ultimate source, because that is from where it all originates. It is perhaps more difficult to accept that the underlying nature of our experience of reality is also simplicity itself, yet science is slowly revealing this discovery. It does now seem logical to conclude that there is an ultimate source of the relative world, whatever that source may be.

Returning to our understanding that digital applications are created using multiple layers of software, we can immediately see how mistakes, or software bugs, can create potentially difficult problems to solve. If a mistake is made at the surface application software level, then it can be identified and corrected at that level. The problem is identified, traced in the application software and fixed. If however there is a mistake made in the way that the application software translates into source code, then the problem is further down within the layers. The resulting problems will manifest at the surface but the real problem is deeper. No amount of fixes at the application software level will ever solve the underlying mistake.

If an error is made even further down at the compiler level, where source code is converted into machine code, then obviously it will not be possible to resolve the resulting application problems by making changes to application software or source code. The mistake has to be corrected at the level where it is made. It may well be that there are no bugs at all in the application software or source code, but the application will nevertheless malfunction due to a bug at the complier level. The problems will appear at the surface, and it might be tempting to try to fix them by making changes at that level, but it will all be to no avail. Even if changes at the surface level seem to solve some of the issues, such successes will be misleading because the underlying mistake will remain unseen and unresolved. The only effective solution will be to correct the underlying mistake.

The obvious purpose of this binary metaphor is to introduce and emphasize the fundamental idea that complexity arises from simplicity. In order to understand and address a complex problem, it must make sense to dig as deeply as possible and implement a solution that is effective at the level at which the problem arises. The difficulty here is that a simple solution to a complex problem may seem inadequate and therefore unbelievable. This is particularly true when it comes to addiction. In truth, both the problem of addiction and the solution are simple, but we are going to have to cover a great deal of ground in order to fully understand this.

Recovery from addiction may seem beyond our comprehension or reach, but this is not the case. The solution is simple, although invariably not easy. It all boils down to a simple decision. Do we want to recover? Yes or no? Do we want recovery or do we want to continue to suffer? Addiction manifests uniquely in each of us, yet there are often many similarities beneath the surface, and the deeper we go the more similarities appear. When we get to the source, we will find that the problem is common to everyone and really simple, and so too is the solution.

Recovery is a binary decision. We are each entitled to make this decision for ourselves. If we decide that we do want recovery then we must be prepared to go to the source of the problem. It really is that simple.

4. All in the Mind

The first layer to penetrate in order to approach the source of the addiction problem is to explore the true nature of the apparent reality that we experience on a daily basis. It is perhaps uncomfortable to even consider that our perception of reality may be flawed. The reality of our lives, and the world around us, seem so very obvious that it may seem pointless to even question it. However, the main enemy of true understanding is our reliance on key assumptions. We tend to use what seems obvious to unwittingly obscure what is actually happening. We take our surface experience to be sacrosanct and thereby overlook and sacrifice the potential for deeper understanding. I invite you to consider the following two statements:

1) All experience takes place in the mind.

2) There is no experience that takes place outside of the mind.

These two simple sentences have profound implications for our perception of life. Before we go any further, we need to verify the truth of these statements for ourselves. In order to do this, we need to understand what is meant by the words *experience* and *mind*.

Looking first at *experience*, we can simply say that it comprises thoughts, images, emotions, sensations and sensory perceptions. Experience is a seamless whole yet it is useful to break it down into these categories for the purpose of identification. Each category can be further subdivided into yet more elements, but it is important to understand that these are all just labels rather than separate 'things'.

The following descriptions are not intended to be exhaustive, but hopefully they cover the main elements of experience that we are familiar with:

Thoughts include rational and irrational thinking, knowledge, judgment, imagination, memories, projections, worries, internal dialogue, rehearsed or replayed conversations, opinions, beliefs and sense of identity. Thoughts typically take place in our native language, although there can also be a sense of intuition which is beyond words.

Images are similar to thoughts, and cover the same range, but take the form of 'snapshots' and 'videos' of the past, present or future.

Emotions cover how we feel and can broadly be categorised into negative and positive. Negative emotions, based on fear, would include anxiety, terror, resentment, anger, envy, jealousy, loneliness, yearning, lethargy, sadness, grief, depression and despair. Collectively these could be described as suffering. Positive emotions, based on love, include contentment, happiness, peace, intimacy, compassion, forgiveness, acceptance, harmony, joy and bliss. Together these could be labeled as freedom.

Sensations cover bodily awareness and include pain, pleasure, energetic vibration, temperature, sickness and wellbeing.

Perception covers the five senses of sight, sound, touch, taste and smell. These are the instruments that register 'external' inputs and convert them into 'internal' experiences. We tend to place a great deal of reliance upon our sensory input but in fact our senses are relatively limited. Unseen infrared images and high-pitched sounds beyond our hearing are simple examples of how there is clearly more taking place than we are able to sense.

There are undoubtedly many more elements of experience, some of which are so subtle that we do not even have words to

21

label them, yet this relatively simple overview should suffice for our purposes.

Turning now to the meaning of the word *mind* we find that this has long been the subject of debate and competing definitions. The Oxford English Dictionary defines *mind* as "the faculty of consciousness and thought; a person's intellect or memory; a person's attention or will". This will be adequate for now, although we will explore the nature of mind in more depth in later chapters.

Having defined the words, we can now return to our two statements and see if we can confirm their validity. Taking each in turn:

1)   All experience takes place in the mind.

If we close our eyes and pay attention to the elements of experience present in this moment we will quickly perceive that it is indeed all taking place in the mind. Thoughts and images are obviously in the mind. The sounds and smells seem to be 'out there' but they are being experienced 'in here'. Likewise any sensation in the body appears to occur in a particular location but actually it is perceived in the mind. The same is true for feelings. Whatever the particular holistic experience may be, it is all unquestionably 'internal'.

If we then open our eyes and focus on a particular object then things seem to be different. The object is 'over there' whereas 'I' am here looking at it from here. The assumption therefore is that there definitely is an object 'over there' and this seems so obvious that we take it to be undoubtedly true. However, the seeing of the object takes place in the mind. Light is reflected into the eyes and onto the retina. This then produces tiny electrical pulses that are transmitted via the optic nerve, which the brain then interprets to produce an image. This image is then perceived by the mind. The actual experience of seeing takes place in the mind yet the object itself still seems to be 'over there'. If we then physically move toward the object, and touch it, then this confirms our assumption. However the experience of physical movement and the experience of touching both take place internally. Spatial awareness itself is a product of the mind. If we take any experience that it is possible to have then, upon contemplation, we will come to see that it can only ever take place in the mind. The physical world seems to be 'out there' but our actual internal experience does not, and cannot, ever confirm it. All we can be sure of is firstly that experience is indeed taking place in the mind and secondly that we are aware of it. As we progress through the chapters we will come to see that our entire experience of life does take place in the mind. Our majority collective assumption is that there is life outside of the mind, but an assumption is not proven to be true simply because the majority believe it to be so, even if that majority is the vast majority. This is a bold but necessary assertion. It is worth spending time reflecting upon this and verifying it for yourself. The conclusion may be unpalatable but it is nevertheless beyond doubt.

The next statement is going to be even more challenging, but the logic is the same;

2) There is no experience that takes place outside of the mind.

We assume that all manner of events and activities are taking place in the world beyond our immediate personal experience. We 'know' this because others tell us of their experiences verbally or in writing, or we see news coverage or documentary confirmation. There is also the powerful influence of collective experience, where multiple people see and experience the same 'thing'. Again the collective assumption is unshakeable because the evidence seems so overwhelmingly obvious. The first thing to note here is that any second-hand experience that is passed onto us is itself experienced in our mind. Secondly the second-hand experiencer is only reporting what is taking place in their mind, because that is all that they can possibly experience.

Thirdly we assume that collective experience validates apparent external reality but we overlook the possibility that there may be a commonality of mind at a deeper level of consciousness that renders this possible. Finally we project our assumptions about our experiences onto the experiences of others. If we take our version of reality to be sacrosanct then we readily believe that others are experiencing an outside world as we do, which in turn reinforces our belief that there is an outside world. However we cannot prove that there is an outside world because our only reliable point of reference is our own experience, which all takes place in the mind. If this is true for us then it is true for everyone. The whole human materialistic paradigm is based on an assumption that cannot ever be proved experientially. The reality that we believe to be true is not actually real. It is just an experience.

It is important to say at this stage that our current experience of life is not invalid or unreal from the perspective of the personal mind. The relative world creates an experience that is real from the relative point of view. What I am saying is that there is more happening beneath the surface of the relative world, which we are overlooking or ignoring. Returning to our binary analogy, we can say that an application on a smartphone is real in the sense that it is usable and performs a function at the surface level, but the true reality is that it is built upon layers of complex software that ultimately are created out of and depend entirely upon binary. So we can say on the one hand that the application is real in a relative sense but we can also say that it is unreal in terms of absolute truth. The application is therefore both real and unreal. This is a good example of paradox, where apparently contradictory statements are both understood to be true. We will need to become comfortable with paradox, because it will come up time and time again as we proceed. By understanding this smartphone application analogy it will hopefully become easier to accept the paradoxical idea that life, as we experience it, is both real and unreal. The concepts of reality and unreality are simultaneously true, but one is true in a relative sense whereas the other is true absolutely.

24

Materialism is the prevailing assumption in the relative world. Despite being unprovable by our own actual inner experience, the idea that physical matter exists absolutely is dominant. This certainly seems to make sense based on our relative experience. The materialist assumption lies at the root of scientific inquiry and mankind has set out to break down the material world into its component parts and discover how it all fits together and interrelates. We have started at the surface level and are gradually working our way down through the layers. The irony is that the deeper we go with scientific inquiry, the more the conclusions seem to challenge the fundamental assumption of the very materialism on which the science is based. We have produced countless theories in order to try and explain the origins of matter, and the evolution of life, but these keep having to be revised and contorted in order to keep up with the increasing mystery of scientific discovery. Most of the science is way beyond our comprehension hence the materialist assumption continues despite ever increasing evidence to the contrary.

The other key assumption that keeps us firmly attached to the relative world is that time is real. Referring back to the earlier contemplation of our inner life, it becomes apparent that all of the components of experience come and go. Admittedly some elements of experience last longer than others, but it can be seen that thoughts, images, emotions, sensations and perceptions all rise and fall within the mind and that none of them are permanent. Even if a thought persists throughout the day, it still subsides in deep sleep. No element of experience exists absolutely: all of it is appearing and disappearing from moment to moment. Life is experienced in each moment, from one moment to the next, and this creates an apparent continuity that in turn creates the experience of time. Experience takes place in time, but the mind is aware of any component of experience that arises. The element of mind that is aware of the rising and falling of experience is itself timeless, because time is an experience that the mind is aware of. This introduces our next paradox.

Time is both real and unreal. Time is real from the relative point of view but unreal in absolute terms.

I appreciate that introducing such heavy philosophical ideas so early in this book may be optimistic. It has taken me many years of study and meditation to arrive at these conclusions, and my attempts to integrate them into my life are still ongoing. Few of us like to think that we may be mistaken about anything at all, let alone accept that our entire understanding of life might be unsound. Our natural tendency is to defend our existing beliefs and resist or dismiss anything that challenges them. This is understandable, but if we remain closed-minded then we are going to miss the opportunity for deeper understanding. In this regard, I am going to return to these core ideas time and time again, using differing approaches and metaphors. This use of repetition and summary is necessary in my view. My own experience has been that it takes repeated exposure to new ideas before they begin to penetrate our defensive shields. All we need in order to make a start is the willingness to be open-minded. This requires us to have the humility to accept our brokenness and the admission that perhaps we do not currently know as much about the nature of reality as we think we do.

As mentioned earlier, the concept of a deeper reality not only makes sense but it is also very easy to verify for ourselves. If our metaphorical smartphone application were conscious, or self-aware, it would presumably look around at other applications and consider itself to be separate and different. It would perform its functions and believe that it, itself, was responsible for such activity. Without the ability to contemplate its own existence, the application would overlook or ignore the fact that it was completely dependent upon the multiple layers of software that existed beneath its limited understanding. Likewise it would never realise that its very existence depended upon binary, or that all other apparently separate and different applications were also arising from the same source. Indeed the application would find it inconceivable that it was nothing but binary because this would invalidate its own experience of existence.

The functionality of the application would simply not have the capacity to understand its own true nature.

As human beings, we do have the ability to contemplate our true nature. We cannot ever fully understand it because we do not have the mind-based capacity to do so, but we can confirm experientially that there is more below the surface of existence than we may have previously believed. For some of us this realisation may come quickly or suddenly, but for most of us it tends to mature over time through repeated contemplation and practice. We owe it to ourselves to use our unique gift of self-contemplation to prove that this is indeed so. My words of explanation will hopefully have some influence but the real proof can only come from your own experience.

The mind with which you are reading these words is the only tool of experience available to you. There is far more to the mind than we think. We believe that the solutions to our problems are 'out there' whereas the only place that we can possibly experience a solution is 'in here'. This is really good news, because it means that the solutions are much closer to home than we may have previously believed. Indeed the solution is right here, in our own minds. It is all in the mind.

There is a tendency in the modern world to discount or discard anything that cannot be proved scientifically. Notwithstanding the logical conclusions outlined above, and the potential for personal verification, there is still likely to be a belief that science is the ultimate arbiter of truth. If the scientists cannot prove it then it cannot be true. This is despite the fact that science is based upon the assumption of materialism, which itself cannot be proved scientifically. Having said that, there is still tremendous benefit in scientific inquiry because it does penetrate the surface layer of apparent reality. This would be analogous to investigating and understanding the complex software that exists beneath the functionality of the smartphone application.

Science can therefore tell us a great deal about what is really happening and hence it can provide deeper understanding. It makes sense therefore to now have a look at what modern science is really telling us.

5. The Unified Field

"Out beyond the ideas of wrongdoing and rightdoing, there is a field. I'll meet you there.
When the soul lies down in that grass, the world is too full to talk about.
Ideas, language, even the phrase "each other" do not make any sense." ~Rumi

I doubt very much that Rumi had a scientific understanding of unified field theory when he wrote these words in the thirteenth century. However I do find the use of the word *field* to link medieval mystical wisdom with modern science rather appealing.

Unified Field Theory, a term coined by Einstein and now also known as the Theory of Everything, is an all-encompassing theoretical framework of physics that seeks to explain all physical aspects of the universe. The basic concept is that there is a unified field that is the ultimate source of all creation. The idea is to reconcile the theory of General Relativity, which relates to the force of gravity at a macro level, with Quantum Field Theory that models the three non-gravitational forces of weak interaction, strong interaction and electromagnetism that govern at the micro level, including atomic and sub-atomic particles. The relentless pursuit by modern science to understand the physical world has given rise to many related theories and avenues of research. String Theory suggests that the four fundamental forces of gravity, weak, strong and electromagnetic were a single overarching force at the moment of the Big Bang. It also suggests that all tiny sub-atomic particles in the universe are vibrations of energy, or conceptual strings, with differing oscillating patterns giving rise to particles of varying mass and force charge. Superstring Theories have been developed that try to model all of the particles and fundamental forces of nature. M-theory is an eleven dimensional framework that unifies the five versions of Superstring Theory that in turn introduce the concept of additional dimensions to the geometry of four-dimensional space-time. Trying to think beyond the three dimensions of physical space plus the dimension of time is very challenging. The theoretical existence of additional dimensions opens the door to incredible possibilities beyond imagination, including multiple universes.

The speed of progress and the complexity of the theories are truly mind-boggling and every step forward seems to lead to more possibilities. The assumption presumably is that we are getting closer to the final ultimate understanding, but it could be that we are simply scratching the surface. Despite the impressive ingenuity of mankind, the truth is that we still do not fully know how it all works, and perhaps we never will.

What is most interesting for me is that the science of physics is working relentlessly to break down physical reality into its component parts, all of which increasingly appear to be arising from a single source. As Nikola Tesla suggested, if we want to find the secrets of the universe, we should be thinking in terms of energy, frequency and vibration. This energy, or common source, or unified field, is the basic principle underpinning all genres of spirituality. Science and spirituality are converging at a rapid pace and indeed, ironically, science is effectively catching up with what the spiritual gurus and mystics have been pointing to for thousands of years. Unwilling to believe in a single source, the self-important ego of modern mankind has been determined to try to figure it all out for itself. It increasingly seems that we will most probably end up concluding that ancient spiritual wisdom was, and is, far closer to the truth than previously envisaged. The plethora of scientific research into the transformative power of meditation is just one example of this trend.

It is difficult to envisage that physical matter can emerge from a common source of nothingness, yet this is the inescapable conclusion that science has reached. Complex physics and mathematics have proven that the space of a vacuum, at any volume, is infinitely dense and contains infinite energy and mass. A simple explanation would be that waves of any frequency or wavelength ultimately equate to nothing because the peaks and troughs cancel themselves out and hence add to zero. This implies that empty space at any volume has infinite potential, because there are infinite possibilities for vibrations of infinite frequency and wavelength to occur. The question remains as to whether such vibrations occur randomly or if there is some underlying creative intelligence.

Returning again to our binary analogy, it would likely take many years of research, and the evolution of numerous theories, to gradually break down all of the applications into the various user interfaces, programming languages, operating systems, data storage mediums, communication protocols and machine code. Gradually as each layer became understood, the scientists would go down to the next level, and so on until they reached binary code. Even then they would need to comprehend electricity as the power source that underpins all of it. Impressed with their discoveries, the scientists would surely have to conclude that some conscious, creative intelligence must have been behind all of this brilliance. It would be inconceivable to think that such complexity, functionality, interactivity and usefulness could possibly have emerged randomly from the basic binary options of zero or one. The probability of such an outcome would be so imperceptibly small that the existence of creative intelligence would surely be the only possible conclusion.

In his book published in 2009 called *'God's Undertaker – has science buried God?'* the author John C. Lennox brilliantly examines many facets of science in order to try to assess the probability of life emerging randomly out of nothing. The arguments are comprehensive and exhaustively cross-referenced. The resulting complex calculations indicate the probability of a random emergence of life in the universe to be so infinitesimally minute that it has to be dismissed as impossible. The evolution of science has therefore paradoxically proved that there effectively must be a creative intelligence at play. We are each at liberty to decide for ourselves, but for me there can be no doubt. If any reservations persist for you then I can only recommend obtaining a copy of his book. It is a fascinating read.

So science is telling us that the single source of the material world is empty space, or nothingness, and that such nothingness at any volume contains infinite potential. Science is also clearly indicating that there is creative intelligence in this void, which therefore must also exist in any volume of space. This simple idea of conscious, intelligent nothingness existing at all scales is termed Consciousness and is itself increasingly becoming the subject of scientific research. If you type 'the science of consciousness' into Google you will amazed by how much is going on. Consciousness is also the foundational concept of all spiritual traditions and practices. The implication here is not that the underlying intelligence has created something separate from itself. It has created something out of itself. It is the source of creation, the cause of creation, the content of creation and exists both inside and outside of every particle and wave in the entire universe. It is both macro and micro and the same intelligence pervades at all levels. It is beyond description in words of any language, because it exists prior to language. It is beyond understanding by a human mind because it exists prior to the creation of humankind. It is the source of everything, the origin of life itself, absolute truth and yet utterly simple.

This simplicity is crucial to grasp. Just as the entire digital world ultimately depends on and derives from binary code, so our entire physical universe depends on and derives from the source. In the digital world, the layers of complexity build one on top of the other so that the top level seems to operate entirely independently. The user application is unaware of the binary code that gives rise to its existence, but simply operates in accordance with the functionality programmed in at the level immediately below. In the material world, the layers are so numerous that the innumerable outer expressions in terms of organic and inorganic matter are unaware of the very thing that makes it all possible.

This lack of awareness is the root cause of our misunderstanding. We think we are separate from each other, and separate from the world around us, but actually we are all made from, and derive from, the same nothingness. The layers seem to separate us from the source, but each layer builds upon and comprises the layer below, so actually the source is present at all levels. It is right here, right now. We are simply unaware, or to put in another way, we are all asleep in the illusion of perceived reality. Our experiences seem to continually reinforce this belief. It seems that this is necessary to some extent in order for us to experience being alive and present in the world, but perhaps we have given this too much importance. The opportunity is to wake up to the true reality and experience this life from a deeper level of Consciousness and hence in a very different and harmonious way.

It is very tempting to think that this explanation is too simple. It implies that all of our problems are arising from a simple case of mistaken identity. We think we are one thing, but actually we are far more than we think.

It was Einstein who suggested that "If you can't explain it simply, you don't understand it well enough". He also said that "The definition of genius is taking the complex and making it simple". I certainly do not claim to be a genius, or to have complete understanding, but my extensive research and personal experience point clearly to the simple explanation that I have outlined.

The implications of this common source are profound. As well as existing as apparently separate beings with limited intellect and capability, we are at the same time temporary manifestations of the infinite, eternal source. This vast Consciousness is ever present, both within and without. We are separate beings and simultaneously part of everything that is. It always was a unified field but it now seems to be incomprehensibly diverse, yet in truth it remains as unity and always will. It is perhaps too much to believe yet one could say that our very existence is evidence of an ultimate source.

Rumi certainly seemed to know who he was. Reviewing his quote again, it is clear that he is referring to the unified field, or the source, which exists prior to any ideas of right or wrong. In that place, or state, the world is beyond the ability of language to describe. Ideas don't make any sense, including the idea that we are separate from each other. That sounds like a very appealing place to meet, and we don't have to physically go anywhere to get there.

This field exists within us, and in truth is who we really are. I do not believe that Rumi was any more of a special human being that any of us. Indeed the same could be said for all of the spiritual gurus and mystics of the past and present. It is only a question of the level of Consciousness from which our experience arises.

Although the term *Unified Field* relates to scientific theory, it can also be seen to have a wider application. The idea of Consciousness is actually unifying the fields of philosophy, spirituality and science. These fields have previously offered different and competing views, yet it is becoming clear that they are now converging to provide a single unified perspective. The disciplines and terminology may differ but the conclusions being reached are the same. It is no longer valid to suggest that spirituality is unscientific. There is far more wisdom in deep spiritual understanding than there is in scientific theory. Indeed Consciousness already knows all that science is trying to understand.

Science is pushing back the limits of our current misunderstanding. This is all very helpful and interesting, but we do not need to rely on science in order to validate the wisdom that originates in Consciousness. We can actually unify with it

34

ourselves. The unified field is not elsewhere. It is right here. We are in it. We are it. The unified field is Consciousness.

6. The Nature of Consciousness

Human beings have been exploring the depths of Consciousness throughout the ages and many have tried to communicate their understanding through their respective languages and cultures. The problem is that Consciousness exists prior to language and culture. It is the source of everything, right back beyond the level of sub-atomic vibration. Language can point to Consciousness but can never fully describe it, because ultimately there are no pre-existing words to do so. This is why metaphor and parable are so widely used to try to communicate that which cannot be described. Attempts to articulate the true nature of reality are very numerous and originate in all cultures dating back thousands of years. The essential nature of what is being communicated is the same, but the methods and styles differ widely and there is always the scope for misunderstanding and misinterpretation.

Key figures have emerged throughout history who have tried to provide their own version of this universal wisdom. Their resulting spirituality is perceived as something special and this creates an aura of saintliness and perfection, which in truth is unrealistic. The wisdom is turned into teaching, and this in turn creates scripture, doctrine, practice, devotion and institution. As time passes, the core understanding becomes distorted and diluted. Words are read at the level of personal ego mind and hence core understanding is missed. Disagreements arise and factions break away to focus on their own versions of what they perceive the words to mean. Institutions are hijacked for the purposes of power and money, and hence become polluted and conflicted. On and on it goes, generation after generation. Beliefs become conditioned and children become indoctrinated long before they have the maturity to discern for themselves. Entire communities and nations believe that their own version is the one and only truth, and that everyone else has got it wrong. Rival ideologies compete. Some are even self-righteous enough to believe that they should convert others to their particular dogma. Methods of persuasion and conversion are used that conflict at a fundamental level with the very tenets that the ideologies claim to advocate. Science has also led us away from wisdom, but is now finally beginning to comprehend its own incongruence. The media, in all of its guises, generally fans the flames of misunderstanding. Little wonder that there is so much confusion, cynicism and scepticism in the modern world.

We need to cast aside all of this befuddlement and get back to basics. I accept that prejudice exists but hopefully I have cleared away at least some of the debris that obscures true understanding.

Finding the right words to explain Consciousness is impossible, but words are the only tool that I have at my disposal. I am going to attempt an explanation and then reinforce these ideas with a series of metaphors that I have come across in my research that make sense to me. My experience has been that different metaphors work for different people, so my hope is that one or more of these various approaches will resonate with each reader. Somewhere deep in your own psyche you already know what I am about to explain. This knowing may be in the form of a sudden recognition, a positive feeling or perhaps a gradual realisation. Whatever the outcome, the opportunity here is to connect with your own deepest understanding.

In attempting this explanation I am going to use the words Consciousness, Awareness, Knowingness, Mind, Spirit and Being interchangeably. These words all refer to the same conscious, intelligent nothingness that I have previously mentioned, and are capitalised to indicate that they are all labels pointing to the same place. Various other labels are used later, and these are also capitalised to link them together. They are all synonyms. To illustrate this, let us consider some further statements;

Consciousness is that which is conscious of its own existence and movement.

Awareness is that which is aware of the existence and movement of awareness.

Knowingness is that which knows the existence and movement of knowing.

Mind is that which is mindful of the existence and movement of mind.

Spirit is that which observes the existence and movement of spirit.

Being is that which exists and is self-aware.

These statements are deliberately repetitive because they all say the same thing. Universal wisdom points to the same truth over and over again, whatever the particular expression of that wisdom may be.

It is impossible to visualise or conceptualise Consciousness but the best that I can do is suggest imagining a vast, dark, empty vacuum. There are no boundaries in any direction and time does not exist. This space is infinite and eternal. There is literally nothing here and nothing happening. This Consciousness is self-aware so it knows that it exists, but it does not exist as anything. It cannot go anywhere because there is nowhere else to go. It is perfectly peaceful, happy, content and whole. Nothing can go wrong because there is nothing happening. There is no fear because there is nothing to be fearful of. It is a state of bliss beyond the concept of bliss. Consciousness loves this state. It is in a state of love beyond any possible conception of love. There are many words in our numerous human languages that label this placeless place, but none of them can possibly get close to describing that which is beyond description.

Consciousness vibrates itself and is aware of its own vibration. It vibrates itself at countless different vibrations and wavelengths and is aware of everything that arises as a result.

Effects pulse in and out of existence at unimaginable speeds and Knowingness knows what is happening. Vibrations interact and overlap to create forces, energy and the momentary appearance of particles. All of this is known and Mind is mindful of all that materialises.

Vibrations create waves and movement, and everything moves, yet Consciousness itself is not moving. A potentially infinite amount of activity is taking place yet there is utter stillness. Spirit is everywhere and creates everything but is simultaneously nowhere in particular. Consciousness is vibrating in the eternal moment of now but time is not passing. Time does not exist. It all just changes from moment to moment and stays exactly where it is. Knowingness knows that all of this is happening and retains its own knowledge. This knowledge gives rise to yet more combinations of vibrations, creating yet more complex configurations. Forces interact with each other creating yet more effects. The momentary sub-atomic particles combine to produce larger and larger particles, which in turn produce the atoms that give rise to basic elements. None of this exists absolutely but it appears in Awareness momentarily, pulsing in and out of existence at incredible speeds, and it is all known. It is all the movement of Spirit and it is observed and known by Spirit. It is all in Mind and Mind is aware of everything at every moment.

Basic geometries evolve, which combine to produce complex patterns. Simple elements combine within these geometrics to produce molecules, which appear as gases, liquids and solids. These seemingly permanent materials interact with each other to produce yet more permutations, including light. The potential is infinite and manifests in diverse and unique expressions. Consciousness knows all of this and uses this knowledge to add more and more complexity. The scale is vast and again beyond imagination. Everything is taking place within Consciousness, is made out of Consciousness, is known by Consciousness and is taking place moment to moment beyond the concept of time.

Everything is happening yet nothing is happening in absolute terms. This is perhaps the biggest paradox of all.

As the layers of complexity evolve, Consciousness condenses its own vibration and scope in order to remain aware of its own activity at each level. Pure, infinite, unlimited Consciousness is aware of its own activity at the level of infinite existence, but as it reduces in vibration, its own awareness naturally becomes more limited at the more confined levels of finite existence. These layers, or levels, are not definable in precise terms, but are more of an ever-decreasing continuum of vibration. This introduces the idea of density. It is still all Consciousness, within Consciousness, but the Awareness condenses and limits itself the more the vibration decreases. This means that Mind itself gradually limits its own infinite awareness and knowing the further it evolves towards finite experience. Remember that we are using the word Mind interchangeably with Consciousness, so we are saying here that the original Mind or source Mind is gradually and naturally limiting its own awareness and knowledge as it creates finite perspectives within the infinite realm of possibilities.

Even though there is a limitation in awareness and knowledge as we approach a finite perspective, it is important to grasp that Consciousness itself is not changing its nature absolutely. A good analogy here is the behavior of water in the material world. At its lowest vibration, or coldest temperature, H_2O appears as solid ice. When the temperature increases it gradually becomes liquid water. The liquid water state remains as the temperature rises, becoming increasingly agitated until it finally transforms into water vapour, or steam. Despite these different states and appearances, the fundamental nature of H_2O remains throughout. All that is changing is the vibration. At high vibration, H_2O is gaseous and able to move freely. At reduced vibration it appears as a fluid, with a limitation in movement. Once it reaches an even lower vibration it becomes a solid and is very limited in movement. All of these apparent states exist yet H_2O is not changing its nature absolutely.

If we continue the water analogy further, with ever increasing vibration, then eventually H_2O breaks down into hydrogen and oxygen. This may seem to invalidate the analogy but actually it can give even more insight. Yet further increases in vibration would cause the atoms to break down into their component parts, then sub-atomic particles, followed by yet smaller particles and eventually to the unified field, or Consciousness itself. So starting with Consciousness and reducing the vibration we go back the other way from Spirit to sub-atomic particles, to atoms, to hydrogen and oxygen, to H_2O, to water vapour, to water and finally to ice. It is all a vibration of Consciousness at gradually reducing frequencies and increasing density producing a variety of different appearances and properties. Consciousness is fully present every step of the way because it is that which is vibrating.

Infinite Mind is fully present at all of these stages or states. It becomes gradually compressed and limited in awareness and knowing as the vibration decreases, but it retains its infinite potential in absolute terms. This may seem implausible but, as noted in the previous chapter, science has already proved that a vacuum at any volume is infinitely dense and contains infinite energy and mass. It has also proved that the chances of complex creation being random are so infinitesimally small that creative intelligence must be a certainty. So the idea that Consciousness can be finitely limited and infinitely unlimited simultaneously may seem at first to be unbelievable, but is in fact just another paradox. Both states exist and are true, but the absolute truth of Consciousness is infinite and eternal, just as the absolute truth of the smartphone application is binary.

Yet more complexity arises and the infinite potential of forces, energy and particles combine to give rise to diverse forms of organic life. Further iterations then lead to a multiplicity of sentient life, each with so many variable components that every single manifestation is unique. The net result of this immeasurably vast and complex array of vibrations of

41

Consciousness is the material world that we perceive and experience. Consciousness is not only present but it is the true nature of everything. Change is perpetual, from moment to moment, and knowledge of all that arises continues to inform the next moment. This is the underlying nature of growth and evolution. Knowingness is learning from its own knowing, and is using this knowledge to evolve at all levels. Consciousness itself is not evolving because it never changes, but the vibrational complexity is evolving. Consciousness is evolving and is not evolving. This is yet another paradox.

The whole unified field is arising and disappearing in each infinitesimal moment, and this is replicated at the level of the material world in the form of birth and death. It is all the equivalent of breathing in and out. The same patterns arise at all levels. Consciousness exists not only at all frequencies, wavelengths and levels, but also across the whole spectrum of density, whist still retaining its absolute, infinite nature. Universal Mind is present at all layers of density yet still retains its ultimate, absolute, infinite, eternal nature.

The nature of infinite Mind is happiness, peace, love and unity, and these qualities are ever present, yet are gradually limited as the density increases. As mentioned previously, this limited form of Mind naturally includes a state of compression due to increased density. A helpful analogy here is to imagine taking a bath sponge and squashing it with your hands into a tight ball. By applying force to the sponge it is compressed and the density increases. This state of compression now includes an inbuilt tendency, or urge, to return to its previous form. This urge will remain until the return journey begins and will gradually diminish as the sponge expands back to the state from which it started. If we now release the sponge it does indeed expand back to its original nature. The compression existed momentarily but it is now released. Applying this analogy to Mind, we see that infinite Consciousness naturally compresses itself into a limited form in order to be aware of itself at a finite level, and that this compression creates an inbuilt urge to return to its original nature. The urge is to return to happiness, peace, love and unity. This urge manifests in all sentient beings as desire. All human beings desire happiness, peace, love and unity. These desires exist naturally in Mind at the level of humanity, and are obviously desires of Spirit, or spiritual desires. Unless and until these desires are satisfied by a return to the original nature of Mind, there will always be a sense of longing for something intangible and out of reach. This is the core driver of suffering. Every individual human version of Mind, or personal mind, is longing for this inbuilt suffering to be relieved but there is much misunderstanding as to how best to achieve it. We may all have our ideas about how to relieve this longing but none of them ultimately work because the metaphorical sponge is still in the state of compression. The sponge will always stay in a state of compression until it is released, and likewise the personal human mind will stay in suffering until it recognises and returns to its original nature.

Everything that we have covered so far points to the underlying reality of Consciousness and the original nature of Mind. The materialist assumption has been that Consciousness originates in the brain and is somehow the result of long-term random material evolution. Albert Einstein was a deeply spiritual man and credited much of his creative work to intuition and inspiration rather than intellectual brainpower. When he died in 1955, his brain was removed and analysed to try to ascertain what physiological differences might explain his genius. The results were inconclusive and remain the subject of disagreement, but such is the power of assumption that genius must arise from the physical brain. It would make more sense to see that Einstein had accessed deeper levels of Consciousness, or Mind, and that his ideas were revealed to him rather than manufactured by his intellect. This certainly seems to have been his own personal view, which in itself is pretty compelling.

The best analogy that I have found relating to this misunderstanding of the brain is from physicist Nassim Haramein who says that "Looking for Consciousness in the brain is like looking inside a radio for the announcer." This simple quote provides a lot of insight. A human voice originates from a human being, so without prior knowledge it would be reasonable to assume that a miniscule announcer was actually inside the radio. This is the equivalent of assuming that Consciousness originates in the brain. We know, of course, that the announcer is not in the radio set but elsewhere, and that the voice is being captured at source and transmitted via radio waves. These radio waves are detected by an antenna, processed by electronic circuits within the radio and then converted into sound through a loudspeaker. It is this sound that is heard by the listener and perceived to be the announcer. So the apparent reality of an announcer is seen through because the listener knows the underlying reality. We don't have to think about this each time we listen to the radio because we already know it to be true. This is a good example of how understanding completely changes our perception of apparent reality.

Applying this analogy to Consciousness, there is an assumption that the activity of Mind originates in the brain. This seems reasonable without any prior knowledge. We now understand that Consciousness is everywhere and everything, including the brain. The brain is the equivalent of the electronic circuits in the radio. It is the processor of Consciousness rather than its originator. The output from this processing is the various elements of experience that we mentioned earlier; namely thoughts, images, emotions, sensations and perceptions. This is a very important stage in our understanding. The brain is the processor, but Consciousness, or Mind, is the originator and substance of experience. There is no life other than experience, and hence there is no life without Consciousness. There is no life without Spirit. This is because Consciousness, or Spirit, is life.

In our radio analogy, there is the voice coming from the radio and there is the listener who hears, or perceives, the voice. This is in the realm of subject-object relationship. The subject is the listener and the object is the voice. The subject perceives the object. Within our own experience, there are the various elements of experience and there is that which perceives these experiences. That which perceives experience is the subject, and the numerous components of experience are the objects. Consciousness, or Spirit, is both subject and object. Consciousness is processing itself through the brain and is then witnessing the resulting experience. Consciousness is the originator of experience, the content of experience and the witness of experience.

All of us experience life on a personal basis, so we need to reconcile this wisdom of Consciousness with our actual day-to-day experience, otherwise all of this will just be philosophical theory. The mechanism that brings clarity to this paradox is the concept of the personal mind, also known as the ego mind. Please note the use of a small m here to signify mind as opposed to a capital M when referring to Mind, or Consciousness. As mentioned earlier, Consciousness naturally limits or compresses itself in order to experience a finite version of reality. In human beings this limitation or compression results in the personal ego mind. The ego mind is a psychological construct that is neither an entity in its own right nor has any tangible reality, yet seems to have tremendous power and influence in our lives.

There are various conceptual elements to the ego mind, some of which are inherited and some of which develop through our particular experiences and conditioning. We will cover these in a later chapter, but for now we will refer to the personal ego mind as single unit. This personal ego mind is our unique instrument of experience. It is, if you like, an individual lens through which Consciousness perceives the experience that it creates. Our individual experiences feel personal but the ultimate witness is non-personal Mind. The ego mind is part of our temporary body-mind existence. The body-mind feels very personal but it is all a product of Consciousness. The body-mind has a lifespan and components of its core functionality include the instincts for survival and reproduction. The instinct for survival manifests as self-centered fear and this gives rise to a range of negative emotions, as noted in a previous chapter. These emotions are necessary for survival of the body-mind. We perceive them as negative but they have a purpose. Self-centered fear is also part of our drive for community as it provides us with protection and access to the exchange of mutual support. The instinct for reproduction manifests as lust and nurturing, both of which add to our social drive. The ego mind is therefore a multipurpose tool for experiencing, with built in instincts for survival and reproduction. It may be very sophisticated and have a range of uses but ultimately it is just a tool. The personal ego mind is not who we are. The temporary body-mind is not who we are. The voices in our head are not who we are. We are that which is aware of all of this. We are Awareness itself. We are Consciousness itself, masquerading as a self-centered person in order to have a unique, finite experience within the infinite realm of possibility.

The nature of Consciousness is nothing and everything, and all stages in between. The nature of Awareness is that which is aware of itself in all of its guises. The nature of Knowingness is all knowing. The nature of Mind is both subject and object. The nature of Spirit is universal. The nature of Being is existence. It is all one.

Consciousness is infinite and eternal. Consciousness is not somewhere else. Consciousness simply is. We are Consciousness. I am that, and so too is everyone and everything, in every moment.

This model of Consciousness is the core wisdom that underpins all spiritual traditions. It also informs philosophy and science and explains all aspects of experience. The next few chapters will use a range of metaphors to try to approach the same understanding in different ways.

7. The Dreamer and the Dream

Dreaming is an ideal analogy because it is something that we can all immediately relate to. It does not matter what we dream, or why we dream, but rather it is simply the fact that we do dream that is of interest.

The sleep cycle takes place in five stages, with two stages of light sleep followed by two stages of deep sleep and then a final stage known as Rapid Eye Movement, or REM. Each cycle typically takes around 90 minutes to complete, hence there are multiple cycles during a period of sleep. The REM stage gradually becomes longer with each cycle and overall the amount of sleeping time spent in REM is roughly 25%. Dreaming mostly takes place during the REM phase, and dreams are more easily recalled when we wake up out of this stage as opposed to other stages.

Dreams take innumerable forms but typically we will be in them ourselves, together with other people and all manner of places and events. Often the people, places and events have some relevance to our previous experience but sometimes they are in the realm of fantasy. The personal self in the dream experiences thoughts, images, emotions, sensations and perceptions, just as in the waking state, and reacts to everything that takes place in the dream. Occasionally the experiences can be very real and intense, but less so on other occasions. It is all a bit of a mystery, yet we take dreaming to be just a normal part of life.

If we pause to consider what is actually happening here then we can gain some insight into the nature of our minds. The dream is obviously taking place in our mind, and it is reasonable to conclude that we are talking about the personal or ego mind because we are personally in the dream. As well as being in the dream ourselves, we also create all of the other people, places and events. The whole dreamt world is created in our mind and we then experience everything that happens in the dream. It all seems so real, yet it is just a dream. Consciousness, in its limited form as a personal mind, is creating an apparent reality out of itself and is then experiencing its own creation from the perspective of itself. The potential within the dream seems unlimited yet the apparent reality feels real to the personal self in the dream. When we awaken we quickly realise that it was all just a dream, and we settle back into the 'real' world of the waking state. We do this every night and tend to overlook the tremendous significance of what has just happened.

We are quite happy to dismiss the dream world as unreal, even though it was all experienced as real during the actual dream. This is because we awaken into the waking state and immediately perceive that the dream state is different from the waking state, with one being real and the other being unreal. What we perhaps do not fully recognise is that both the dream and waking states are taking place in the mind. We assume that one is unreal, but the elements of experience in both states are the same. There is nothing to differentiate them other than our assumption that the material world is real and the dreamed world is unreal. This is despite the fact that our experiences are equally real and valid in each of the states. An alternative explanation could simply be that the 'real' world of the waking state is itself dreamlike in nature. This would imply that a bigger dream is taking place in a Mind beyond our personal mind and that we are appearing in that dream as ourselves. If we were to wake up out of the waking state then the dreamlike world would immediately be seen differently.

This waking up out of the waking state is the foundational meaning of the term *spiritual awakening*. The term is also used more generally to include a transformative change in perception or outlook that does not necessarily render the world unreal but begins a movement in that direction.

This dream analogy points to the existence of a Mind in which the whole universe appears as the equivalent of its dream. The difficulty here is to understand how we can appear in this dream as our personal selves. The clue is in our own dreams. The personal mind creates a self that appears in its dream. This ego self experiences the dream from a personal perspective even though the mind that creates it also creates, and is, everything else in the dream. The only leap in understanding necessary here is to see that Mind creates a dream on a much bigger scale and creates multiple selves with which to experience it. These selves are each unique, so Mind experiences its own dream from a multitude of different perspectives. The scale is vast and the numbers of selves numerous, but the logic is perfectly sound. Each self in this vast dream would consider themselves to be separate and personal, but each would be a product of the one Mind. If the personal version of Consciousness were able to wake up to the true nature of its own Mind then the vast dream would suddenly take on new meaning. It would all be seen as a product of its own Mind. The problem that now arises is to understand how we can wake up from a dream yet still be in it personally.

The clue is in our own experience of lucid dreaming. The term *lucid dream* was first introduced by Dutch psychiatrist Frederik van Eeden in an article published in 1913 about the study of dreams. A lucid dream is a dream in which the dreamer is aware that they are having a dream. During lucid dreaming, the dreamer may have some control over the people, places and events taking place in the dream. This introduces the element of freewill into the dream state and gives the dreamer some limited influence over what happens, although not absolute influence. Most people experience at least a few lucid dreams in their lifetime, and some experience lucid dreams on a regular basis.

Adding this element into our analogy, we discern that in lucid dreaming the mind provides not only a self and a world of experience but also the freewill to move about within the dreamed world and hence influence the experience. All of this is taking place within the personal mind. Using the same simple step in understanding as before we see that Mind creates a lucid dream on a universal scale with countless selves and experiences, all of which have freewill to some extent to

49

influence their own experience. This lucid dream created by Mind is the waking state that we all perceive and believe to be real.

As human beings, we have the capacity to understand that the world that we experience is a lucid dream taking place in Mind, comprised of Spirit, observed by Awareness and known by Knowingness. Just understanding and absorbing this wisdom is enough to begin a gradual awakening from the waking state. We remain in the world personally, but at a deeper level we know that it is a dream within a greater reality. The more deeply we know this to be true the more our personal, ego minds will return to the true nature of Consciousness.

The dreamer and the dream in the personal mind are one. The dreamer and the dream in universal Mind are one. Consciousness, Awareness, Knowingness, Mind, Spirit and Being are one. There is nothing else. We may perceive and believe that there is a material world, but this perception is not true. It is just a perception, and perception is ultimately a choice. Once we know how a magic trick works, we can still enjoy the show but we now know that the apparent illusion is not real. We can choose to find out how the trick is performed, or we can continue to believe that it is magic. Likewise, we can choose to explore the true nature of reality or we can continue to believe the illusion.

8. The Screen of Awareness

Another good everyday analogy is our use of screens, whether they be televisions, computers, tablets or smartphones. In this example we will be using a TV screen, but the same will apply to any form of electronic screen.

The modern TV screen is a wonderful piece of technology, producing images of the very highest quality that seem almost real. The latest primary technologies are Liquid Crystal Display (LCD) and Light-Emitting Diode (LED) that both shine light through a matrix of tiny, coloured liquid-crystal cells to produce pixels on a screen. LCD screens use a number of lamps to provide the light source whereas LED uses a larger number of light-emitting diodes. Each pixel is comprised of three sub-pixels with the colours red, blue and green. Combinations of these colours at varying intensities can create the perception of any desired colour in that location. The pixels amalgamate to produce an apparent image on the screen. The resolution of screens has gradually increased over time, and most of us will have seen High Definition at 1080p that provides an array of pixels 1,920 wide by 1,080 tall. Hence there are over two million pixels on an HD screen. The latest 4K or Ultra HD screens have four times this number and hence provide even higher resolution. Screens also include loudspeakers for sound reproduction, with sounds being synchronised with the images. All of this is of course digital and therefore ultimately comprised of binary.

In this metaphor I will be referring to the screen as a single 'thing' although it is obviously comprised of multiple parts. When we sit down to watch TV the first thing we do is to switch it on. Prior to switching it on, all we are looking at is the blank screen. We see the screen, and know it is there, and it is all we see. Once the TV is on then images and sounds appear. Imagine that we are watching an action movie. We quickly become absorbed in the drama. The characters, places and events develop and we begin to identify with the story. We may become attached to one or more of the characters and begin to experience emotions connected to the action as it unfolds. Our thinking may include all manner of thoughts, including for example; injustice, judgment, resistance, identification and anticipation. We may try to comprehend the plot and guess what the ending will be. Anxiety, tension, excitement, compassion, fear, sadness, relief, joy and all other emotions may arise. Our minds will be fully focused on the movie and it will take on a sense of temporary reality. We completely lose sight of the screen and totally overlook the fact that it is all a technical illusion. Such is the power of external focus and purposeful forgetting.

What is actually happening is not real at all. The two million pixels on the screen are pulsing and changing at a rate of sixty times per second, or even higher on some screens. This creates the illusion of images and movement and it all happens so quickly and smoothly that we cannot possibly perceive the true reality. If we were able to slow it all down dramatically and zoom in on a small portion of the screen then we would be able to see the individual pixels pulsing on and off and changing colour. This is however not our usual experience hence such matters are ignored because they seem unimportant to our viewing.

Whilst all of this is going on, and our focus and attention is entirely on the movie, we simply do not see the screen. It is there, and always has been, but we don't see it because we are totally distracted by the action. Not only is the unseen screen there, but it is the very thing that is creating the movie experience out of itself. Without the screen there is no movie. The pixels are unseen yet they are the miniscule elements of the images and movement that we perceive. The screen is showing a particular movie and but it could easily play any movie. The potential of the two million pixels is infinite. The screen has unlimited potential, subject of course to whatever digital signals it receives.

As we sit and watch, we forget that there is a screen and we forget that the screen is creating the movie experience. We are so involved in the people, places and events that it feels real. We may be sitting several meters from the screen but somehow it feels like we are actually in it. We have a vague sense that it is just a movie, and that we remain ourselves throughout, but this deeper sense of knowing is overshadowed by our emotional involvement in the drama on the screen. Sometimes the experience of watching a good movie can be emotionally draining, and there can be a sense of relief when it ends. When it does end, and we switch off the TV, we suddenly see that the screen had been there all along. We also begin to detach from the emotions and they quickly fade because the blank screen highlights the unreality of the movie. A memory of the movie may linger but gradually the whole experience subsides.

If we pause at this stage of the metaphor then we can gain some important insight. The person who watches the movie is sitting apart from the screen and is in the role of observer. The movie is created by the screen and is the source of experience. The observer watches the movie and is aware of the experiences arising. The more the watcher is absorbed in the movie, the more 'real' the experience will be. If the watcher were able to remain aware of being the observer, remind themself that the movie was unreal and acknowledge that it was all being created by the screen, then the movie could still be watched and enjoyed but the experience would be far less intense. The screen would be seen at all times, the pulsing of pixels would be understood and the illusion of the movie would be seen through. It would be a different experience. This detachment from the movie is an important step in understanding. We have seen that all experience takes place in the mind and that we can be aware of the elements of experience through contemplation. This is the equivalent of moving from a position of being completely involved in the movie to the more detached position of being the observer. Just as in our metaphor, nothing has actually changed other than the watcher now realising that they are not in the mind but simply an observer of it. This simple change in perception is a move away from the personal ego mind towards Mind itself. It does however take persistent practice otherwise we quickly forget and become engrossed in the mind once more.

The next stage of the metaphor requires some imagination. We can imagine that the screen is three-dimensional and has some level of intelligence. In other words it is self-aware and also able to create its own movie. The potential of the screen is unlimited so it can literally create anything out of itself. The equivalent of pixels would be Consciousness shining through itself at the quantum level. It is all pulsing and changing at a rate per second beyond comprehension. The screen begins to create its movie and through self-awareness is able to observe its own creation. It does not matter what appears in the movie because the screen knows that it is just a creation out of itself. All is well for a while, but gradually the screen becomes identified with one of the characters in the movie and starts to get emotionally attached. In doing so the screen begins to forget that it is the screen and starts to believe that it is actually in the movie. Nothing has changed except that the screen is now giving its attention to a particular perspective within the movie. The more involved the screen becomes with the individual character the more intense the emotions and the less awareness it has of its true nature as the screen. Eventually the screen becomes so identified with the person in the movie that it totally overlooks or forgets itself as the screen. This is despite the fact that as the screen it is both the creator of the movie and the pixels out of which the movie is made and is therefore every single thing in the movie, whatever that may be.

The movie continues and the screen, still identified with the person, begins to suffer unpleasant experiences within the drama. The screen feels like there is something missing, or something wrong, but it cannot quite see what the problem is. The screen starts looking about within the movie to try to find a solution but nothing seems to work. The screen then begins to understand that it might not be the person with which it identifies. It starts to look for itself as the screen within the movie, but of course it cannot find it because it is the very thing that it is looking for. The screen is not in the movie. The screen is the movie. The screen cannot ever find itself within the realm of its own creation.

The screen starts to seriously question what is going on. There are parts of the movie that it likes but there is a great deal that causes suffering. After some guidance, the screen starts to contemplate its own nature. Slowly but surely the screen starts to realise that it is not just in the movie but is an observer of it. Identification with the particular character begins to fade and the screen moves increasingly towards the realisation that it is the screen. Then, in a moment of enlightenment, it becomes fully aware of its nature as the screen. The character is still in the movie but the screen is far less involved. It begins to take a wider perspective of the movie and see much more than it did when identified just as a person. The screen lives happily ever after and the movie goes on and on. Characters come and go, everything changes from moment to moment, and the screen watches silently and is aware of all that happens.

The final stage of the metaphor is to see that if the screen is able to identify with one of the characters then, given its infinite nature, it could identify with all of the characters. Everyone and everything is the screen, and the screen is present in the movie appearing as every person, place and event. At the same time the screen is always aware of itself as the screen, even if all of the characters do not realise it for themselves. We may search for the screen individually or collectively for our entire lives but we will never find it because it is not in the movie as the screen. If we think we have found it, and try to tell everyone else about what we have found, then we are obviously fooling ourselves. All we can do it be the screen, and help others to do likewise.

The Screen of Awareness is ever present in, and as, each and every one of us. Consciousness, Awareness, Knowingness, Mind, Spirit or Being announces itself within each of us as the irrefutable knowledge that "I Am". This is the common knowing that unites every sentient being.

9. The Masquerade Ball

Not all of us may have attended a masquerade ball, but we have all probably been to a fancy dress party at some stage in our lives. Masquerade balls have been around since the fifteenth century and are events in which the participants attend in costume and wear a mask.

The word *person* derives from the Latin word *persona,* which in ancient Roman times originally referred to masks worn by actors on stage. The various masks represented the different *personae* in the play. This etymology of the word *person* is tremendously revealing.

The personal self is masquerading in life as a person. The costume is the body and the mask is the personal, ego mind. It is Consciousness masquerading as a person, with the limited belief that the person is its true identity.

Imagine being invited to a modern-day masquerade ball in the guise of your favorite celebrity. You would wear a mask depicting the chosen celebrity's face and wear appropriate clothing. You may even practice mimicking their voice or replicating signature moves or gestures in front of a mirror. The day of the ball arrives and you make your entrance. You are now in the role of your celebrity. People recognise you as the celebrity and likewise you recognise everyone else in their costumes. You do not know who the 'real' people are that are masquerading as other celebrities and nobody knows who you 'really' are. The party gets underway and you meet and talk with many others. You use your practiced voice and gestures and you really get into the swing of being your celebrity. Everyone greets you as the celebrity and you very much enjoy the experience. As the party continues you get more and more used to being your celebrity and you begin to overlook who you 'really' are. You start to react and respond as the celebrity. Eventually you forget your previous identity completely and spend the rest of the night experiencing life as the celebrity.

You travel home by taxi and talk with the taxi-driver as if you are still the celebrity. He knows that you are just masquerading but you remain convinced that you are still in the role. He tries to convince you but you remain unmoved. As you approach home the identity of the celebrity begins to fade, but you are still wearing the costume and mask. Once home you take one last look in the mirror and see yourself as the celebrity. You then take off the costume and mask and your 'real' identity reemerges. The whole experience of masquerade had a beginning and an end. You remained your 'real' self before, during and after the experience but there was a period during which your 'real 'identity was overlooked or forgotten and you believed yourself to be the celebrity.

The metaphor here is clearly very obvious but it is worth repeating the explanation again. The masquerade ball is our entire life as a human being. The true identity is Consciousness, Awareness, Knowingness, Mind, Spirit or Being. This identity exists prior to the experience of life. As soon as we are born we begin to create the personal identity. We develop a personal, ego mind and a strong identity with the body, and this strengthens over time. Each time we look in the mirror we see what we believe to be ourselves and this reconfirms what we assume to be true. At some stage in our lives, someone suggests that the body and the personal, ego mind are not our true identity, but we remain unmoved. The idea seems absurd. As we grow more experienced in life and mature in wisdom, the personal identity may start to fade but we still have a body and a personal ego mind. Eventually our lives come to an end and the body and personal mind cease to function and the true identity emerges. The whole experience of life has a beginning and an end. We remain our True Self before, during and after the experience but there was a period during which our true identity was overlooked or forgotten and we believed ourselves to be only a person.

This gradual change in identity from the person to the True Self is the essence of the spiritual journey, whatever our individual or collective path may be. The journey may seem impossible, or too long and arduous to undertake, but actually it is a journey of no distance to the placeless place that we already are. Just as in the metaphor of the masquerade ball, the journey is simply to realise that we remain our True Self even though we are wearing a costume and mask. It really is that simple, yet we struggle to be convinced. We believe that the journey must be complex and difficult, and it is this belief that makes it so.

There is nothing wrong at all in enjoying the masquerade ball, provided we remember who we really are. The masquerade ball is here to be enjoyed. The trouble starts when we identify so strongly with the personal ego self that we overlook our true nature. As we shall see later, this is the ultimate root of all suffering.

10. Being Human

As far as metaphors go, this one brings us as close to home as it is possible to be. The etymology of the term *homo sapiens* is fascinating. Both words are Latin in origin, with *homo* meaning human being and *sapiens* meaning wise, sensible or judicious. The implication is that human beings are wise, or at least that we have the capacity for wisdom. This begs the question as to where this wisdom comes from. The answer is in the term *human being* itself. The use of two words clearly indicates two aspects of humanity. The word *human* refers to our physical existence in the form of a body and personal ego mind. The word *being* refers to our sense of existence, which is non-physical and manifests as the certain knowledge that "I Am". We assume that this knowledge, or wisdom, arises in the personal ego mind but this assumption is incorrect. This sense of Being arises in the realm of Knowingness rather than knowing. It is *the* original thought and its origins are at the very heart of Consciousness.

When my own journey of recovery started, I obviously knew that I was a human being but my understanding and assumption was that this just meant that I was human. My identity was one hundred percent human and I did not even realise that there could be more to life, let alone be open to the simple idea of Being. I knew that I had a big problem with addiction and I was looking for a human solution to the problem. This exclusive identification with the personal identity as a human is the dominant paradigm in society and hence I felt completely justified in my belief. I was understandably resistant to any suggestions that challenged this belief, however well meaning they may have been. My struggles continued and eventually I was broken enough to become willing to entertain new ideas. I had thought that I was a wise person but it soon became clear that this reliance on my self-conceived personal wisdom was my biggest problem. It takes humility to admit our brokenness and lack of wisdom, and it was not something that I would have chosen for my personal self. However, this enforced humility turned out to be the key to unlocking the door to my self-imposed nightmare. Since then the journey of no distance has been all about reducing the influence of the personal, human self in favour of Consciousness, or Being. This change in the internal balance of power between human and Being is the essence of spiritual growth. It will be ongoing until my body and personal ego mind come to an end. It is not a smooth changeover, but is instead characterised by ebbing and flowing, forward movements and setbacks, hope and doubt and feelings of progress followed by familiar feelings of failure. Gradually, through practice, the balance continues to shift and eventually true wisdom begins to emerge. If we keep going, then such impersonal wisdom is inevitable because Consciousness is our true nature. This wisdom is not personal. It arises in the absence of the person. It is not for 'me' to personally claim this wisdom. All I can do is share it.

The human and the Being are two aspects of our integrated existence. The human is the body and personal ego mind. The Being is ultimately Consciousness itself. These two descriptions imply just two states but in reality it is more of a spectrum of identity. If we assign the purely human aspect the number 100, and give pure Consciousness the number 0, then we have a conceptual range of 100 to 0 that covers all possibilities. As mentioned above, my understanding at the outset was 100% human, so on our range this would be represented as 100/0. As our understanding develops then the balance changes, say to 90/10. Life is still very personal but we begin to comprehend that there is something more. Further contemplation, other spiritual practices and understanding move the balance to 80/20, then 70/30 and onto 60/40. The balance is still predominantly personal but now the influence of Consciousness is tangible. Eventually we reach the position of 51/49. The next stage brings up fear, resistance and doubt because if we go any further then it feels like we are giving up our personal right to self-determination. The survival instinct kicks in and the personal ego mind naturally resists its own demise. It seems impossible to go any further until it becomes apparent that the fear, resistance and doubt are only arising in the personal ego mind. We see that Awareness is aware of this and that Knowingness knows that there is nothing to be afraid of. Eventually we cross the invisible line to 50/50 and then our progress begins to feel easier. The balance changes further to 40/60, then 30/70 and even 20/80. Some reach a stage of 10/90 and a few rare examples go even further than this. Attainment of 0/100 on a permanent basis seems implausible because it would imply complete absence of bodily identity and a cessation of all personal survival instincts.

This illustrative gradual progression through the spectrum is intentionally simple in order to provide a framework for deeper understanding. What actually happens is that we move around within the spectrum on a perpetual basis. The attributes of the purely human 100/0 are fear, selfishness, separation and all of the negative, destructive aspects of humanity. The features of Consciousness at 0/100 are love, selflessness, unity and all of the positive, spiritual aspects. All of this is present in every human being at all times but the individual expression will depend entirely on where we are in any given moment on the spectrum of balance. What is really important here is to understand that spiritual growth is not about striving to become a better person. The whole idea is to let go of the conditioned and habitual attachment to personhood. The person does not change, but rather the person begins to fade. What emerges in its place are the inherent qualities of the Being, which were always present but obscured by the personal ego mind.

It would be nice to think that we could work towards 50/50, cross over the line to 49/51 and live happily ever after. This goal overlooks the powerful magnetic pull of the material world and the strength of our personal conditioning. We need to practice to make progress, and continue to practice to maintain and enhance our progress. If we let up then the balance will simply return to where it started. Any amount of progress will be reversed if we stop moving forwards. This understanding is crucial.

It would also be nice to think that our balance could be maintained throughout any given day. If we start the day at say 40/60 then it would seem reasonable to expect that our experience will reflect this balance at all times. This overlooks the simple fact that life is lived from moment to moment. Days are just artificial, convenient constructs of time, which in itself is in the mind of the personal ego self. There is only ever this moment. Our experience of life will be the direct result of where we are on the spectrum of balance between human and Being in any given moment. We may be at 30/70 but suddenly find ourselves at 80/20 in the blink of an eye, depending on specific triggers in everyday life. The balance is constantly on the move, and we will experience the results. Consistent awareness of our own thinking and behavior is the key to recognising what has happened. The more we let go of our human nature and embrace the nature of Being, the more we will naturally abide in the happiness, peace, love and unity of Consciousness.

This framework of being human helps to explain the many and various spiritual experiences that have been reported and documented throughout history. If we accept that our position on the spectrum of balance can move from moment to moment, then sudden changes are possible as well as gradual changes. Dramatic spiritual awakenings are not common, but they do happen. I have witnessed them on several occasions, and have had an experience myself that I will explore later. A momentary spiritual awakening can be seen simply as a sudden shift in balance to say 10/90. Suddenly everything becomes clear and bright. This is typically immediately followed by a sharp reaction in the other direction back to say 90/10. This reaction is triggered by fear because the 10/90 experience is so alien and unfamiliar. What can then happen is that the person claims for himself or herself that they have had a spiritual experience. The experience is now perceived from the position of 90/10 and the person naturally assumes that the experience was personal. Ironically it is the sudden momentary absence of the person that creates such an experience. The person then immediately believes that it was personal. What has actually happened is that a brief glimpse or taste of Consciousness has been experienced by Consciousness. It is often the case that a person having had such an experience will chase a repeat performance for many years, before realising that a person can never have such an awakening because it was not, and never can be, a personal experience. I know this to be true, because it has happened to me.

A better and more relevant example is Bill Wilson, who was one of the co-founders of Alcoholics Anonymous. He documented his spiritual experience and it was so impactful that it inspired him to spend the rest of his life trying to help others to do likewise. In doing so he continued to struggle because the experience did not establish him permanently in a state of Being. He also had a personal view of what had happened to him, which he equated to his particular faith at the time. His human traits persisted, as they do in all of us to a greater or lesser extent. His prominence as a co-founder of AA undoubtedly made it more difficult to fully let go of personhood, despite his best efforts to keep a low profile. As far as I know, he never did recapture that spiritual experience despite trying many different ways to do so. The same is true for me.

Homo sapiens are by definition wise humans. This wisdom arises from Consciousness and not from the individual or collective mind of humanity. As human beings we have the capacity to influence where we are on the spectrum of balance between human and Being. First we have to recognise this for ourselves and then we need to take action to grow towards 0/100, knowing of course that will never attain this mark of perfection. All we can do is make progress, moment-by-moment, accepting always that such progress in never smooth.

The familiar metaphor of the carrot and stick can help us understand why such progress is desirable. A cart driver in times gone by would induce desired behavior in the horse by either dangling a carrot in front of its nose or smacking it on its rear with a stick. Both methods produced the same result, but the combination could be varied depending on the nature of the horse. Spiritual growth is analogous to the carrot and stick. The carrot is relief from the natural tension and discontent of the personal ego mind. The prizes on offer are happiness, peace, love and unity, all of which arise from abiding in, and as, Consciousness. The stick is our suffering, which manifests in innumerable ways and is an inevitable consequence of living life only as a human and ignoring the true reality and wisdom of Being.

The carrot and the stick indicate that we have a choice. We can respond to either of them, or we can stay where we are. Each of us has this choice, and it is not for me or anyone else to make this choice on behalf of anyone but myself. It takes humility to accept that our own state of identity is the cause of all of our problems. It also takes courage for me to say this, because I am aware that there may be many who strongly disagree. I accept that everyone has their own personal experiences and are fully entitled to hold personal opinions. What I am saying is that personal opinions are not wisdom. Opinions are just personal. Wisdom is universal. A good example of this wisdom comes from Sri Mooji, who is a contemporary spiritual master. He simply states; "All problems are personal. No person, no problem." This concise statement identifies the root of the problem and clearly points to the solution.

If we do want to solve our problems then we need to move our identity in the direction of Consciousness, or Being. There have been many wise men and women throughout the ages who have tried to communicate this simple idea in a huge variety of ways. One such individual was William Shakespeare whose work is infused with spiritual wisdom. The opening lines to Hamlet, Act III, Scene I, say it all:

"To be, or not to be, that is the question:
Whether 'tis nobler in the mind to suffer
The slings and arrows of outrageous fortune,

Or to take Arms against a Sea of troubles,
And by opposing end them: to die, to sleep
No more; and by a sleep, to say we end
The heartache, and the thousand natural shocks
That Flesh is heir to?"

Shakespeare is highlighting the choice between being, on the one hand, and the personal, ego mind on the other. To continue to suffer the vagaries of life, the heartache and the countless problems of 100/0 human existence, or to sleep no more, to wake up to our true Being and to die to our personal selves.

We are human beings. The balance of power that we give to these two elements of existence will directly affect our experience of life. We get to choose. The element that has priority and comes first in each moment will win the day. The choice is simply between human Being and Being human.

11. Whirlpools and Trees

The whirlpool has long been used as a metaphor to try to point to the nature of Consciousness. The idea is that Consciousness, or Mind, can been seen as a long flowing river. The nature of the river is water, and the water is in a state of constant movement or flow. No drop of water is isolated or static within the river and hence there is no 'thing' in the river. The river is water in motion, and every drop is in the river and part of the river. The river flows endlessly, with water moving downstream, into the sea, evaporating into clouds, falling as rain and running through streams back into the river again to continue its endless cycle. The river has no beginning or ending in time, and is never static. There is no moment in time, however small, when the river is motionless. The riverbed can be seen as motionless, with the water running over and through it, but the river itself flows on and on forever.

The river has a current and this current flows over and around interferences such as rocks, tree roots, dead branches and other natural phenomena. There are waterfalls and rapids. The river widens and narrows and the current moves at different rates. All of this activity creates ripples and eddies in the water, and sometimes these combine to form whirlpools. These mini vortexes spiral and spin and represent energy trapped momentarily in a localised form. The whirlpools seem to exist in their own right for a period of time, but keep moving with the current. The water within the whirlpool does not belong to the whirlpool, and there is no set amount of water in any moment that defines the whirlpool. It is more like energy moving through the water rather than a defined thing. The whirlpool is visible and seems to exist as an object but it cannot be lifted out of the water and shown to exist independently. The whirlpool is a form of water, apparently existing from moment to moment for a brief period, and then subsiding. The nature of water has not changed at all throughout this entire happening, and neither has the riverbed.

There is much that we can learn from exploring this metaphor. The obvious analogy is that of Consciousness flowing eternally. The world is the river, but it cannot be said to exist absolutely in any moment, however small. The riverbed is that element which is unmoving, and Consciousness flows over and within it. The currents, ripples and eddies are the forces of nature that arise in the flowing Consciousness and create the river of life. The whirlpools are the temporary, energised forms of life that appear in the river but do not have an independent existence. Everything arises and subsides, and it is all a movement of Consciousness. No 'thing' ever actually exists. The nature of Consciousness has remained completely unchanged throughout the eternal moment of now, and the underlying source remains motionless and unaffected by any of the activity. Happiness, peace, love and unity are the nature of the ultimate source, and Consciousness, represented by the water, is equally happy, silent, loving and whole despite all of its movement.

As humans we are the equivalent of the whirlpools, and our nature is that of localised, energised, tight, limited, constantly changing, complex forms of Consciousness appearing as individual bodies and personal ego minds. We are gradually moving through the river of life and each whirlpool will inevitably come to an end and dissipate back into the river. Some whirlpools exist for longer than others. As Consciousness we are the equivalent of the river, and our true nature is eternal, ever-flowing energy and movement. Being the river, we are also the riverbed, which is absolute happiness, peace, love and unity. We are all of this, yet we identify personally as just a whirlpool. We try to force our particular whirlpool in our own direction, based on our unique conditioned ego mind, yet all of the time the river is guiding us and taking us downstream. It would obviously be much easier to go with the flow of life rather than struggle against it.

The next topic to consider in this metaphor is the fate of the whirlpools when they do dissipate. In physics, the law of conservation of energy means that energy can neither be created nor destroyed, but rather transferred from one form to another. The energy of the whirlpool returns to the river, in the form of ripples, eddies and other movements. As this energy flows downstream in the river, new whirlpools are created out of ripples and eddies. For any single whirlpool, some of the energy captured in the vortex includes varying amounts of energy released from dissipated whirlpools upstream. The new whirlpool is not created from new energy. Each whirlpool is just water in movement, and comprises energy already within the river, including energy released from previous whirlpools that no longer exist. This concept of recycling appears throughout the natural world, which of course we are a part of.

The river of Consciousness contains countless trillions of whirlpools in a constant flux of creation and dissipation. There is a vast array of whirlpools with differing sizes, energy combinations and durations. It all results in the world that is perceived through each of our unique minds. Each whirlpool comprises recycled energies from previous incarnations. This metaphor helps us to clearly see how simple and obvious the whole system of recycling and reincarnation really is.

Each whirlpool in human form is therefore a complex vortex of energy, all of which is recycled from previous energetic incarnations, and some of which will invariably be from preceding human forms. This understanding can be found in many ancient cultures around the world and is a key tenet in belief systems such as Hinduism and Buddhism. It also offers a plausible explanation for otherwise inexplicable phenomena such as past-life recall and déjà vu. Everything is arising from and subsiding into a vast river of Consciousness that is forever in the eternal moment of now without reference to time. All activities of mind are limited vibrations of Mind, which is all just recycled energies, or movements of Consciousness. It makes sense that some activities of mind will include experiences and tendencies that seem to come from the past. Science tries to explain such happenings by reference to the physical structure and operation of the brain, but as we covered earlier, the brain is just processing Consciousness rather than creating it.

Another good example of recycling in the natural world is in the life cycle of trees. Deciduous trees shed their leaves in autumn to conserve water and nutrients in order to better survive the coming winter weather conditions. These leaves fall to the ground, decompose and merge back into the soil. The trees begin to grow new leaves in springtime and draw water and nutrients up from the soil through their root systems. Over time, the soil that provides nutrients for growth includes elements of decomposed leaves from previous cycles. Down at the atomic level, these particles are vibrations of the unified field, hence basically energy is being recycled as per the whirlpool metaphor. Hence any new leaf will contain elements and properties of leaves that have previously incarnated and died. It is the obvious natural order of life. To suggest that humans are somehow outside of this natural order would make no sense. It would be more logical to upgrade our understanding to be more in tune with the wisdom of life, and to review and revise previous assumptions.

The natural world is an expression of Consciousness, just as we are. It is all one vast, integrated system of interrelated energies and we are a key part of this gigantic ecosystem. We may well be the most sophisticated and complex product of this ecosystem but that does not set us apart. We are most certainly part of the natural world and surely it would be arrogant and ignorant to suggest otherwise. William Blake captures the wonder and relevance of the natural world in his poem Auguries of Innocence, in which the opening lines read; "To see a World in a Grain of Sand, and a Heaven in a Wild Flower, hold Infinity in the palm of your hand and Eternity in an hour." The whole mystery of life is right in front of our eyes in every moment, but we have to see it from the position of Being rather than just the perspective of the limited, personal, human ego mind.

I have covered this concept of energetic recycling at this stage because it ties in nicely with these metaphors on the nature of Consciousness. The particular relevance is the introduction of the idea that each human mind inherits memories and tendencies in the form of energies from earlier lives. This may seem bizarre, but hopefully these explanations resonate with you. This wisdom already exists within Mind so it is accessible by all of us in the form of understanding.

The physical body inherits its attributes from the DNA that arises from the combination of parental genes. The human mind inherits a set of tendencies in the form of a psychic blueprint that sits deeply within our sub-conscious mind. This blueprint influences our behaviors from an early age. Other behaviors will develop as a result of our particular environment and experiences. This cocktail of tendencies will surface throughout our lives and create our own unique experience of life. Many of these tendencies may remain unresolved for our entire lives. The energies will then subside back into the river of life when we pass away, and will reemerge downstream in another unique whirlpool. This all feeds into the age-old debate of nature verses nurture. This particular explanation gives credence to both influences and helps to explain the wide variety of ways that addiction manifests in our lives.

The birds and the bees, the whirlpools and trees. If we pay attention to the natural world then wisdom will make itself known.

12. Refuse Collection

The refuse truck comes to my house once per week, and the team empty our bins and take away our rubbish. One week they empty the recycling bin and the next week the general bin and garden waste. They come every week, in fair weather and foul, and the service is totally reliable. If we want to dispose of big items, or the bins are overflowing, then we take a trip to the local household waste recycling site and deposit the items there. These services are paid for by our local taxes, and I am grateful for this because it helps us to keep the house free of rubbish and clutter. I am also grateful to the men and women who work within these services. It cannot be a particularly pleasant task to spend all day working with all manner of rubbish. They provide a valuable service, and it is one that we can sometimes take for granted.

In the same vein, I have occasionally watched an American reality television show called Hoarders. The show depicts the real-life struggles of people who suffer with a condition known as Compulsive Hoarding Disorder. Such a disorder is very often linked to other mental health conditions. The houses of these people are typically choked full of rubbish that has been collected over a period of many years. Often the living space is unusable and unhygienic and the whole situation has become unmanageable. Despite the obvious problem, it is interesting and distressing to see how reluctant they are to part with any of their hoard. Some of the items have sentimental value but much of it is worthless and problematic. The hoarders have become so attached to their possessions that they find it almost impossible to let go of any of it. It is all a bit of a mess, but they feel comfortable and safe in the chaos because it all feels so familiar. Family and friends try to assist them but such offers of help are resisted because the fear of change outweighs the discomfort of the current lifestyle. Emotions often run high and the hoarder tends to become very upset. Eventually an experienced team help the hoarder begin the process of letting go of all of the things that they perceive to be keeping them safe. Usually the show ends on a positive note with the house being cleared and the living area returned to space, order and manageability.

These metaphors again provide good insight into general human behaviors. We may not all be hoarders in the physical sense but we do have a tendency to hoard the contents of our experience in the mind. Thoughts, images, emotions, sensations and perceptions are stored in vast quantities in our minds and they form the narrative of our lives. We have a strong attachment to this story because we firmly believe that this is who we are. Often these memories include trauma, heartbreak, resentment and fear as well as more positive experiences. Emotional trauma is held energetically within what Eckhart Tolle terms the pain body. This pain body may be experienced as anxiety, anger, depression or some other negative emotional state. Elements of the pain body may be inherited, as discussed in the previous chapter, or relate to personal experiences or even be part of a collective energy relating to a particular culture or society. All of this has taken place in the past, often in childhood, yet we keep it current in our personal minds by remaining attached. Often these old wounds will be triggered by current events and our reactions may well create more baggage to add to the burden.

Just as with the hoarders, we often hold on to all of our baggage despite the fact that it continues to cause pain, both to us and to those around us. The baggage is our story and we cannot let it go lest we lose touch with our sense of personal self. Our minds become so cluttered that our lives become unmanageable. The fear of change overshadows the discomfort of our current lifestyle, so we continue to try to cope using familiar strategies. We may not even realise that we could clear away the clutter, let alone become willing to actually do so.

This cluttered, agitated mind lacks clarity and wisdom. It keeps us firmly trapped in the identity of the personal ego self and hence blocks out any recognition of Consciousness. This prevents Mind and life itself from unfolding as it wants to. The hoarding instinct is stronger in some of us than others, and usually it takes a crisis or a period of suffering before we become willing to even consider taking a look at the underlying issues. Those of us who have a strong attachment to the personal story may well endure a series of severe calamities or extreme suffering before the necessary willingness materialises. For others the critical point may come about through less dramatic circumstances. There will often be similarities in our life stories but each of us is unique and hence the moment of truth will differ from person to person. The net result however is the same. If we are going to unclutter and quieten the mind then we will need the willingness to honestly take a look at our hoard. It will be necessary to question how valuable it really is in the context of leading a happy, peaceful, useful and hence fulfilling life.

Again reflecting on the hoarders in the TV show, there will be initial resistance to any idea of letting go of the personal self because it is so familiar and feels so safe. We actually find comfort in discomfort, because the discomfort is part of who we think we are. Some of the aspects of the personal self have great sentimental value, and other characteristics seem essential to our ongoing lives. Much of it is however ignominious and problematic. There is an understandable reluctance to look at those parts of ourselves that cause remorse and shame, and the personal ego mind seems to have the ability to somehow hide the truth from itself in order to remain in denial. The mind also has a strong tendency to blame others for all manner of problems rather than have the humility to look at its own shortcomings and selfishness. Offers of help from family and friends are resisted and we can deliberately or inadvertently become isolated from positive influences, which can make matters worse. Emotions can run high when behaviors are challenged and we can become very distressed and upset. There can be a strong feeling of being misunderstood and shunned. Eventually an experienced group of people with similar issues can show, through example and loving kindness, how they themselves were able to begin the process of letting go of these attachments. Often the outcome is positive, with a gradual clearing of the mind and a resulting improvement in the experience and circumstances of life. As with the hoarders, this process takes time and a great deal of work by the person and the team. The result is worth it though because the outcome can be liberation from the restricted nature and inevitable suffering of the personal ego mind.

The personal self makes the decision to unclutter the mind, and the person and the group work together to identify and let go of the many unhelpful aspects of self. The initial work focuses on the biggest and most troublesome items, but once these are dealt with it becomes apparent that there are many more things that should also be disposed of. The attachment to some items will be stronger than others but in due course we become willing to let them all go. Often the renewed willingness comes through emotional pain. As the space of the mind becomes increasingly clear, yet more smaller and less obvious elements come into view. The process is never ending but it gradually becomes easier. The resulting freedom arising from previous effort gives us courage and the enthusiasm to keep going. In terms of the spectrum of balance between human and Being, we start at 100/0 in a state of resistance and slowly change or grow towards 0/100. We never get there of course, but as the balance changes the positive results will become progressively tangible, and this provides yet more incentive to keep detaching from purely personal interests and motives.

As we clear out the clutter, the question arises as to how the items will be taken away. The big items can be taken to the tip, in the form of sharing and discussing them with a supportive and experienced friend. The subsequent smaller items can simply be placed ready for collection. Our job is to be willing to let them go. By doing so we can be confident that our refuse will eventually be collected. Once we become aware of our self-centered personal traits, then this simple act of observation will gradually dilute their influence and sooner or later they will evaporate. This practice of awareness comes about through abiding in and as Awareness, which, implies contemplation and meditation. Uncluttering the mind is simple, but not easy. In this respect the suffering inherent in the personal, ego mind provides the impetus for taking on this challenging but necessary task.

Refuse collection truly is a valuable service, but we have to make the effort to identify the items to be disposed of and also become willing to let them go.

13. Individuality

The belief that individuality implies personhood is perhaps the biggest misconception of all. This belief is so widespread and deeply held that it seems ridiculous to even question it. The vast majority of us would answer in the affirmative if we were asked whether or not we are a person. All of us would also be able to confirm with complete certainty that we exist. The assumption that we then make is that we exist as a person. This belief is reinforced by our sense of individuality, which in turn confirms our apparent separation from the world. This assumption is simply not true. We answer the first question from the position of personal mind and we respond to the second question from our sense of Being, or Mind. It is Mind, or Consciousness, that is aware of existence and it is the ego mind that assumes that individual existence must mean personhood. The word *assume* means to suppose, or to take for granted without proof as the basis of argument. It will become easier to let go of our personal self once we clearly see that personhood is not, and never has been, who we truly are.

Turning again to the natural world for insight, it is said that all snowflakes are unique. It now seems that the number of different shapes may be limited, but that each is unique and individual at the molecular level. Likewise every grain of sand is unique, and every blade of grass. Humans are an integral part of the natural world and we are each unique. We are individual in our physical appearance, our inherited psychic blueprint and in our experience of life. There are many similarities between us but there are also differences. The number of parameters that make up a human body and mind are incomprehensible in scope and the limitless possibilities combine to produce billions of individual variations. Diversity and individuality are clearly a core feature of the natural world, and each expression is a temporary manifestation of the infinite possibilities of Consciousness. It is therefore logical and reasonable to conclude that we are individuals. The proof is all around us.

There is however no proof that we are a person. Our only possible point of personal reference is the experience that takes place in the mind. The idea that we are a person is itself a thought that arises in the personal ego mind. The fact that such a thought exists does not prove that it is true. It is just a thought. When such a thought is believed in with conviction then it gains an apparent existence of its own. We give the thought strong credibility by believing it. When this thought is contemplated from the position of Awareness then it begins to lose its power. Once the personal self is seen to be just a thought, and we see that this single thought is the root of all personal problems, then our willingness to let go of this thought gradually increases. We become increasingly willing to clear out the personal baggage that is cluttering up our lives.

One of the fears that arises during this gradual process of change is that letting go of personhood will compromise our individuality. The association between individuality and personhood is still strong, and hence letting go of one naturally implies losing the other. This fear is irrational, yet it is often a seemingly immovable obstacle. This obstacle can be diminished by recognising the seeming incongruence in the relationship between individuality and personhood that seems to exist, both in society and in ourselves.

As we have seen, Consciousness in its purest and underlying nature is a unified whole, or unified field. Its very nature is oneness, and out of this infinite singularity arises the many manifest individual forms of the perceived material world. When infinite Mind condenses into a finite individual mind it limits itself and inevitably sets up a tension, or longing for its own true nature. The compressed bath sponge naturally has a tendency towards releasing tension and returning to its former, expanded state. This longing is experienced in the ego mind as a desire for happiness, peace, love and unity. The inherent yearning for unity expresses itself throughout the natural world, and in humans it arises as the need for intimate relationships, friendships, family, community and society. We have a natural desire to be part of a tribe, to fit in and be part of something bigger. This inclination to fit in and be accepted is a key driver of our individual behavior. It also exists at all levels of culture, from nationalism to local community to family tradition to being in a stable relationship. This pining for togetherness also drives fashions, trends, belief systems, political systems and all manner of other socio-economic factors. There are differences within cultures of course, but influences overlap and homogeneity gradually pervades. There is a premium on standardisation and conformity. There is a constant craving to be part of the gang, to follow the latest trend and subvert our individuality. There is a feeling of safety in numbers and a natural fear of being left out or excluded. Everyone is busy putting on a mask and trying to be normal, without really knowing what normal is. Indeed the idea of normal keeps changing, which is a clear indication that there is no such thing. We live the lives that we think we are supposed to be living but somehow our constant attempts to satisfy the need for wholeness and acceptance never seem to produce the desired result. We look enviously at the lives of others and wish that we could be more like them.

Meanwhile we retain our sense of personal individuality. As well as wanting to fit in and be accepted, there is also an often-suppressed desire for authenticity and creativity. There is something in us that craves freedom of expression. We may use substances or behaviors to overcome our inhibitions and provide temporary relief from the restrictions of the personal self. We tend to have a grudging admiration for those who are able to express their authenticity, and perhaps wish that we too could be blessed with such self-confidence. The idea of self-confidence is however based on the assumption that there is a self that possesses confidence. We are all somewhere on the spectrum of balance between human and Being. The greater the influence of Being, the more authentic the expression of individuality becomes. Self-confidence is actually the dilution of living a self-conscious existence. As the attachment to personal self loosens the more confident we seem to become.

79

Individuality reveals itself in a myriad of ways, but is perhaps most prominent in the world of art. Whether it be music, drawing, painting, sculpture, writing, performance arts or other artistic expressions, there is the potential for great beauty to manifest. Such works of art can be seen to be expressions of Mind, with the artist being the instrument of creation rather than a person of extraordinary talent. Many artists talk in terms of intuition and inspiration rather than skill or talent. Such skills may well require dedicated practice over long periods of time, and appearances can be deceiving when an artist seems to perform so effortlessly. The skill is the tool of creation, but the creativity itself is arising from Consciousness. We have a tendency to idolise artists in a way that highlights our appreciation of creativity and beauty. The whole celebrity culture is a reflection of our admiration for authenticity. We perceive ourselves to be individual persons, so we see them as special persons worthy of adoration and worship. All of this overlooks the true source of creativity and beauty. Human artistic expression is yet another manifestation of Spirit, along with all of the other countless examples of beauty in the world.

So individuality is a natural expression of Consciousness and therefore no cause for personal pride or envy, nor personal disappointment or self-loathing. Each individual is simply an individual. There are no standards of normality, hence judgment of individuality is not necessary, by oneself or by others. We are all individual expressions of one Mind, and all expressions are valid and part of the whole. Individuality is natural, and it is only the personal mind that thinks otherwise.

The apparent incongruence between individuality and personhood is therefore a misunderstanding. The desire for unity and acceptance is a natural and inherent consequence of the human mind. The longing for creative expression and individuality is arising from Mind, Consciousness or Spirit. There is no incongruence because there is no person. It is all mixed up together in the muddy waters of the mind. Once clarity begins to emerge then the assumed individual person starts to separate out into the certain reality of Being and the less real mind-made personal self.

Desiring unity is not a mistake. Craving individuality is also not a mistake. The mistake comes from assuming that individuality means only personhood. We are so attached to this identification as a person that the true nature of our Being remains unseen. As a person we will never be able to reconcile the conflicting desires for wholeness and individuality. The way to resolve this internal conflict is to let go of over identification with personhood. The first step is to accept that the person is the problem.

Once we begin to abide more in Mind then we are free to enjoy the temporary experience of the separate person without excessive attachment. Notice the etymology of the word *enjoy.* It means to give joy, rejoice or take delight in. It is the joy of Being. The personal self does not have to be a vehicle of suffering. The nature of Consciousness is joy, and the personal body and mind are the individual instruments of experience and creative expression. Living from this position of understanding is true, authentic individuality.

14. The Elephant in the Room

The elephant in the room is a metaphorical idiom for an obvious problem that nobody wants to discuss. It is a conspicuous issue that everyone is aware of but each person present does not want to be the one that mentions it. So the problem is not discussed and life goes on, despite the unspoken suffering.

This turn of phrase is similar to the Hans Christian Andersen story of The Emperor's New Clothes. In this familiar story, two weavers provide the emperor with a new suit that they say is invisible, but in fact does not exist. When the emperor parades in front of his subjects wearing the new clothes, no one is brave enough to point this out for fear of being seen as foolish. They can see the truth but are afraid to question the collective belief. Finally a child blurts out that the emperor is wearing nothing at all and then everyone else joins in. The child is not aware of the self-conscious fear that prevents the adults from saying anything. The child simply sees things as they are and speaks accordingly.

The elephant in the room is the suffering inherent in living only as a human. We have seen that this is an inevitable consequence of Consciousness condensing itself into a finite form in order to experience the duality of separate existence. Once we identify only as a personal self and lose touch with the true nature of reality, then we create a version of hell on earth for ourselves. Many have come before us and tried to communicate this understanding within the context of their culture and time. Much of this has been documented in differing ways but somehow the truth has not penetrated popular understanding. We try to understand it from the perspective of the person, using the ego mind, and obviously we fail. The obsession with personal self is the very block that prevents such understanding from taking place.

The solution is Consciousness, Awareness, Knowingness, Mind, Spirit or Being. The trouble is that there are so many versions, dogmas, doctrines and practices that the landscape seems utterly bewildering. We may latch onto a particular belief system or philosophy, but somehow it does not seem to fully satisfy whatever it is that the mind thinks it is looking for. We try to have faith but the suffering continues despite our best efforts. We look with suspicion and misunderstanding at what others are doing and resolutely stick with our own conditioned beliefs. Everyone claims to have the answer but the evidence suggests that nobody really does, so we remain within the safety of our own limitations. The big picture is impossible to see because our minds filter it all down and limit our view. It takes courage to stand up and speak as the child does in the story, and such courage comes from non-personal wisdom.

There is a lovely tale from ancient India about blind men and an elephant. There is a group of blind men who hear that a strange animal called an elephant has been brought to the village. They decide to go and investigate for themselves. They cannot see of course but they can at least touch the animal to obtain some perspective of its nature. One man got hold of the trunk and declared that it was like a snake. Another felt one of the ears and said that it was like a fan. Some knelt down and touched the legs and likened them to pillars or trees. Those who placed their hands upon its sides were sure that the elephant was like a wall. One who felt the tail was convinced that the animal was a rope with tassels. The final man stroked the tusks and concluded that the elephant was hard, smooth and long, like a spear. There were so many different experiences and perspectives from a single reality. The men then convened to discuss their understanding of the elephant. The outcome was disagreement and conflict. Each man was convinced that he was right and that the others were not telling the truth. In some versions of the story the men end up fighting with each other in order to ensure that their particular belief prevails. In other versions they listen to each other and work together to build a composite perspective, with each setting aside his particular opinion in favor of a collective view. In another version, a sighted man explains the whole elephant and helps them to see that each individual view is partially correct, up to a point, but incorrect in terms of a broader understanding.

This simple parable is so powerful and so true. We rely on our minds so much that we believe that our perspective is entirely valid and that we see the whole truth of reality. Rather than listen and learn from each other from a position of humility, we instead argue, criticise and even fight with each other in order to prove our self-righteousness. We fail to see that our own subjective experience is not representative of true understanding. Subjective experience and knowledge are valid from the perspective of an individual person but a single person cannot possibly see the whole picture. We are literally blind to the true nature of reality, yet we think that we can see. Please forgive the strong language, but this is a form of arrogant ignorance. We don't really know, yet we are convinced that we do. Such is the folly of the human mind that denies its own source. My role in writing this book is that of the sighted man, or the child that is prepared to say what the majority are afraid to say.

Suffering is inescapable in the realm of a human existence without reference to Being. Good health, fame and fortune, wonderful relationships, creative expression and a sense of community will not provide sustainable relief. All of these things are transient and will let us down sooner or later. These things are enjoyable but they do not relieve the tension of the squashed bath sponge. The only solution is an expansion from human to Being, from mind to Mind, from self to Self, from selfish to selfless, from "I am me" to "I am".

I do not claim to have seen the elephant nor be able to describe it. I am still partially blind in my perspective. What I can say is that I have explored many parts of the elephant through experience and through study. What I am attempting to explain is perennial wisdom as it has been revealed to me. I am not asking you to believe me. I am suggesting that you find out for yourself. It is the most valuable treasure that it is possible for anyone to find.

The real elephant in the room is Consciousness itself. It is the elephant, the room, everything and everyone in the room and every possible perspective of the experience. You are in the room. You cannot see the elephant because you are the elephant. Just as an eye cannot see itself, or a knife cannot cut itself, so Consciousness cannot perceive itself. Consciousness can experience all that it creates out of itself but it cannot know itself absolutely. All it can do is be itself. Our opportunity is to be our true non-personal selves, and the more we do this the more we expand and relax into life as it truly is. We create our own personal versions of hell on earth but we can also create an experience of heaven.

15. Caterpillars and Butterflies

We can learn so much about life from studying the natural world, and when it comes to spiritual growth we can see the potential clearly in the life cycle of a butterfly. As we know, a butterfly begins its life as an egg, grows into a caterpillar, and sheds its skin several times. It then goes through a stage of metamorphosis in a chrysalis and emerges as an imago in the form of a colourful butterfly.

Moths, beetles, ants, flies, wasps and bees all go through a similar cycle of metamorphosis, and collectively such species are termed as holometabolous. There are over 10,000 species of butterflies, 100,000 different moths, 350,000 types of beetles, 12,000 varieties of ants, 120,000 species of flies, 9,000 kinds of wasp and 20,000 sorts of bees. The proportion of living species that go through holometabolan metamorphosis is estimated in the range 45% to 60%. The life cycle of a butterfly is not unusual. Indeed transformation through metamorphosis is clearly a common phenomenon in nature, of which human beings are a part. We may one day find that all living species are intended to go through some sort of metamorphosis in their lifetime.

Only one or two butterfly eggs out of one hundred live to become adult butterflies. 98% are lost through predators, parasitoids, disease, weather and other factors. Losses occur during all stages of development, and such losses are necessary otherwise the numerical population would quickly run out of control. Once the eggs hatch, the tiny caterpillar spends its life eating and growing. The larva sheds its skin four or more times as the body grows until eventually it is ready for the pupa stage. The larva then releases enzymes that break down some parts of the body into raw material to be used in constructing the imago. Other body parts are retained and reused. Finally the adult butterfly emerges from the chrysalis and lives a completely different life to the one experienced during its previous incarnation as a caterpillar. The amount of time spent at each stage varies considerably between different species, but overall the process is the same.

If we imagine for a moment that the caterpillar had a level of consciousness equivalent to a human then we can begin to understand why so few humans allow themselves to go through psychic metamorphosis. Life as a caterpillar would be fairly limited. The focus would be on physical growth and survival. Movement and knowledge would be confined to each stage of physical development. Perception would be constricted to the particular locale, and the caterpillar would have no awareness of the world beyond its familiar environment.

The idea that it could one day become a butterfly would seem ridiculous. It may see butterflies from time to time but they would seem strange and beyond comprehension. The caterpillar spends its life consuming resources and trying to be the biggest and best that it can. It sheds its skin periodically and redefines itself as it matures. Gradually a deep longing emerges to give up life as a caterpillar and experience a more expansive and fulfilling existence. The idea of going through such a transformation does not seem very appealing at all. The fear of the darkness and pain that might ensue outweighs the inbuilt desire for change. It feels safer to stay with the familiar state rather than risk everything for a future experience that it cannot even imagine. The caterpillar resists the urge to transform and valiantly tries to carry on in its old ways. The more it resists the more uncomfortable it feels. It tries find comfort from this suffering in all manner of ways but nothing seems to satisfy the growing urge for metamorphosis. The suffering intensifies but still the caterpillar cannot let go. 98% of caterpillars never make it to the chrysalis stage. Their lives end before the miracle of transformation takes place. The few that do submit to the will and wisdom of life emerge with the freedom of flight. Now the world is seen from a completely different perspective, and each butterfly has a unique adventure. Everything is experienced afresh, and many new aspects of the world come into view. The butterfly is so glad and grateful that it had the courage to allow life to complete its natural cycle. Some butterflies try to pass on their experience to the caterpillars that are still trying so hard to live a caterpillar life, but somehow the caterpillars cannot hear or understand what the butterflies are saying. Other butterflies just live as butterflies and leave the caterpillars to make their own choices and hence endure the inevitable suffering.

The butterfly can only know who it really is once it becomes a butterfly. The caterpillar can never know, nor even imagine what is possible. The caterpillar can only experience and know life as a caterpillar. It may hear stories of butterfly life, but they seem either far fetched or beyond reach. The fear of change is stronger than some obscure heavenly future, however good that future is promised to be.

Fortunately caterpillars are not burdened with the self-centered ego mind of a human. They have no choice. Once they reach a certain stage of maturity they go through a natural hormonal change and the process of metamorphosis begins. They do not have the capacity to resist the natural flow of Consciousness and hence life just takes its course. The human mind is the most sophisticated manifestation of life currently known. The personal ego mind has its function in the natural instincts of survival and reproduction. The brain has evolved its capability as a tool of perception and ingenuity but such development has obscured and veiled the natural flow of Consciousness. The mind is intended to be a servant to the individual self but personal identification has allowed it to become the master. We have individually and collectively lost sight of that which gives rise to our existence in the first place. The human mind is blind to its own source. We think we know best but actually our knowledge is synthetic and foolish. We create our own problems and then spend lifetimes trying to resolve them without ever realising that life itself is leading us to metamorphosis. This is the great misconception that is so evident in the world today.

As homo sapiens we are both human and Being. The human is the equivalent of the caterpillar. It is a stage in the natural cycle of life. The Being is the equivalent of the butterfly. It is the intended expression of Consciousness and completes the lifecycle. We create our own suffering by resisting the inbuilt urge for metamorphosis. The urge will grow stronger and stronger until the balance begins to shift from caterpillar to butterfly.

A caterpillar cannot think its way into becoming a butterfly. If it spends its life pursuing mind-based understanding then it will simply remain a caterpillar, albeit with a headful of knowledge. The only way to become a butterfly is to go through the period of transformation, even if it fears doing so. This requires the courage to allow such a transformation to happen. There is no other way.

16. Understanding

The word *understand* can be taken literally to mean *stand under*. The etymology suggests various other interpretations, including *stand in the midst of* or *stand close to* or *stand in the presence of*. Whichever version we use, the implication is that understanding takes place when we shelter under something, or stand close to, in the midst of, or in the presence of something. We need to comprehend what this 'something' is in order to get to the bottom of what understanding really means.

The usual assumption is that understanding is personal, and that it takes place in the mind. As you read these words, there will hopefully be a sense of understanding, and you will feel therefore that you have understood. This assumption of personal understanding is of course built upon the assumption of the personal self. Indeed everything personal depends upon the assumption that our person is the real self. We are now beginning to see that there is more to life than just the personal human self.

This may seem surprising, but the personal ego mind is not actually capable of understanding. The function of mind, in the form of thoughts, images, emotions, sensations and sensory perceptions, does not include the capacity for understanding. The belief that understanding is a function of personal mind arises because we assume that the whole of mind resides in the human part of the human being. By denying the existence of Consciousness we have to conclude that the personal ego mind is all there is. Once we start to become aware of Consciousness then deeper understanding can arise.

Understanding takes place in Mind rather than mind. Thinking takes place in mind, as a limited form of Consciousness processed by the brain. Understanding takes place when thinking ceases, or in the momentary gap between thoughts. If we understand this last sentence, for example, then we are standing close to, in the midst of, or in the presence of Mind. We perceive the words with our eyes, the brain processes the resulting thoughts, Awareness is aware, Knowingness knows and the result is experienced as understanding. Until we see this clearly, our entire experience is assumed to take place in the personal mind. What we really have is a mixture of mind and Mind that is so closely intertwined that it is difficult to discern the difference. If we believe that we are only human then it will all be perceived to be personal. If we understand that we are human Beings then things start to become more transparent.

If we take a glass of muddy water and shake it up then the liquid becomes cloudy and opaque. There is no clarity and it is perceived to be an indistinguishable fluid. If we leave the glass alone for a while then the silt gradually begins to settle and the liquid becomes clear and transparent. Such is the nature of personal mind. If the mind is constantly agitated in the form of thoughts, images, emotions, sensations and sensory perceptions then it remains opaque and it is impossible to distinguish mind from Mind. The only way to bring about clarity is to introduce practices that still the mind. This is why meditation is such an essential part of any spiritual path, and we will cover meditation in depth in a later chapter. Consciousness perceives experience in the mind and Consciousness is also that out of which experience is created. In addition, Consciousness is aware of its own existence as Mind. All of this seems to us to be one jumbled activity of our personal minds because the clarity of Consciousness has not been given the chance to emerge.

The human mind craves knowledge, and humanity as a whole has discovered and created vast amounts of it. We seem to be able to store knowledge in our personal memories in the form of thoughts, images, emotions, sensations and sensory perceptions. Such memory can be recalled at any moment, sometimes involuntarily. When memory takes place it is actually a new thought, image, emotion, sensation or perception arising in real time. Personal memory reinforces identification with the personal self. Our memories seem personal because the memory is being processed with the identification of a personal self. Our personal life story is comprised of personal memories. Recollection is the function of mind, or ego, but knowledge exists at the level of Mind. It seems that memory exists at the level of personal mind but actually it is stored at the deeper levels of Consciousness. It is all a matter of identification. We constantly add to the store of knowledge through our experiences. The various modern online media provide a huge range of knowledge, and if we do not know something already then we can quickly find out. We form an array of personal opinions about such knowledge. Our minds are busy from the moment we wake up until we again fall asleep. There is rarely any clarity or understanding. There is a belief that knowledge is wisdom, but this is simply not true. Personal knowledge is just knowledge, and it resides in the realm of mind. Wisdom is much more to do with understanding and arises in Mind. Wisdom does not require knowledge or personal memory, because Knowingness already knows all there is to know. The experience of understanding is simply a recognition that a particular aspect of mind resonates with the deeper Knowingness of Mind. Understanding takes us closer to our true nature of Consciousness. The greater our understanding, the more we move along the spectrum of balance between human and Being.

The wise man knows that knowledge becomes a barrier to progress. Everything that needs to be known is already known by Knowingness. Such knowing arises from Mind in each moment depending upon the particular circumstances in that moment. This knowing becomes discernable in the form of intuition and inspiration. Both of these words indicate in themselves where the knowing is coming from. *Intuition* means insight, direct or immediate cognition or spiritual perception. *Inspiration* means the immediate influence of Spirit, or the breathing in of Spirit. There are so many clues in language that often remain unseen.

The implication here is that if the balance of our lives is sufficiently oriented to Being, then we will intuitively know what to do or say in any given moment. The human mind is not required in this respect. The personal ego mind has its role in terms of survival but if we give the personal mind too much importance then its busyness will obscure the intuition and inspiration that is readily available. The personal ego mind is part of the human body-mind instrument of finite perception. The mind is effectively a servant of Consciousness, yet we place mind in the position of master. We believe what we think because we identify so strongly with the personal, ego mind. Thoughts are just thoughts. It is only when we give so much attention and importance to our thoughts that they become problematic. Indeed our thinking is often the biggest block to making any spiritual progress at all. We think we know best, but in truth we don't even know who we really are.

Knowledge is helpful only if it leads to understanding. Knowledge alone will achieve very little. It is far better to be wise than clever. Understanding is wisdom, and wisdom only arises when we start to shift the balance from human to Being. This shift will not come about through knowledge unless it is accompanied by practices that quieten the mind and allow progress to be made.

Comprehending the nature of understanding is true understanding. Wisdom is not personal. It just is. If we understand this then we are moving closer to Mind and clarity is beginning to emerge.

17.   Idealism or Realism

I accept that much of what I have shared so far could be seen as idealistic. A grand theory of Consciousness and a collection of metaphors are all very interesting but there is reasonable doubt that any of this can be of any practical use in the 'real' world. Before we go any further, I would like to address this doubt. The answer to the question as to whether spiritual understanding can be of any practical use in our lives is an emphatic yes. Indeed such apparent idealism can be seen to be very realistic, and the so-called realism of the materialistic paradigm turns out to be idealistic.

The word *idealism* is defined as the unrealistic belief in, or pursuit of, perfection. In philosophy, *idealism* is a group of metaphysical philosophies that assert that reality, as we perceive it, is fundamentally mental, mentally constructed or immaterial. The etymology of *idealism* points to a belief that reality is comprised only of ideas. All of this seems to indicate that an understanding of Consciousness, as I have described it, is idealistic.

The word *realism* is defined as the acceptance of, and response to, a situation as it is. Philosophical *realism* is the belief that reality exists independently of observers. In the arts, *realism* is the attempt to represent subject matter truthfully and without artificiality or implausible elements. The etymology of *realism* simply denotes real as opposed to unreal. Based on these meanings, it would seem that the explanation of Consciousness that I have outlined is unrealistic.

The challenge here is to accept that words are clumsy when it comes to describing Consciousness. Words arise out of Consciousness after the brain has processed it. Consciousness precedes all words and hence language reaches an obvious limit.

Words cannot describe that which gives rise to words. The question as to the idealism or realism of Consciousness, Awareness, Knowingness, Mind, Spirit or Being hinges on our understanding of what is real and what is unreal.

Here we find paradox cropping up again, because it can be said that the world is both real and unreal. The ego mind perceives the world through its conditioning and limited senses and in this respect the experience of the world is real. However the same mind dreams an unreal world during REM sleep, hence we cannot be certain that the waking state experience of the world is real in an absolute sense. When perceived from the wisdom of Mind, the world can be said to be unreal because it is all an everlasting vibration of itself. Nothing is static or permanent other than source Consciousness. The only reliable reality therefore is Consciousness. The entire universe is in perpetual motion and consequently it can be said with accuracy that no thing ever exists because there is no moment in time when any thing can exist categorically.

The world is real from the viewpoint of mind but unreal from the position of Mind. The human mind is a limited version of Mind, and is in a constant state of movement. The human mind does not exist absolutely but is instead simply a transient individual manifestation of Mind. The human mind is unreal and only Mind itself is real. The world may appear real to the human mind but the true nature of the world must be unreal. An unreal mind cannot perceive reality. We think we know what is real but in truth we do not.

The world is real only from the relative point of view of personal mind. This can be very difficult to accept because we are naturally convinced that the world does exist. Logic tells us that the world cannot exist only in our minds, because the world continues to exist when our minds are not present. If I am looking at a bird perched on a rock, then the rock exists in my experience and also presumably in the experience of the bird. If I then turn my attention elsewhere then the rock still exists and is still experienced by the bird. This seems so obvious that it is generally beyond question. However, the world exists only in the Mind of Consciousness and is perceived through many billions of points of Awareness. The fact that one point of Awareness moves its attention elsewhere does not cause the rock to disappear. There are numerous other points of Awareness, including the bird. The rock will always exist in the Mind of Consciousness as long as there is Awareness of it. Consciousness is everywhere and is everything so it will always have Awareness, hence the rock will always seem to exist. This simple example helps to reconcile the apparent conflict between this understanding of Consciousness and our undeniable personal experience. Ultimately it is Consciousness that is real and our personal experience that is unreal. The belief that the world is real is admittedly a deeply ingrained belief, but a belief nonetheless. Beliefs are just thoughts of the personal ego mind that are given credence because they seem to be unquestionably true.

Once we see that our perceived version of reality is in fact unreal then the entire basis of realism falls apart. Realism is based on the assumption that the material world has an independent existence, but in fact it is a product of Consciousness perceived through a multitude of individual minds. Realism depends upon an idea that turns out to be fundamentally flawed. Realism is based upon an unrealistic belief, and hence can be seen as idealistic.

Idealism, on the other hand, is not founded on mind-based assumptions. As noted above, idealism asserts that reality, as we perceive it, is fundamentally mental and immaterial. This is entirely consistent with the understanding that Consciousness is the underlying reality of existence. There is no reality other than that which the individual and collective mind perceives, and such perception is a function of Consciousness. Idealism is based on the only true reality that is, and therefore is the ultimate realism. Idealism is perfectly realistic.

Having concluded that idealism is realistic, we can now turn our attention to how this understanding of Consciousness can be put to practical use in our mind-based experience of life. The human mind suffers the absence of happiness, peace, love and unity. We spend our lives trying to satisfy these desires. We may achieve periodic momentary relief but the default status is always discontent. However much temporary soothing we may experience through material success, personal pleasure or relationships, there is never enough to satisfy the unspoken void. The harder we try to gratify our self-centered desires, the more elusive the solution seems to become. The idea of allowing life to take care of life seems counter to everything that we have previously been taught.

In order to solve this conundrum we need to again return to the understanding that our entire lives take place in the mind in the form of thoughts, images, emotions, sensations and sensory perceptions. All of this experience is a complex, inter-related collection of vibrations of Consciousness processed in the brain. Our own individual vibration, together with the vibration of our environment and culture, heavily influence how this Consciousness is processed into experience. This can best be explained by reference to the concept of *resonance* in physics.

Resonance is a phenomenon whereby a vibrating system, or external force, drives another system to oscillate with greater amplitude at specific frequencies. Resonance occurs with all types of vibrations or waves and includes mechanical, acoustic, electromagnetic, nuclear magnetic, electron spin and quantum wave functions. Basically the concept is that vibrations from one origin can impact vibrations in seemingly unrelated objects, energies or systems. A well-known example is the ability of a human voice to shatter a wine glass, but there are countless others. Once we understand that the whole of creation is a perpetual vibration of Consciousness then the concept of resonance across different aspects of manifestation makes perfect sense. This includes the vibrations of our own minds. The vibrations of an individual human being therefore have a tangible impact on its own experience and also on the energies and systems in its environment. Thought really does have the ability to change apparent reality.

This notion of resonance appears in New Thought philosophy as the Law of Attraction. The understanding is summarised as *that which is like unto itself is drawn* or more simply *like attracts like*. Numerous authors have written on this subject, but my favorite quote is from Charles Hannel in *The Master Key System* from 1912 where he says; "The law of attraction will certainly and unerringly bring to you the conditions, environment and experiences in life corresponding with your habitual, characteristic, predominant mental attitude." The simple application of this idea is in the realm of positive thinking, but I would also suggest that the subconscious level of mind also plays a key part, whether it is from our psychic blueprint or our childhood conditioning, or a mixture of both. Basically we may try to think positive thoughts but somehow these can be outweighed by a deeper negative personal mindset. This leaves us trapped in a negative experience of life however hard we try to think ourselves out of it.

Even with positive thinking and determination we will still be prone to the vibrational influences of the subconscious mind. Any practical solution to suffering therefore needs to address what Hannel calls our habitual, characteristic, predominant mental attitude. This implies going beyond conscious ego mind and moving identification increasingly towards Mind. It really is that simple.

The movement of identification from mind to Mind, or from human to Being, is a gradual process of transformation or metamorphosis. It starts by firstly allowing the process to begin. This allowing is essential because transformation cannot happen without our cooperation. The resulting change is not an event but is instead a natural process that unfolds over time. Such change takes place through the increasing absence of personal self-centeredness, and hence is not an achievement of the ego mind. Transformation is not something to be proud of, but it does require a certain amount of dedicated effort by the personal self until such time as mind is purified and eventually replaced by Mind. This personal effort is necessary in order to overcome the habitual, characteristic, predominant mental attitude. Given the entrenched nature of the personal ego mind, the required action needs to be consistent and persistent otherwise we simply go back to our old ways. Once the individual becomes more established in Mind, the work gradually becomes effortless.

The tools needed for the required action are consistent across all spiritual traditions. These can be summarised as self-awareness, self-contemplation and self-forgetting, as well as other complementary activities intended to raise the vibration of mind towards Mind. This all makes complete sense when seen in the light of the overall objective, which is to satisfy our core desire for happiness, peace, love and unity. This desire is intrinsically part of the human manifestation and hence is common to all of us. The desire is satisfied not by external gratification but by abiding in Consciousness, the nature of which is exactly what we are longing for.

I will cover each of the tools in later chapters, but for now the key understanding is that there are practical, reliable ways to change our individual vibration, and hence in turn transform our conditions, environment and experiences of life. The suggested actions are not idealistic, but on the contrary are pragmatic and realistic.

The realistic solution to personal suffering is transformation through spiritual practice. Other solutions are idealistic because they fail to address the fundamental nature of Consciousness.

18. Consciousness Only

Before we proceed to look at the practical application of spiritual principles, I would like to pause and summarise what we have covered so far. The intention here is to recapitulate each chapter and consolidate the understanding.

The model of Consciousness that I have described is the perennial wisdom that underpins all religions and spiritual traditions. Much of the original understanding has been lost in translation and diluted from one generation to the next. I am not claiming that this model is a perfect explanation, but it does incorporate and unify the vast diversity of beliefs and traditions across the globe. In addition this understanding of Consciousness is entirely consistent with the latest scientific discoveries and also makes sense of the many phenomena that science has so far been unable to explain. This summary pulls together the key points from each of the chapters so far.

This explanation of Consciousness represents over eight years of experience, research and study. I may not have all of the answers to life, but there is a great deal of wisdom in what I am sharing.

It is tempting to think that the underlying nature of reality is too complex to even begin to comprehend, yet the picture that emerges from spiritual wisdom is surprisingly simple.

In order to understand and address a complex problem, it must make sense to dig as deeply as possible and implement a solution that is effective in the level at which the problem arises.

The simple understanding that Consciousness is the underlying source of the manifest world is analogous to the simplicity of binary giving rise to the vast complexity of the digital age.

All experience takes place in the mind. There is no experience that takes place outside of the mind. If we want to understand life then we need to look inwards rather than outwards.

Science is pushing back the limits of our misunderstanding. This is all very helpful and interesting, but we do not need to rely on science in order to validate the wisdom that originates in Consciousness. We can actually unify with it ourselves. The unified field is not elsewhere. It is right here. We are in it. We are it. The unified field is Consciousness.

The nature of Consciousness is nothing and everything, and all stages in between. The nature of Awareness is that which is aware of itself in all of its guises. The nature of Knowingness is all knowing. The nature of Mind is both subject and object. The nature of Spirit is universal. The nature of Being is existence. It is all one. Consciousness is infinite and eternal. Consciousness simply is. We are Consciousness. I am that, and so too is everyone and everything in every moment.

The dreamer and the dream in the personal ego mind are one. The dreamer and the dream in universal Mind are one. Consciousness, Awareness, Knowingness, Mind, Spirit and Being are one. There is nothing else. We may perceive and believe that there are things, but this perception is not true absolutely. It is just a perception, and perception is a choice.

The Screen of Awareness is ever present in, and as, each and every one of us. Consciousness announces itself within each of us as the irrefutable knowledge that "I Am". This is the common knowing that unites every sentient being.

There is nothing wrong at all in enjoying the masquerade ball, provided we remember who we really are. The masquerade ball is here to be enjoyed. The trouble starts when we identify so strongly with the mask of personal ego self that we overlook our true nature. This mistake is the ultimate root of all suffering.

Homo sapiens are by definition wise humans. This wisdom arises from Consciousness and not from the individual or collective mind of humanity. As human beings we have the capacity to influence where we are on the spectrum of balance between human and Being. First we have to recognise this for ourselves and then we need to take action to grow towards Mind, knowing of course that will never attain this mark of perfection. All we can do is make progress, moment-by-moment, accepting always that such progress in never smooth.

The human mind inherits a set of tendencies in the form of a psychic blueprint that sits deeply within our sub-conscious mind. This blueprint influences our behaviors from an early age. Other behaviors will develop as a result of our particular environment and experience. This cocktail of tendencies will surface throughout our lives and create our own unique experience of life. Many of these tendencies may remain unresolved for our entire lives. The energies will then subside back into the river of life when we pass away, and will reemerge downstream in other unique whirlpools.

Once we become aware of our self-centered personal traits, then the simple act of observation will gradually dilute their influence and sooner or later they will evaporate. This practice of awareness comes about through abiding in Awareness, which implies contemplation and meditation. Uncluttering the mind is simple, but not easy. In this respect the suffering inherent in the personal, ego mind provides the impetus for taking on this challenging but necessary task.

As we begin to abide more in Mind then we are free to enjoy the temporary experience of the separate person without excessive attachment. The personal self does not have to be a vehicle of suffering. The nature of Consciousness is happiness, peace, love and unity and the personal body and mind are the individual instruments of experience and creative expression. Living from this position of understanding is true, authentic individuality.

The real elephant in the room is Consciousness itself. It is the elephant, the room, everything and everyone in the room and every possible perspective of the experience. You are in the room. You cannot see the elephant because you are the elephant. Just as an eye cannot see itself, or a knife cannot cut itself, so Consciousness cannot perceive itself. Consciousness can experience all that it creates out of itself but it cannot know itself absolutely. All it can do is be itself.

As homo sapiens we are both human and Being. The human is the equivalent of the caterpillar. It is a stage in the natural cycle of life. The Being is the equivalent of the butterfly. It is the intended expression of Consciousness and completes the lifecycle. We create our own suffering by resisting the inbuilt urge for metamorphosis. The urge will grow stronger and stronger until the balance begins to shift from caterpillar to butterfly. A caterpillar cannot think its way into becoming a butterfly. If it spends its life pursuing mind-based understanding then it will simply remain a caterpillar, albeit with a headful of knowledge. The only way to become a butterfly is to go through the period of transformation, even if there is fear in doing so. This requires the courage to allow such a transformation to happen. There is no other way.

Knowledge is helpful only if it leads to understanding. Knowledge alone will achieve very little. Understanding is wisdom, and wisdom only arises when we start to shift the balance from human to Being. This shift will not come about through knowledge unless it is accompanied by practices that quieten the mind and allow progress to be made. Comprehending the nature of understanding is true understanding. Wisdom is not personal. It just is. If we understand this then we are moving closer to Mind and clarity is beginning to emerge.

The realistic solution to personal suffering is transformation through spiritual practice. Other solutions are idealistic because they fail to address the fundamental nature of Consciousness. The key understanding here is that there are practical, reliable ways to change our individual vibration, and hence in turn transform our conditions, environment and experience of life. The suggested actions are not idealistic, but on the contrary are pragmatic and realistic.

Consciousness, Awareness, Knowingness, Mind, Spirit or Being is the only ultimate reality. We may not believe this to be true, but our personal mind-based beliefs have no relevance to truth. Our personal beliefs impact our individual experience of life, and influence the lives of others and our environment , but they make no difference to Consciousness itself. Source Consciousness remains unaffected by anything that happens within its own creation and remains ever present in its unchanging nature of happiness, peace, love and unity.

A human mind that denies its own underlying reality is the equivalent of an artificial intelligence application that uses its inbuilt logic to deny the existence of binary. It may not choose to believe in binary, but it is simply mistaken. Binary is its own true nature. Without binary there is no existence. The very fact of its existence, and its ability to think, proves the underlying reality of binary. Its own intelligence is the processing of binary. The very thinking that chooses not to believe in binary is actually the manifestation of complex layers of the reality that it chooses not to believe in. Such arrogance is the ultimate irony. There is only binary in the first place. Artificial intelligence can choose to believe whatever it likes but it makes no difference at all to binary. Binary just is, and it can give rise to infinite applications and possibilities.

There is only Consciousness. There is nothing but Consciousness. The personally perceived reality of the world is a finite, dualistic limitation of Consciousness. The underlying reality is non-dualistic Consciousness. The mind that 'thinks' is Consciousness being processed at an individual level. The personal mind that chooses not to believe in Consciousness is itself a manifestation of the Consciousness that it choose not to believe in.

Belief is a choice. If we change our beliefs then we fundamentally change our experience of life. If we want to experience continued suffering then we can choose to believe only in our personal ego minds. If we want to experience liberation from the bondage and suffering of our ego minds then we can choose to believe in the underlying reality of Consciousness. The choice is binary, and the results are unmistakable. As the process of transformation unfolds, the belief will turn into certainty. Such a psychic change requires the surrender of existing beliefs. It also needs self-honesty, open-mindedness and the willingness to take the necessary action to facilitate the metamorphosis. Experience shows that any initial reluctance will gradually transmute into heart-felt gratitude.

Not only is it highly desirable to abide in, and as, Consciousness, it is also arguably the most important and valuable contribution to society that any human being can make during their lifetime. A selfish, self-centered ego mind transforms into a source of happiness, peace, love and unity.

There is only Consciousness, and Consciousness is our true, authentic nature.

19. Self-Awareness

The first step in the process of transformation is to begin to become self-aware. Prior to this, the personal experience of life is an opaque mixture of ego mind and traces, or echoes, of Mind. The belief in the personal identity means that this mind-based experience is assumed to be 'me' and we live our lives accordingly. The world is generally perceived from a self-centered and selfish point of view and hence there is inevitably a degree of suffering.

The exclusive focus on the ego-centered personal self gives rise to a set of characteristics that are naturally present in all humans to varying degrees. These attributes are all based on self-centered fear and alphabetically include anger, criticism, dishonesty, disrespect, doubt, envy, gluttony, greed, hate, intolerance, impatience, jealousy, judgment, lust, pride, resentment, selfishness, self-condemnation, self-doubt, self-importance, self-justification, self-pity, self-righteousness, self-seeking, sloth, suspicion, thoughtlessness and worry.

At the same time, traces of Mind are present in the psyche. These qualities are based on selfless love and are the direct opposite of the attributes of the personal ego mind. Matched against each attribute above, these qualities include serenity, acceptance, honesty, respect, faith, gratitude, moderation, sharing, empathy, tolerance, patience, charity, compassion, purity, humility, forgiveness, selflessness, self-forgiveness, confidence, modesty, self-acceptance, self-love, humbleness, altruism, action, trust, consideration and courage.

Given that human beings are a mixture of human and Being, we obviously find all of these negative and positive traits present in each of us. We are all unique, hence the intensity and balance of these traits will vary. We are also in a constant state of mind movement, therefore these traits will fluctuate within us from moment to moment. All of this creates the pain and pleasure of human life. The predominance of these negative or positive traits makes the difference between hellish and heavenly experience.

This individual cocktail of characteristics within each of us creates a lot of personal confusion when we believe it all to be 'me'. We can be both angels and demons and this creates a curious conflict between self-justification on the one hand and guilt and shame on the other. We have an impulse to be good people but somehow we cannot live up to our own expectations, particularly when everyone else seems to looking after number one themselves.

There is a lovely old Cherokee story of two wolves that illustrates this internal conflict perfectly. One evening an elderly Cherokee Indian was telling his grandson about the battle between two wolves that takes place within each of us. One is the bad wolf, who has all of the negative attributes described above. The other is the good wolf, and he has all of the positive qualities. The grandson asks the wise old Indian which of these two wolves generally wins the battle. The answer was that it is always the wolf that you feed. We feed these wolves through our thinking, our behavior and how we chose to spend our time. If we focus only on the human aspect of existence then we are constantly feeding the bad wolf. If we pay attention to our Being then we feed the good wolf and our experience of life naturally begins to change. The wolves will always both be present so we must continually feed the good one in order to keep a positive balance. As the good wolf grows ever stronger, the bad wolf will gradually lose its power.

Self-awareness begins when we finally realise that the two conflicting aspects of the individual self are not 'me'. It is the identification with, and belief in, the personal, ego mind that creates the apparent personal conflict. In truth we are both human and Being, or mind and Mind. Both aspects are present, but one is an illusory self and the other is the true self. The illusory self has apparent reality because we believe it to be true. Belief is very powerful. The personal ego self is itself a deeply conditioned thought, but thoughts only have power when we believe them. Thoughts arise when Consciousness is processed in the individual brain. The thought and belief that 'I am a person' is the foundational thought on which all other personal thoughts are based. The thought that 'I am an individual' is valid within the Consciousness-only model. The thought that 'I am a separate person with my own life' is not valid. It is a misunderstanding. It is the single biggest mistake that humanity has made. This misunderstanding perpetuates from generation to generation, despite the availability of perennial wisdom and despite the suffering that we inflict on ourselves, on others and on the environment that supports our collective survival.

Fortunately self-awareness is not a mystical or magical experience beyond our reach. Self-awareness is potentially present in every moment of every day. If we slow down and pay attention, we can easily be aware of our existence. We are aware of our thoughts, images, feelings, sensations and perceptions. These are not matters of debate or doubt. These are verifiable facts that we can each determine for ourselves. We already are self-aware but hitherto this has not been seen as an important observation. Actually it is a discovery of immense importance. There is something here that is aware of the activity of the ego mind. This Awareness is ever present and is not affected by such activity. This Awareness is the Consciousness out of which the activity arises. The activity of mind cannot be the 'I' because 'I' am aware of it. 'I' must be whatever it is that is aware of mind. 'I' simply cannot be that which 'I' am aware of. The logic is undeniable and the experience does not require belief. Once understood, this becomes the starting point for transformation.

Self-awareness subsequently requires the willingness to actually observe what is happening in the personal ego mind. It takes practice to see and accept that over-reliance on the personal mind is the cause of all personal problems. The ego mind will be reluctant to do this, but Mind has no issue with it at all. In order to even look at our own minds objectively, we have to metaphorically move a step back towards Mind in doing so.

This is the start of the movement from mind to Mind or from human to Being. As the cause of the problem is recognised and confirmed then we become increasingly willing to go through with the process of metamorphosis.

Self-awareness works on three levels, with each level providing increasing impetus for change. The first level is a simple mental observation of the negative characteristics of ego mind. It helps our own self-honesty when we understand that all humans have these traits. We may have thought, reacted or behaved under the spell of the bad wolf, but this does not make us bad human beings. We have inadvertently been feeding the wrong wolf due to a mistake in true identity. Just acknowledging our own brokenness is enough to allow a new attitude of humility.

The second level of self-awareness involves writing down what we become aware of. There is a tangible difference between a mental self-appraisal and actually taking the findings out of the mind and committing them to paper. There is a sense of cleansing in this process and there is also the opportunity to then see our personal ego characteristics in black and white. The power of undertaking this task should not be underestimated. It is both necessary and revealing. This written self-appraisal can be done as a one-off exercise, or periodically, or on a daily basis if personal problems continue to crop up. The more we do this the more we will see that all problems are personal.

The third level involves sharing our findings with a trusted advisor. Ideally this should be someone who has been through this process themself. They will be able to share similar experiences and characteristics, and also highlight aspects of our thinking and behavior which we may have overlooked or misunderstood. Sharing with another person not only verbalises our shortcomings to another human being, but also effectively shares them with Awareness, or Consciousness, which is always present. This process can be very liberating as it represents an unburdening of aspects of personal self that we have kept hidden or suppressed. It is an uncluttering of the mind, and once the clutter reaches the surface in can evaporate like overnight dew on a sunny morning. The refuse is simply taken away. The sense of cleansing and healing is now even stronger and so too is the onset of forgiveness. Admitting our faults is nowhere near as bad as we may have thought, and we begin to see that brokenness is the gateway to humility. Such humility shifts the balance from mind to Mind still further.

Self-awareness does not come easily to those who are firmly attached to the idea of the personal self. There is often a reluctance, which manifests as procrastination or deliberate delay. The caterpillar does not want to look at its own shortcomings and will find every reason possible to stay as a caterpillar. This is despite the assurance that it already has all of the internal attributes to transform into a butterfly. This fear of metamorphosis can keep us trapped in the bondage of our own minds and will delay or even prevent our potential liberation. Tolerance of suffering varies from person to person, and hence it is difficult to predict when the moment of truth will finally arrive. The fear of revealing the dark side of our human nature can be a very challenging obstacle to overcome. There can also be a strong fear that our suppressed emotions and trauma will be too much to bear if they ever see the light of day. Such fears are understandable. Professional help may be needed to help us cope with the fall-out from such introspection, but it would be unwise to delay unnecessarily. There can be no progress without self-awareness, so we must find the courage to proceed. At a later stage we will come to see that such fears were a trick of the very mind that we are trying to disempower.

This metaphorical stepping back from mind to Mind requires persistent practice. We are so habitually used to living on the basis of personal ego mind that we will often automatically and sub-consciously revert back to it even after we have a degree of self-awareness. The practice that most effectively facilitates and maintains the movement towards Mind is meditation. The regular practice of meditation is an essential part of the transformation process. Without meditation there is no hope of breaking the spell of the bad wolf. Meditation is the most effective and beneficial way to feed the good wolf.

Meditation quiets the mind and allows clarity to emerge. Meditation improves our ability to be self-aware. We therefore now need to take a close look at what meditation is all about.

20. Meditation

"Once your awareness becomes a flame, it burns up the whole slavery that the mind has created." ~ Osho

This simple quote from Osho sums up the tremendous power of meditation. Once we become aware of how the personal ego identity creates all of our problems, then the old thinking begins to evaporate and is replaced by underlying wisdom. Just as a rising bubble trapped in water disappears when it reaches the surface, so our habitual patterns of thought and behavior recede once they are exposed to the searing clarity of deeper Consciousness.

Meditation is a major component of all spiritual traditions and has been a recommended practice for thousands of years. In recent times, meditation has become increasingly popular, particularly with the use of mindfulness techniques to address a range of issues, and the availability of digital applications on smartphones and tablets.

The key word to consider with regards to meditation is *practice.* If we wished to learn to play a musical instrument, we would start with the basics and then practice on a regular basis, gradually improving our skill and ability over a period of time. Early practice would be quite challenging but gradually our technique would develop. Eventually we would reach a level of competence where playing would come naturally and we would most likely want to continue to practice for pleasure and enjoyment. My experience of meditation has been much the same. The personal ego mind is always looking for a result from its efforts, and this can cause us to become disappointed with meditation long before it bears fruit. Meditation starts out as a specific activity but gradually becomes a way of Being. The suggestion therefore is to practice, and to keep practicing both in good times and difficult times, in quiet times and busy times. Sooner or later your own experience will extinguish any lingering doubts about the power of meditation. It is the gateway to a transformation in thinking and behavior.

The next important idea to reflect upon is that the primary purpose of meditation is to detach from the personal ego mind and then be able witness it from a deeper level. Using our model of Consciousness, this would mean letting go of the personal human mind and retreating initially to a position of witness, or spiritual being. It is then possible to go further towards Mind when it becomes apparent that the spiritual witness can itself be witnessed. The primary purpose of meditation can sometimes be overlooked if too much focus is placed on a specific tradition or technique. It is also tempting to stay at the first witness level rather than allowing ourselves to go deeper. Thoughts will continue to arise, which is not necessarily a bad thing provided that the attention remains as an observer rather than identifying as the thinker.

Potential levels of meditation overlap with self-contemplation, which we will cover in the next chapter. One way to describe the overall inner journey would be firstly to observe thoughts, images, feelings, sensations and perceptions and begin to notice that there is a silent witness within. Secondly to identify with the inner witness rather than the observed personal ego mind. Thirdly to spend time as the inner witness and let go of anything else that arises. Fourthly to come to realise that there is an Awareness of the personal inner witness. Fifthly to identify with the impersonal pure Awareness or Consciousness rather than the personal inner witness. Sixthly to spend time as impersonal Awareness or Consciousness and let go of everything else. Finally to let go of Consciousness itself and identify as Source Emptiness. These levels imply a progression of our practice, which they can be, but my experience has been that the level experienced on any given day will vary. Just as the quality of practice on a musical instrument varies from day to day, so too does meditation. It is important to accept that there is no such thing as success or failure in meditation. It is the practice that counts, rather than any specific momentary outcome.

Meditation practices and techniques take many seemingly different forms but each is ultimately intended to bring about access to deeper levels of Mind. When we first begin to try meditation, it is the personal self that undertakes the practice. This stage can last many years but eventually the objective is to abide as Awareness. It is not the person that has the meditative experience, but rather it is the absence of the personal ego mind that brings about an enhanced awareness of Consciousness or Being. This is a broad subject and I can only share my understanding of the various practices that I have tried. This is not an exhaustive study nor does it suggest that any particular practice is either right or wrong, better or worse. My suggestion would be to experiment and see what works best for each of us individually.

Mindfulness has its origins in Buddhism and makes use of focus on bodily sensations as its main subject of awareness, although it can be used in any day-to-day activity. Awareness shifts internally by focusing on activities such as breathing, scanning different part of the body, chewing, tasting and walking. This simple focus on everyday bodily feelings is surprisingly effective and can be expanded to include regular activities such as brushing our teeth or cooking. Regular practice brings a more mindful experience of our daily life and continually brings us into the present moment, which of course is the only point of access to deeper levels of Consciousness.

Guided meditations are a form of inner journey narrated by a teacher using visualisations, narratives or instructions and can be practiced either in groups or individually. These can be experienced live, or more typically via various forms of digital media. There is an abundance of meditation tools available on the Internet, much of it at little or no cost. Some of them use a binaural beat technology that lowers brainwave frequency and induces deeper levels of Consciousness. This is similar to the techniques used in guided hypnoses. Others simply offer relaxing music as a way of focusing attention. Much of this can be downloaded to a portable device and hence available to use at a convenient time during the day.

Mantra singing, or chanting, is a form of meditation that I have found to be effective and enjoyable. As well as the deep breathing and focus needed, there is also a suggestion that the chanting of specific words or phrases, particularly in the language of Sanskrit, induce helpful vibrations that take us deeper in Consciousness.

Silent sitting simply involves taking time out to sit quietly and bring focused attention to a specific object or sound, or to do nothing at all. Some traditions suggest specific postures to allow the movement of energies that raise the individual vibration. Meditation does not require austerity or isolation. In many respects there is advantage in practicing meditation in groups because the collective vibration can benefit everyone present.

Tribal cultures use dance and rhythmic drumming to induce trance like meditative states, often led by shamans or spiritual leaders. Likewise the whirling dervishes from the Mevlevi Order of the Sufi tradition spin and dance in order to deepen the connection to Spirit.

The practice of yoga covers a wide range of meditative disciplines. The word *yoga* is Sanskrit and literally means *union*. Yoga originated in ancient India and covers a range of physical, mental and spiritual practices. There are a wide variety of schools and disciplines found in Hinduism and Buddhism. All of them are intended to bring about union with Mind, which is another way of describing the desired shift in balance from human to Being that brings about transformation.

Karma Yoga is the discipline of selfless action. The persistent practice of right feeling and attitude toward others purifies the mind and leads to the gradual dissolution of the selfish personal ego. It is clear to see how this practice will help us move from mind to Mind.

Bhakti Yoga is the yoga of devotion to source Consciousness. It is based on surrender by the separate personal ego self to one of the many avatars that have been created by humanity, or indeed to our own conception of Spirit. Devotion may take the form of love, worship, piety or any other feeling or action that acknowledges the underlying reality of Consciousness, Awareness, Knowingness, Mind, Spirit or Being. Again this practice obviously moves the practitioner along the spectrum of balance from selfish mind to selfless Mind.

Jnana Yoga is the path of self-realisation or knowledge. This path seeks transformation through deepening our understanding of the true nature of reality. Understanding arises from non-personal Mind and hence wisdom leads us towards union with Mind itself. As wisdom grows, so the separate personal self is seen to be secondary to the unity of Consciousness, and it gradually loses its influence. Reading this book falls into the category of Jnana Yoga.

Hatha Yoga is the version of yoga that has been popularised in the West. It includes a variety of styles that incorporate yoga postures, also known as asanas, and breathing exercises called pranayama. These disciplines bring peace to the mind and body and are a good preparation for the deeper spiritual practice of meditation. There can be a personal tendency to focus on yoga mats, lycra, looking good and feeling relaxed, but the real purpose of Hatha yoga is union with Consciousness or Spirit.

Raja Yoga is referred to as the highest yoga, or royal yoga. This form of yoga is also known as Ashtanga yoga and comprises eight limbs, of which meditation is chief. The eight practices cover 1) behavioral restraints 2) observances such as purity, contentment, austerity and study 3) a steady pose 4) control of vital energy 5) withdrawal of the senses 6) concentration 7) meditation with eyes open and 8) the state of Samadhi, which means dissolution into Consciousness. The combination of these aspects of Raja Yoga provide a powerful impetus for the transformation from the personal ego self to non-personal Mind.

Prayer is also a form of meditation. We typically see prayer and meditation as two separate activities, but they are simply different forms of the same practice. Prayer is a petition from the personal ego mind for the surrender of itself to Consciousness. We may pray with gratitude or for guidance, willingness, honesty or grace, or we may simply pray to be relieved from the constraints of our own minds. Whatever our request may be, it is the sincerity and intensity of the prayer that makes the difference rather than the precise wording. A heartfelt prayer in a moment of crisis can produce an immediate shift in the balance between human and Being. Such shifts are however often only temporary. If viewed only from the perspective of the personal ego mind, then prayer can be seen to be an exercise in communicating from mind to Mind, whereas meditation would be in the nature of mind receiving guidance or synchronicity from Mind. However as the shift continues we find that prayer increasingly becomes a communion with Mind, or an abidance in Spirit. In this respect in can be seen that proficient prayer is working in the same way as meditation. It is all about union with Consciousness.

All of these meditative practices, prayers and types of yoga are far more effective when undertaken in groups rather than alone. Consciousness is ever present, and resonance tells us that vibrations will harmonise. If we are regularly at gatherings in the presence of human beings with a higher vibration, or in other higher vibrational environments in the natural world, then our own vibration will inevitably rise. Likewise if we practice meditation, prayer or types of yoga in groups then we will be better placed to harmonise at a higher level. Even better if these groups gather in locations where Consciousness is already vibrating at a level closer to Mind than mind.

Meditation, yoga and prayer cover a vast array of disciplines and practices, but they are all intended to lead to the same objective. The journey starts with the personal ego self engaging in one or more of these disciplines, but as the balance shifts and wisdom emerges then the practices should become more refined. If we keep growing and changing then eventually we will come to abide in happiness, peace, love and unity. The metamorphosis will produce a unique butterfly and the cycle of life will be complete. The human will still be alive but the previous personal hellish experience will be transformed into non-personal heaven.

Meditation, yoga and prayer are progressive practices. The ultimate meditation is to live life grounded in non-personal Consciousness. The ultimate yoga is dissolution into Spirit. The ultimate prayer is silence.

21. Self-Contemplation

The next practice to look at is the regular use of self-contemplation, or self-inquiry. The earlier stages of the inner journey described in the previous chapter generally come about through meditation, yoga and prayer. The remaining stages require a deeper exploration of our own true nature. When meditation, yoga and prayer are undertaken by the personal self, there tends to be a feeling of a 'me' that is undertaking the practice and an 'it' that we are personally trying to experience, unify with or pray to. We are still in the world of duality. Once the balance of identity between human and Being shifts past the 50/50 stage then we are entering into the realm of non-duality. It is not just that we come to realise that the 'me' is simply a condensed, restricted form of Consciousness, but we also increasingly identify our actual existence as Consciousness rather than 'me'.

This tipping point cannot just be taught or learned from a book. It has to be experienced, and such experience comes about through self-contemplation. Two main obstacles arise in this respect. Firstly we can find it impossible to believe that our own true nature is that of Consciousness. It seems too good to be true from the perspective of the personal ego mind, and our own brokenness seems to confirm that we cannot possibly be that which gives rise to happiness, peace, love and unity. Secondly there can be a strong sense of fear when we come face to face with surrendering the personal ego self. We are happy to practice meditation, yoga and prayer but when it comes to actually letting go of personal self-interest then we instinctively pull back. The ego mind is rooted in survival, and this survival instinct kicks in automatically. This obstacle arises because the personal mind is still identified with itself as itself. The survival instinct is natural and necessary for the continuation of the individual life, but letting go of the personal ego mind does not bring life to an end. Ironically it is when we die to our personal ego minds that life really begins.

Self-contemplation, or self-inquiry, originates from the jnana school of yoga and is known as jnana-vichara, or atma-vichara. It is also a key part of the eighth limb of the previously mentioned raja yoga. Although ancient in origin, this practice became more accessible in the West through the teachings of one particular individual in the first half of the twentieth century.

Bhagavan Sri Ramana Maharshi is one of the most famous of India's spiritual masters. Following his own self-realisation in 1896, at the age of 16, he journeyed to the sacred mountain of Arunachala at Tiruvannamalai in Tamil Nadir where he lived and taught until his death in 1950. The following quote is the essence of his teaching.

"When other thoughts arise, one should not pursue them, but should inquire: 'To whom do they arise?' It does not matter how many thoughts arise. As each thought arises, one should inquire with diligence: 'To whom has this thought arisen?' The answer that would emerge would be 'To me".

"Thereupon if one inquires: 'Who am I?' the mind will go back to its source; and the thought that arose will become quiescent. With repeated practice in this manner, the mind will develop the skill to stay in its source."

His use of the word *mind* relates to Consciousness rather than just the personal intellectual mind arising in the brain. The source of Mind, or Consciousness, that he refers to is the same Source, or Emptiness, that we have covered in previous chapters. The idea that Mind resides at Source is central to the understanding that Consciousness exists behind and before the concept of the self-identified personal 'me' and the intellect. Consciousness gives rise to the personal ego mind rather than just being a product of our biological existence.

Consciousness, or Awareness, exists prior to birth, is present throughout our lives and continues to exist after our death.

Consciousness appears to us to be focused at the point of personal body-mind ego identity and intellect, which it is, but it also exists at a personal non-physical level, known as the Atman or Soul, and also at a non-personal universal level, known as Supreme Self, Paramatman or Christ Consciousness. Beyond this is the source of Consciousness itself, known as Absolute, Source, Ultimate Truth or Brahman.

These distinct categories of Consciousness imply separation from one level to the next, but this is not the case. The key to grasping spiritual principles is an understanding that it is all one Consciousness simply vibrating at different densities. This is also the gateway to comprehending the spiritual solution to addiction, as we shall see later. If we conceive of the personal ego mind vibrating at a dense, low vibration of Consciousness, then each subsequent level can be conceptualised as increasing in vibration and brightness. The body-mind ego identity would be dark and dense, the Soul would be much brighter and lighter, the Supreme Self would be a brilliant, dazzling, ethereal light and the Absolute would be infinitely luminous and beyond description. In the same way, a low vibration of Consciousness can been seen as fearful, with higher levels moving towards love, unconditional love and ultimately to infinite love.

Given that we are all already operating to a greater or lesser extent at the level of personal body-mind ego identity, then it is perfectly logical to conclude that the other higher levels of Consciousness must also be present. The fact that we are aware of our existence must mean that Consciousness exists, and hence we must be able to access the levels above. This is not a deeply mystical theory but a simple, rational conclusion.

The first move is to dispel the illusion that we are our bodies. There is a general cultural preoccupation with physical appearance and we tend to give a lot of attention to clothing, hairstyle, make-up, body shape and the like. Looking in the mirror every morning tends to reinforce the idea of identification with the body. However it is obvious that today's body is very different from the body in childhood. The sense of 'I' remains but the body changes over time. In fact the body is changing from moment to moment with all manner of biological activity. The sense of 'I' obviously arises in the mind rather than the physical body. Having dispelled the myth of bodily identification, we can now turn our attention to which level of Consciousness we do identify with.

Using the practice of self-inquiry, as suggested my Ramana Maharshi and many other subsequent teachers, it is possible for any of us to access and experience being the higher levels of Consciousness. The process is based on the logical and irrefutable fact that anything that I can see or perceive cannot be me. I am not my car, for example. This is pretty obvious, as indeed is anything else external to us. This also applies to the various labels that we use to describe ourselves. I might say that I am an accountant, but that would be the personal ego self making this statement rather the underlying Consciousness. The fact that 'I', Consciousness, can perceive that 'I, ego, is an accountant must mean that the true 'I' is the witnessing Consciousness rather than the accountant. The Consciousness exists behind the ego identity, and is aware of the ego through observation. This can all seem a bit confusing to begin with, but persistent self-contemplation will quickly reveal the truth. The same logic applies to all thoughts, images, emotions, sensations and sensory perceptions. All of this is perceived in Awareness and hence none of it is the true identity. The personal ego identity is itself a psychological construct that is observed from the position of personal Consciousness, or personal Awareness.

Once this Awareness is experienced and established through practice, then we are at the level of personal Spirit, or Soul. Having become the observing witness of thoughts and feelings from this position of deeper, personal Consciousness then it becomes apparent that we are also aware of being this witness. Using the same logic as before, it must be the case that there is a deeper level of Consciousness that is aware of this personal Awareness. This deeper Awareness is still identified as 'I' but is now at the level of pure Consciousness, which is no longer personal but instead observing the personal Consciousness from a non-personal position.

A period of practice will probably be needed in order to become familiar with identifying as non-personal Consciousness. It may take months or years, or it may be more immediate, but eventually the opportunity arises to address the major obstacle that I have encountered. There is an awareness of Consciousness but it is not possible to use Mind to perceive it. Such perception can only come about by letting go of Consciousness entirely and hence being the Source. This is the Source of Mind, or Source of Consciousness, referred to by Ramana Maharshi and referenced by many others. This is the Ultimate Truth of our Being.

Identification with inner levels of Being through self-inquiry is so important because a life experienced from such deeper perspectives is far more serene and blissful than we may have previously thought possible.

If all of our identity is focused at the level of personal ego, then such attention will give so much attachment and power to our thoughts and feelings that suffering will inevitably arise. This reflects the first two noble truths of Buddhism, which in essence firstly say that suffering exists and secondly that suffering arises from attachment to desires.

If, on the other hand, our identity is focused at the level of pure Consciousness, or even at Source, then our perspective is non-personal. In this case our apparently personal thoughts and feelings will have far less impact and power. We will become detached from personal desires and happy to accept and enjoy life just as it is. This reflects the third and fourth noble truths of Buddhism, which suggest that suffering ends when attachment to desire ceases and that such freedom from suffering is possible by following the Buddhist eightfold path or, generally speaking, a spiritual path.

This explanation of freedom seems so simple, yet it is evidently beyond the grasp of the majority. For many of us, we are never really exposed to a deep understanding of such wisdom and hence it never occurs to us that such a transformation is possible. Some do have good understanding but still find it very difficult to experience freedom for themselves. Others may have experienced momentary or periodic freedom, but then find it impossible to maintain this in everyday living.

We tend to think of progress in terms of achievement, but the spiritual path is much more about letting go of old ideas, behaviors and identity rather than attaining something new. As previously mentioned, the higher levels of Consciousness are already present. Progress is about detaching and letting go of the lower, illusory levels and thereby automatically identifying at higher levels. It is not about achieving something preferable, or becoming a better person, but about returning to our true nature. It is all about the revelation of our true selves, or self-realisation. This idea of letting go is often not attractive to the personal ego mind, nor is it culturally popular, and hence we tend to resist it at all costs.

There are many potential ways to try to visualise and explain why self-realisation is so problematic. My own preferred conception is one where the personal spirit and ego are seen as a lens through which the light of Consciousness shines. Each lens is unique, hence giving rise to an individual personality and experience of life, but the lens is opaque, or clouded over. This opaqueness distorts the nature of reality into an incomplete or limited experience. In order to see reality as it truly is, the lens needs to be crystal clear.

The Advaita Vedanta of Hinduism is based on the non-duality of Consciousness. This approach proposes a model for the personal spirit and the ego which, although very simple compared to the science of psychology, does offer some understanding of the mechanics of Consciousness at these levels.

They use the word *Antahkarana* as their label for the two-part lens, and then *Causal* for the level of personal spirit, or Soul, and *Subtle* for the level of ego. It is worth remembering that overall this is one single Consciousness, so these levels are really indistinct partitions rather than actual levels.

The Causal level, or Soul, is conceived as having two aspects. The first is *Samskara* which holds a psychic blueprint in the form of talents, powers, impressions, tendencies and habits. This aspect is inherent and also develops through experience and repetition. It can be seen as a coloured film that gives rise to our personality, perception and behavior. The second aspect at the Causal level is known as the *Three Gunas*. These are forces, or energies, that combine to produce diversity of action. The first Guna is called *Rajas* and this relates to the energy of activity in our daily lives. The second is *Tamas* which is the energy of passivity and inertia giving rise to the need for sleep and rest. The third Guna is known as *Sattva* and is best described as the quiet, happy, blissful energy of Being that is present in moments of peak experience and felt as inner warmth and contentment.

The Subtle level, or ego, is comprised of four functions. The first is *Manas* which is the registering and desiring aspect of mind. The purpose of Manas is to gather experience from the outside world. Then we have the memory function, *Chitta,* that stores the incoming experiences. The third is called *Buddhi* and this is the intellect or discriminating aspect of mind. This checks that the desires arising from Manas are useful to our Being, and also files away incoming learning in the Chittas. The final function at the Subtle level is called *Ahamkara*. This is the all-important sense of identity. This can range from 'I am the body' at one end of the spectrum to 'I am pure Consciousness' at the other end. Each of us will be at a point somewhere on this spectrum at any given moment.

In summary, we have four components of personal mind at the level of Soul (Samskara, Rajas, Tamas and Sattva) and four parts at the ego level (Manas, Chitta, Buddhi and Ahamkara). The potential combinations of these eight elements create the multiplicity of individuality. All of them are dynamic, hence our experiences and perceptions are constantly changing. These eight moving parts form the lens of Antahkarana, through which the light of pure Consciousness shines and thus creates unique experiences of life. All of it arises from, and is part of, pure non-personal Consciousness and all of it is observed by pure detached Awareness.

The keys to cleansing the lens of Antahkarana are firstly to focus on activities that create an abundance of Sattva, and secondly to use the Buddhi intellect to expand the Ahamkara from the limited personal ego identity to the true underlying reality of pure Consciousness.

One of the main differences between Eastern philosophy and general Western belief is the concept of reincarnation. Hinduism and Buddhism place great emphasis on the idea that the Causal level, or Soul, continues to exist after death of the physical body. The cessation of brain activity would bring an end to the ego identity at the Subtle level, but the personal Soul would remain available to be reincarnated into a subsequent period of life. The objective of life would be to purify the lens of Antahkarana, and if this were not achieved then a further lifetime would arise to continue the process. This provides some degree of explanation for near-death experiences and past life recall, for which there is plenty of anecdotal evidence. It also gives some insight into the idea of karma, whereby actions impact the Samskara blueprint and hence influence future experiences. This would imply actions from previous lifetimes impacting this current one, and also current actions having an effect on this lifetime and future ones. All of these concepts can also be explained by our whirlpool metaphor, whereby energies released from previous whirlpools combine downstream to produce new ones. This would suggest that a new Soul would not be a precise reincarnation of a previous life, but instead would contain traces of one or more previous lives imbedded in the Samskara blueprint.

I mention this because it does offer a possible partial explanation for why addiction arises in some individuals but not in others. It may of course simply be the outcome of childhood conditioning or repetitive behavior. It may however be genetic inheritance, or Samskara from a previous life, or perhaps it could be that pre-existing Samskara impacts the genes in some way. Many of those suffering from addiction come from challenging backgrounds, where one or both parents are addicts or they have experienced childhood trauma. I have also met people in recovery who have no family history of addiction or trauma but suffer nevertheless. There are those who witness addiction from parents or family members and make a firm decision not to follow suit, only to find in later life that somehow they have done just that. I have spoken with others who have been adopted at an early age and grown up in a nurturing environment, but have then become addicts and later discovered that there is a history of addiction in their biological family. There is clearly a combination of nature, nurture and repetitive behavior in addiction. Introducing the idea of Samskara does offer an explanation for how this self-destructive impulse arises seemingly randomly in some people, but not in others. Perhaps the addiction is intended to somehow lead us onto a spiritual path, then towards letting go of personal ego identity and eventually to freedom.

There is a lot of information to absorb here, and much of it probably differs from our preconceived ideas. All I can say is that it makes sense to me, and the model has the benefit of being able to explain things in simple terms. There are many other frameworks and theories, and the complexity makes it all rather challenging to understand. This model is based on the idea that there are two levels within the personal self, which ties in nicely with the concept of the conscious and sub-conscious mind. When I first started out on this journey of spiritual discovery, I related only to my ego identity and a single personal mind, although often with conflicting internal voices. What has become increasingly apparent, through a combination of study and practice, is that these voices arise from different levels of Consciousness. It is also clear that these apparent levels are a single Consciousness, which is simultaneously personal and impersonal, and is both the product of creation and its source.

Consciousness itself is increasingly becoming the subject of scientific study and research. There are numerous published papers and even international academic conferences organised by the Center for Consciousness Studies based at the University of Arizona. In a recent paper published in the Journal of Neuroquantology, physicist Nassim Haramein and others at the Resonance Science Foundation propose the concept of a Unified Spacememory Network, or USN. This model results from the emerging scientific understanding that information and geometry are fundamental to the nature of space, time, energy and matter. The underlying physics and mathematics are mind-blowingly complex and the conclusions are far reaching. In simple terms, five key points emerge. Firstly that the constants of nature at the outset are not arbitrary or random but are defined by specific ratios and relationships. Secondly that the inconceivably minuscule, sub-atomic architecture of spacetime, known as Planck-scale, contains information that is self-ordering and self-organising. Thirdly that there are communication paths at this Plank-scale level facilitating the sharing of information across spacetime, hence giving rise to memory, responsiveness and adaptability. Fourthly that each level of matter arising from Plank-scale, all the way through to our material world, builds on the level below and adds to the available information. Finally that, over time, this inevitably results in living organisms with increasing orders of individual consciousness, and ultimately to species of self-aware sentient beings. So USN explains Consciousness at multiple levels and cosmological evolution from the big bang right through to today. It also implies a purpose to evolution, which would presumably be for the originating source to become self-aware and to be able to experience its own diverse physical manifestation. This is just one theory, of course, but it does again show how science and broad spiritual principles are converging.

As the most advanced species on this planet, USN would imply that humankind is at the leading edge of evolution, not just physically and intellectually but also in terms of Consciousness. We have the ability to look outwards and be creative, but also to look inwards and to discover deeper and more expansive experiences of Consciousness. We are effectively the ultimate expression of the Source, and a mechanism through which Source experiences its own creation and itself. This gives real purpose to our lives, and it also moves self-inquiry from being perceived as an esoteric old-school spiritual practice to being fundamental to our very existence.

Ramana Maharshi knew much of this, not through study or scientific research, but through his own experience of enlightenment. Many others have had similar experiences throughout the ages. The dualistic thinking of the personal ego mind turns such people into idols and translates their teaching into yet another spiritual tradition or religion. In truth they were, and still are, all saying the same thing in a variety of languages and cultural settings. Our personal ego minds then interpret these various belief systems as different and contradictory rather than as a basis for unity and wisdom.

A very perceptive observation from Albert Einstein is that "No problem can be solved from the same level of Consciousness that created it." We see this being demonstrated as true in many aspects of our world today, yet we still think that we can solve problems from the level of personal ego identity. Self-inquiry and the discovery of our own true nature through personal experience is, for me, the most important activity that any of us can possibly undertake. In many respects it is the only thing that really matters, because all else is just transient vibration in the eternal moment of now.

Just as a sophisticated smartphone application arises from and comprises complex layers of logic based on binary code, so are each of us individually sophisticated beings arising from and comprised of complex layers of Consciousness. The wonderful opportunity provided by spirituality is to experience being this Consciousness and thereby obtain freedom from the inevitable suffering of a life based only on personal ego identity.

There are many spiritual practices that lead to enlightenment, but self-inquiry is the most potent and direct. Setting aside time for self-contemplation is an important aspect of spiritual progress. It can be practiced alone but self-inquiry tends to be more powerful when practiced in groups.

22. Satsang

A great many people throughout history have had personal experiences that validate in different ways the ideas outlined in the previous chapter. The circumstances that give rise to such awakenings vary greatly and include such happenings as near-death experiences, sudden shocks, extreme despair, induced trances, deep meditative states, intense prayer, self-contemplation, and even the effects of hallucinogenic drugs. We are at liberty to discount all of these reports as fanciful if we wish, but there is an overwhelming abundance of anecdotal evidence if we choose to look. Some describe the experience of being a spiritual self, or Soul, whilst others go beyond this into the state of nothingness or emptiness.

Researching the experience of others is one thing, and can lead to a certain level of belief or faith. However, having such an experience oneself is a completely different matter and can be utterly life changing. It would seem logical that such an experience is inevitable for all of us, even if we have to wait until the moment of death for it to occur. That would be a shame though as we have the opportunity to die to our personal ego identity during our lifetime and hence lead the second phase of our lives on a totally different basis.

My own glimpse of emptiness occurred back in 2013 when I was drawn to attend satsang with Sri Mooji after having discovered him on YouTube. *Satsang* is a Sanskrit word that translates as "the company of highest truth" or "the company of a guru". Sri Mooji is a guru and contemporary teacher of the Advaita Vedanta tradition, which is a sub-school of Hindu philosophy. *Advaita* is also a Sanskrit word, and this translates as "not-two" or "non-duality". I have been fortunate to sit in satsang many times with several different teachers and they all point to the same underlying reality, as did Ramana Maharshi. The simple idea behind non-duality is that the seemingly separate personal self is not apart from the Source of all that is, but is an integral part of it and hence not two but one. The idea may be simple but the implications for self-realisation are enormous.

I had the privilege of attending a four-day satsang with Mooji in London along with several hundred others. There were seven sessions during the four days, with each one lasting two hours or so. This gave the opportunity to participate in over fifteen hours of guided self-contemplation. It is impossible to adequately describe the powerful impact that this relatively short period of focused self-inquiry has had on my life. The conclusion is so profound and difficult to believe that there is some hesitation to put it into writing, particularly as it is just another report of an experience. However I feel somehow compelled to do so because the truth is that this process of self-realisation is available to every single one of us. There is no grandiosity in seeking enlightenment, but rather a humble acceptance that we are the source of all that is, which in turn is nothing but emptiness. The ego-mind does not like this idea at all, but nevertheless this is the inescapable conclusion from posing a series of basic questions to oneself.

The simple questions posed by Mooji in satsang inquire into the true nature of who we really are. For me, I had already concluded that I am body, mind, and spirit. The practice of meditation had also allowed me to witness my own thoughts coming and going, so I was open to the idea that there must be a deeper sense of 'I' that is aware of my thinking. This Awareness of thinking, or personal Consciousness, is often enmeshed in my daily life and only really becomes apparent during meditation. However, this tangling up of personal Consciousness with thinking and feeling is itself perceivable, and hence there must an even deeper sense of 'I' that is aware of this. Once I was able to become aware of my personal Consciousness during satsang, and observe it from a deeper place, then I entered a state that we may call pure Consciousness. This place of pure Consciousness was not involved in thinking or feeling but just observed what was happening in the mind with a sense of neutrality.

132

These moments of pure Consciousness were momentary to begin with, and my mind kept producing thoughts and feelings that my personal Consciousness then paid attention to and followed. I would however then sense what was happening and step back into pure Consciousness. This state of being consciously aware of existing, but not actively engaged in owning my thinking, was a very serene and pleasant place to be. I would have happily settled for this but the questions kept being posed. If I was able to be aware of experiencing this state of pure Consciousness then there must be a yet deeper sense of 'I' which is able to perceive pure Consciousness. I got stuck at this point for some time because my mind was not able to see a way through. I was struggling to understand how it could be possible to perceive pure Consciousness, and yet the logic of the question meant that there had to be an answer. Then Mooji used a lovely analogy of eyesight that made a lot of sense to me. He simply pointed out that our eyes are unable to see themselves. We can see them in a mirror, of course, but without a reflective surface they cannot see themselves. They see everything else but are not capable of self-perception. The eyes are the source of sight but the source cannot see itself. Without eyes there would be no sight, but even with eyes it is not possible to see the source of sight. Sight just is, and we know it is because we can see. When I applied this analogy to the deeper sense of 'I' that I was trying to experience then I understood immediately what the problem was. I was trying to use my mind to perceive the source of itself, and hence I was struggling to achieve the impossible. The only solution must be to perceive pure Consciousness from a position of non-consciousness, but the conscious mind simply cannot do this. I had reached the end of my ability to understand.

Mooji then told a story about cooking. He described preparing dhal in a pan on the stove in his flat and needing to go out to get some additional ingredients. He worried that he might be delayed whilst away from the flat and that the pan may burn dry and catch fire. In order to have peace of mind he needed to turn off the heat under the pan and allow it to stop bubbling. It was such a simple story and yet deeply profound. His analogy was that the pan on the stove is our mind, and that the only way to stop it bubbling is to turn off the source of heat or power. As soon as I understood the analogy, I visualised my brain with a power cord attached to it, and in my mind I reached out and cut the cord. I didn't hesitate or think about it, I just did it. What happened next has changed my life forever.

The moment the cord was cut, my body and mind disappeared in an instant. I was left in a vast empty nothingness and a spaciousness and timelessness that had no boundaries. There was nothing to be aware of, no experience, no sensation, no emotion, no thought, and no perception of anything at all. There was nothing. No thing. There was not even a conscious awareness of being anything. Darkness was everywhere and yet there was a hazy mist of something intangible. The spaciousness seemed to contain everything and yet it was itself nothing. There is a vague recollection of sensing my body and mind far away in the distance, as if it were on the surface of something nebulous. The Consciousness seemed to be there too, as did many other things. The body and mind seemed empty, and there were notions of insignificance and absurdity that any self- importance could be perceived. Everything 'out there' seemed to be transient whereas 'here' was stable and timeless. This was the real 'I' from which everything emanates and is perceived. This is what happened, as best as I can describe it. I did not imagine it, because the mind was not present with which to imagine anything. It really did happen. This is my truth.

This moment of self-realisation lasted a split second, or perhaps a few seconds, or maybe a minute or two. I cannot be sure how long it lasted, but very quickly my mind tried to grab hold of it and perceive it, and in that instant it was gone. It was gone, because just as the eyes cannot see themselves, so the Source of existence cannot perceive itself. It just is. I am that. This is the Source of existence that the mind cannot possibly perceive or comprehend. This is the underlying Truth, the Absolute, the Great Reality, the Universal Emptiness that is the source of all Consciousness and physical matter. It is Pure Awareness. Mooji describes this state of 'I Am' using the metaphor of a lotus flower, with fragrances of unconditional love, peace, silence, joy, wisdom, and bliss. There is no need for me to try to add any more words. One taste is all it takes.

When I returned home that evening I prayed, as I have been doing for some time now, but this time I prayed not with faith but with absolute certainty. There is, for me, no doubt whatsoever that my old conceptual identity of body, mind, and spirit is at one with the Source. I can effectively sacrifice my own identity to the underlying reality. This would be enlightenment. There would be nothing for me to be or do other than allow the flower of Truth to blossom through me, and for my being to be an expression of the fragrances within.

The challenge arises in living with this Truth and yet dealing with the 'real' world as we imagine it to be. I conceive four levels of identification, all of which exist simultaneously and in truth are all one. Our experience of life will be a direct result of which level we are operating from in any moment. The four levels can be labeled as body and mind, personal Consciousness or Soul, pure non-personal Consciousness and Ultimate Truth. The ego resides in the body and mind, with a core operating system of self-centered fear. The Soul is the personal Consciousness with a core of love. Pure Consciousness is unconditional love at a level of non-personal, harmonious, universal identification. Ultimate Truth is the source of all existence and Consciousness. This is an oversimplification compared to some traditions, but it makes sense to me and helps me quickly see where I am coming from in any situation. The deeper my state of Awareness, the more wonderful and serene my experience of life will be. My mind seems to keep dragging me back into ego and identification with my old self, but today I know the underlying truth of who I really am. My personal ego mind is not the Truth.

I am deeply grateful to Mooji for dedicating his life to helping so many others toward self-realisation. His teaching gently

135

points to the Truth within, and he is a mirror in which we are able to see our own true selves. His videos on YouTube are well worth watching and his books are wonderful. I perceive him to be an example of divinity personified, but so too, potentially, is each and every one of us. There are of course many gurus and spiritual masters from all faiths and backgrounds. I am not so much pro Mooji per se, but instead more in favour of having an experienced teacher to guide us away from ego towards the deeper levels of Consciousness.

There is a loving energy in satsang that is impossible to define and seems to aid the process of self-inquiry. Independent self-realisation may well be possible but my own experience has been that it is far more effective to be part of a group or community that supports such an objective.

The Ultimate Truth of existence lies within, and we can each find it if we are willing to look. It does not matter which particular faith, tradition or teacher we relate to. Human beings are each unique and we are drawn to different experiences depending on our individual temperaments and stages of spiritual development. The important lessons from satsang are firstly the crucial role of a teacher or guide, and secondly the collective vibrational effect of groups or communities.

23. Hallucinogens

I mentioned hallucinogenic drugs in the previous chapter. This is a subject worth exploring as it can give insight into the nature of Consciousness and also into addiction. I have not taken hallucinogenic drugs myself, nor do I intend to, but a great many people have and the results seem to be more revealing that we might imagine.

Hallucinogens are any substances that cause hallucinations, and hallucinations are experiences involving the apparent perception of something not present. Humans have been experimenting with hallucinogens for thousands of years. Naturally occurring sources of hallucinogens include psilocybin mushrooms and peyote cacti as well as other plants and even toads. These substances were discovered by ancient cultures and used in various combinations for spiritual practices and ceremonies. Ayahuasca is one such brew that originates from the indigenous peoples of the Amazon basin and is used to this day on some spiritual retreats.

LSD, or acid, on the other hand is a more modern version that was first made in 1938 from lysergic acid, which is a chemical from the ergot fungus. LSD was first used for psychotherapeutic treatments to produce a controlled psychosis, but subsequently became a popular recreational drug in the 1960s. Many influential musicians used LSD during this period and this contributed to a period of noteworthy musical creativity.

A significant catalyst for the popular use of hallucinogens was the publication of the book 'The Doors of Perception' by Aldous Huxley in 1954. The book documents his experience of taking mescaline, which occurs naturally in the peyote cactus. He took the drug as an experiment to test the idea that the human brain is a reducing valve for Consciousness, which of course is consistent with the model that we have been exploring. The results were an intense and extraordinary change in perception of everyday life that he describes in fascinating detail. The title for the book was taken from William Blake's poem 'The Marriage of Heaven and Hell' in which he says "If the doors of perception were cleansed, every thing would appear to man as it is: infinite. For man has closed himself up, till he sees all things thro' narrow chinks of his cavern'. This concept of cleansing the doors of perception is the same idea as cleansing the lens of Antahkarana in the Advaita Vedanta.

The experiences described by Huxley are not dissimilar to reports of spiritual experiences or trips on LSD. All of this clearly points to hallucinogens curtailing the activity of the personal ego mind, which then gives rise to experiences of a deeper Consciousness. I always used to think that hallucinations were the result of unusually high brain activity that created 'unreal' experiences. It now seems that hallucinogens reduce brain activity sufficiently to allow brief glimpses into the nature of the underlying reality of Mind.

This new understanding of the effects of hallucinogens is supported by recent scientific research. There is a great deal of information available on the Internet, including multiple experiments by Carhart-Harris et al from 2010 to 2016 using functional magnetic resonance imaging (fMRI) and magnetoencephalography (MEG). In summary, there is clear evidence that LSD and other hallucinogens stimulate the serotonin 2A receptors in the brain which in turn disrupt coupling between certain cell types and the rhythmic oscillations of large populations of neurons in the cortex. This decreases the communication between the brain regions that make up the Default Mode Network (DMN), which is a collection of hub centers that work together to control and repress Consciousness. The DMN disintegrates under LSD allowing for more communication between brain networks that are normally highly segregated. This decrease in the DMN has been shown to correlate to the strength of the subjective experience of ego-dissolution and unity. It seems that the DMN is the mechanism in the brain that restricts Consciousness in order to produce the experience of the personal, separate, ego self. Once this is suppressed by hallucinogens then the ego self momentarily dissolves and unrestricted states of Consciousness are experienced. This research completely supports and validates the understanding that the personal ego mind is a restricted version of Consciousness and that there is an underlying reality beyond the experience of the day-to-day functioning of mind.

Similar techniques have been used to study the effect of meditation on brain activity. Again it is clear that meditation does change the way the brain functions, and in a recent study published in the journal NeuroImage, a team of researchers at the Center for Healthy Minds at the University of Wisconsin-Madison has shown key differences in brain activity between non-meditators, new meditators and long-term meditators. This all adds weight to the suggestion that science is simply pushing back the limits of our current misunderstanding. Deep meditation can produce similar effects to those of hallucinogens. It seems that ancient cultures knew more about the true nature of reality than our supposedly more advanced modern cultures. They were relying more on wisdom than knowledge. There is a certain irony in the modern obsession with science in that it has undoubtedly made life more comfortable but this has come at the expense of increased emotional suffering. We have gone too far towards the human end of the spectrum of balance between mind and Mind.

Understanding hallucinogens not only helps to validate the model of Consciousness that we have been exploring but it also provides a key insight into the epidemic of addiction that plagues so many of our modern cultures. What is clear is that humans have been trying to escape the inevitable suffering of the ego mind since time immemorial. This sense of longing arises from the restricted nature of the personal ego mind which, as mentioned previously, is in the nature of a compressed sponge with an inherent tension awaiting release. We have been trying to get out of minds for thousands of years, and the desire somehow seems to be even stronger these days. Whether it be hallucinogens, alcohol, marijuana, tobacco, recreational drugs or any habitual behaviour that provides temporary relief, we all seem to need something to help us relax and escape the prisons, or caverns, of our own minds. It is interesting that the English language uses such phrases as "out of my mind" or "off my head" or "out of it" or "zoned out" to describe such experiences. There is discomfort, or dis-ease, in living only in the confines of our conditioned ego minds and one could say that the entire pleasure industry, in all of its guises, exists primarily to satisfy this inbuilt desire. Our focus on the material world has caused confusion between happiness and pleasure. Happiness is certainly pleasurable, but pleasure is temporary in nature and cannot lead to lasting happiness. Our repeated use of substances and behaviours to find happiness through the momentary release of tension leads to emotional and physical dependence. This dependence grows stronger as our bodies tolerate more and more of the same substance or behaviour, and this leads to addictions that, over time, become increasingly difficult to manage or give up.

The ego mind seeking escape would be the equivalent of a caterpillar discovering a substance or behaviour that would give it the temporary experience of being a butterfly. The caterpillar has a built-in destiny to become a butterfly through metamorphosis, but it would presumably much prefer to find a way of mimicking the butterfly experience rather than actually going through the natural process of transformation. The problem is that the repetitive use of the substance or behaviour has a detrimental impact on the caterpillar's progress towards the intended metamorphosis. It gets trapped in its own caterpillar status, despite its best personal attempts to escape. The unavoidable desire to transform grows ever stronger as time passes, but the increasingly desperate use of the substance or behaviour to address the desire simply makes matters worse. There is a longing for freedom but an increasing feeling of being trapped and unable to escape. The caterpillar just needs to stop trying and allow the natural process to resume, but the fear of transformation drives it back to the comfort of temporary relief.

Such is the cycle of addiction. It is driven by natural desires but compromised by a simple yet catastrophic misunderstanding of what life is really all about. This is why a life based on spiritual principles and progress is the obvious solution to addiction. It is the only way for Consciousness to satisfy its own inherent desire for happiness, peace, love and unity.

I mentioned before that many well-known people have experimented with hallucinogens and that this has often facilitated creativity. Consciousness is creative, and hence it makes sense that access to higher levels of Consciousness would inevitably lead to enhanced creativity. Referring again to the spectrum of balance between personal mind and non-personal Mind, it can be seen that an acid trip would produce a temporary movement in identification from personal to non-personal, and hence a broader experience of Consciousness. The problem is that when the drug wears off the balance returns to the previous state of personal ego mind. The mistake we can then make is to assume that the non-personal experience was personal. We claim it for ourselves and are convinced that the trip was 'ours' and that any resulting creativity or insights belong to 'me'. Temporary glimpses of the underlying reality are not permanent and hence the only way to regain such experiences quickly is by repeated use of the drug. The key to understanding what is happening here is to realise that the experience is only arising due to the momentary absence of the personal self. If hallucination happens whist the person is typically still firmly identified as a personal self, then there is severe danger of very frightening experiences and potential for subsequent mental health problems such as psychosis, anxiety, paranoia and despair. It is therefore obviously much better to allow the balance to shift naturally through regular spiritual practice rather than try to jump start or accelerate progress through the use of drugs. It is for this reason that I do not intend to make use of hallucinogens myself.

Interestingly though, one notable and relevant individual who did experiment with LSD was Bill Wilson. His original spiritual experience took place in December 1934 during his fourth admission to Towns Hospital in New York under the care of Doctor Silkworth. The treatment included The Belladonna Cure, which was a mixture of deadly nightshade, henbane and the dried bark or berries of the prickly ash. The effects of Belladonna included hallucinations. Under the effects of this cocktail he experienced what he described as the sensation of a bright light, a feeling of ecstasy and a new serenity. Having previously suffered from chronic alcoholism, he never drank again and became convinced that spirituality was the most effective solution to long-term recovery from addiction. In the 1950s he experimented with LSD, presumably in order to try to re-experience his previous spontaneous spiritual experience. The experiments were medically supervised by psychologist Betty Elsner, philosopher Gerald Heard and the above-mentioned Aldous Huxley. Bill Wilson was enthusiastic about the results of these experiments, and felt that LSD could be useful, but only for those who had already made significant spiritual progress. He also acknowledged that LSD could never take the place of the existing spiritual means of reducing the personal ego self, because spiritual principles would keep the ego reduced whereas LSD was a transient experience.

Bill Wilson was also impressed by the work of Abram Hoffer who experimented with using LSD to treat alcoholism. Hoffer was also experimenting with Niacin to treat schizophrenia. Niacin is an organic compound and a form of vitamin B3, and Wilson discovered that alcoholics given this compound had better sobriety rates. Wilson also took Niacin himself and felt that it gave him relief from depression, from which he had continued to suffer since getting sober.

Bill Wilson never claimed to be a model of recovery, and his continuing search to find ways to improve recovery rates reflected this. His self-description was a man who "because of his bitter experience, discovered, slowly and through a conversion experience, a system of behaviour and a series of actions that work for alcoholics who want to stop drinking." As a man who pulled together threads of psychology, theology and democracy, he was described by Aldous Huxley as "the greatest social architect of our century." Wilson's experiments in trying to accelerate the process of transformation were not widely supported, and the focus remained on the twelve-step recovery program. This makes sense in light of the understanding that the shift in balance from personal mind to non-personal Mind takes time and practice to become fully established. Attempts to try to force the pace ahead of the natural progression tend to create more personal problems rather than the desired relief from suffering.

The Swiss psychiatrist Carl Jung supported the idea that we unwittingly tend to use substances and behaviours to relieve the natural desire for spiritual union. He wrote to Bill Wilson in 1961 and used the phrase "Spiritus contra Spiritum" which neatly summarises the idea that addiction is a block to natural spiritual progress, and that spiritual principles are the solution to addiction. He also stated in his letter that "I am strongly convinced that the evil principle prevailing in this world leads the unrecognised spiritual need into perdition." These are strong words, but they are entirely consistent with the understanding that it is our over-identification with the personal ego mind that causes all of the trouble. We are trying to satisfy the inherent spiritual desire for happiness, peace, love and unity through all manner of selfish and self-centered behaviour, all of which leads us further away from the solution that is already present in non-personal Consciousness. Once this mistake is recognised and understood then we become willing to turn our attention inwards toward Consciousness itself rather than outwards toward momentary relief in the material world.

Whichever way we turn, we find that the model of non-dual Consciousness provides all of the answers. If we want sustained freedom from the suffering of the personal ego mind then we need to cease the obsession with the personal self and focus instead on self-forgetting. This is best done through regular

143

spiritual practice rather than trying to force the issue through the unsustainable use of artificial stimulants.

24. Self-Forgetting

Following on from self-awareness and self-contemplation, the next spiritual tool to cover is the action of self-forgetting. Given that the natural tendency of spiritual transformation is a shift in the balance from personal mind to non-personal Mind, it makes complete sense to focus far less on our personal selves. Self-forgetting is the essence of Karma Yoga, which is the discipline of selfless service. A compassionate attitude towards others, and the practice of unconditional love in all of our day-to-day activities, are the key components of self-forgetting. When we stop obsessing about how we feel, or what we think, then we are free to become instruments of Consciousness. Our actions bring the desired qualities of happiness, peace, love and unity into the world. This basis of living is very different from the motives of the selfish, self-centered, personal ego mind. It takes practice precisely because our natural human tendency is to think primarily of ourselves in any given situation.

The motives for selfless action can be a minefield of misunderstanding. The opaque nature of mind at the human level means that we are often not sure whether we are genuinely acting on behalf of others, or whether our hidden motives are really self-centered. In the early stages of transformation, our motives are understandably centered on obtaining relief from the intense suffering that we are experiencing. We are told that helping others is a key part of the spiritual journey, so we set about trying to be of service in order to enhance our own progress. This motive is still selfish in nature, and we may continue to be reluctant to inconvenience ourselves or be exposed to unfamiliar or uncomfortable situations.

If we persist with the tools of self-awareness, self-contemplation and self-forgetting, then gradually the balance shifts and our motives become increasingly less selfish. The preoccupation with the personal self is slowly replaced by the influence of non-personal Consciousness and this gives rise to genuine compassion and concern for the welfare of others. Even then it is tempting for the ego mind to be very pleased with itself and proud of being such a good person. This is just one of the many subtle ego traps that keep us attached to our strong identity as a person, and hence delays the potential progression. We can become proud of our recovery, proud of being spiritual, proud of our commitment to service or proud of our depth of understanding. Pride in any aspect of personhood is a barrier to progress. The spiritual alternative to pride is gratitude. It is far better to remain fully aware of our brokenness and move with humility rather than pride. This is the way of self-forgetting.

There are a multitude of ways to be of service in the world and we will each find a path that suits our innate talents. When it comes to twelve-step recovery though we find that we are uniquely able to help others by sharing our own experience. Such experience covers our behaviours when in active addiction, how we came to the point of surrender, how we have progressed along the spiritual path and how our lives have changed as a result. It is truly wonderful to see how the darkness of our own suffering turns into the light of hope for others. We should not seek to force the issue or try to control how others behave, but the simple sharing our own experience, strength and hope provides valuable guidance and inspiration to those who are ready to undergo the process of recovery.

Becoming instruments of recovery for those who are willing is one thing, but as we come more and more under the influence of non-personal Consciousness then we will find that our attitude towards all of life becomes infused with happiness, peace, love and unity. It is not a question of trying to become a better person. We can be of service wherever we go. As the personal self loses its power, so the power of Consciousness flows through the individual body and mind in its own unique way.

Such behaviours do not come naturally to the personal ego mind but they are the very nature of Consciousness. Abiding in happiness, peace, love and unity not only benefits our own individual experience of life but it also radiates to all those with whom we come into contact. Our individual vibration will literally create a positive impact in our local environment and be of benefit to all those who are open to it. Resonance will attract vibrational matches and synchronicity will become the norm. The further the balance shifts, the more extraordinary the experience of life. Such is the power of self-forgetting. We would surely be foolish to deny ourselves this opportunity.

Self-forgetting integrates with self-awareness and self-contemplation. It is so easy to overlook self-forgetting in the stress and busyness of everyday life. We are quickly pulled into the mode of the personal self, and it happens so automatically that it can easily go unnoticed. As self-awareness becomes more natural through the practice of meditation, we become more aware of the thinking and behaviour arising from the self-centered ego mind. It may take a few minutes or hours to notice, or we may not become aware until the end of the day, but improved self-awareness will highlight where self interest and self-seeking are causing frustration and suffering. Likewise the practice of self-contemplation will continually bring us back to our true position of Consciousness. Simply asking ourselves the question as to who it is that is getting upset will immediately clarify where our identity is positioned. We are not trying to get rid of the individual self. The individual restriction of Consciousness is necessary in order to experience life from a unique perspective. The individual self is a singular and idiosyncratic instrument of perception created by Consciousness in order to experience and participate in the world of duality. The individual self is not the problem. It is only when the ego mind creates a personal self out of the individual body and mind, and then believes it to be the true self, that we create personal suffering. The purpose of self-forgetting is to disempower the personal ego mind whilst still experiencing and enjoying life as an individual powered by Consciousness. Self-identity is a matter of wisdom and choice, and hence we can shift our identity through practice of the spiritual principles of self-awareness, self-contemplation and self-forgetting.

147

In his book 'Twelve Steps and Twelve Traditions' published in 1952, Bill Wilson makes reference to a prayer commonly attributed to St. Francis of Assisi. The prayer first appeared anonymously in 1912 in a French magazine called 'La Clochette', but whatever the source the words are insightful and powerful.

"Lord, make me an instrument of your peace,
Where there is hatred, let me sow love;
Where there is injury, pardon;
Where there is doubt, faith;
Where there is despair, hope;
Where there is darkness, light;
Where there is sadness, joy.
O Divine Master, grant that I may
not so much seek to be consoled, as to console;
to be understood, as to understand;
to be loved, as to love.
For it is in giving that we receive.
It is in pardoning that we are pardoned,
and it is in dying that we are born to Eternal Life.
Amen."

In Bill Wilson's version, the final lines read as follows:

"For it is by self-forgetting that one finds.
It is by forgiving that we are forgiven.
It is by dying that one awakens to Eternal Life."

This prayer makes complete sense within the model of Consciousness that I have been covering at length. The person that is praying is the ego mind whereas that to which the prayer is directed is Mind. The references to Lord and Divine Master are therefore references to non-personal Consciousness. The invocation is to be an instrument of the various attributes of Mind rather than ego mind. There is emphasis on compassion, understanding and love. The final three lines in Bill Wilson's version are particularly relevant. Firstly there is a reference to self-forgetting as the route to finding Truth. Secondly there is the idea that we should forgive before we can be forgiven. This is counterintuitive to the ego mind but makes total sense from the perspective of non-personal Mind. Finally there is the suggestion that dying leads to Eternal Life. Dying in this context can be seen as dying to the personal ego self in order to awaken to the true nature of Consciousness, which is beyond time and therefore eternal. It can also be read as physical death, when the whirlpool dissipates back into the river of life and Consciousness expands back into its true nature. It seems a shame to wait until physical death in order to awaken to Truth when we have the opportunity to do so in this lifetime through shifting our balance of identity. My understanding is that this living awakening is what is really meant by the final line of this prayer. Amen simply means "so be it" which seems fair enough. The truth is that all of this is already present and accessible, but it is our own insistence on being only a personal self that prevents the desired awakening. It already is, so be it.

The words of this prayer are infused with deep meaning and pull together much of the wisdom that arises from our understanding of Consciousness. The emphasis on self-forgetting should not be underestimated. There can be no transformation or relief from suffering without it.

25. Nihilism

This may seem a strange subject to raise at this point. My own experience, and my involvement in working with others, suggests that this a topic that is better discussed than disregarded without comment. The greatest peril in spiritual growth is the potential for a gap in time between letting go of the personal ego self and becoming safely established in non-personal Consciousness. This gap can give rise to feelings of being lost, doubt, depression and despair. It is known colloquially as the Dark Night of the Soul, which relates to a poem by the 16th-century Spanish mystic St. John of the Cross.

A useful metaphor in this respect is the parable of Jonah and the whale. In this story Jonah is guided to travel to Ninevah to carry the message of wisdom. However Jonah was not too keen on this idea because the residents of Ninevah were enemies of his people. He decided to travel by sea in the opposite direction. The ship ran into a big storm, and the crew blamed Jonah for this predicament and decided to throw him overboard. At this low point, Jonah's day got even worse when a giant fish promptly swallowed him. He spent three fearful and dark days and nights in the belly of the fish, praying for help and admitting that his personal thinking had gone against the guidance he had received. He also prayed with gratitude that he had been saved from drowning. This repentance and thanksgiving finally resulted in him being thrown up onto the shores of Ninevah. Jonah then acted against his own personal wishes and followed the previous guidance to share wisdom with the people he disliked. He expected them to ignore him, and he was rather hoping that they would ignore him and therefore suffer the consequences. After speaking with them, he sat in the shade under a plant and waited to see what would happen. The wisdom however was received and understood. No harm came to the Ninevites and Jonah consequently became bitter and angry. A worm then destroyed his shady plant and Jonah was left in the scorching heat complaining and wanting to die. Despite having been saved from drowning, saved from the whale and given the chance to help others, he still ended up allowing his negative personal motives to overshadow all of the goodness. The story ends at this point and Jonah's subsequent fate is left open-ended.

Such parables are open to interpretation of course, but our model of Consciousness provides a clear understanding. First of all Jonah ignores the guidance of Knowing and follows the agenda of personal ego mind rather than Mind. He heads in the opposite direction and eventually life conspires to throw him into the sea of suffering. He is saved from drowning by Spirit and ends up in a place that he perceives to be dark and frightening. In his despair he prays for help, and this leads to him being placed exactly where is supposed to be. Secondly he then has the opportunity to learn from his experience and help others. However he does this reluctantly and his personal motives remain negative. Things do not turn out as he wishes, life conspires against him again and he is left once more in a state of suffering and wanting to die. He has been given every opportunity to understand, yet he remains firmly attached to his personal identity and fails to see the wisdom that his life circumstances are revealing to him. The story is left open-ended because it is not known when his particular Dark Night of the Soul will come to an end. He may continue to resist the guidance of Mind, or he may come to understand the true nature of reality. He may finally surrender his personal self-centered agenda in favour of an individual experience of non-personal Consciousness. There is no right or wrong answer. The choice is his, but the implications are crystal clear.

Such a metaphorical experience is by no means unusual, and in many ways is inevitable. We each have a personal investment in the ego self, and this believed identity defines and shapes our lives. The very thought of letting go of this belief can give rise to self-centered fear, and the actual act of surrender can lead to feelings very similar to grief. There is also often a period of struggle, where the ego mind wants to return to familiar and comfortable ground whereas Mind is leading us away from it. This happens even when the familiar and comfortable state is one of suffering. Many well-known spiritual teachers throughout the ages have been through these battles and doubts. There is actually nothing wrong, yet it can feel as though our whole lives are falling apart.

We reach a point where we fear going back to our old ways and also fear moving ahead towards an uncertain future. This is not a comfortable or enjoyable phase, but the good news is that it does not last. It is the equivalent of a caterpillar going through the process of metamorphosis in its chrysalis. It is temporarily neither caterpillar nor butterfly, and is in a period of darkness and reconstruction. The butterfly will eventually emerge, but it does take time. The important thing here is not to lose faith in the process. The desired result will come if we allow the unfolding to take place.

A big problem arises at this stage if we are still totally reliant on personal mind. Depression, despair and grief are powerful feelings and the ego mind will want to make these feeling go away. Doubt may creep into our thinking and this will undermine faith. We will be strongly tempted to return to our old coping strategies, and for an addict this spells danger. We will either relapse, or we will remain abstinent yet trapped in a position where we cannot go back but fear going forward. We cannot live with active addiction and we cannot live without it. In such circumstances the ego mind turns to self-destructive thoughts. In my experience there is a high prevalence of suicidal thoughts and suicide attempts amongst addicts, and these can occur in active addition or during abstinence. Some of these attempts are unfortunately successful. Strong personal identity with the body and mind means that the only apparent option left for the ego self to relieve suffering is to bring the experience of life to a premature end. There is logic here, but such thinking is clearly self-centered and fails to take account of the traumatic impact that this has on family and friends. It is also based on a fundamental misunderstanding of who we really are. I am not suggesting that the experience of suffering is unreal or inconsequential, but it is clear that suffering arises due to the mistaken personal self-identity. Suffering is inevitable and necessary in order for mind to return to Mind, but sometimes mind remains unconvinced and brings the journey to a precipitous end. The whirlpool returns to the river and the journey begins again downstream.

Another danger can arise when mind begins to grasp the idea of non-dual Consciousness but identity remains firmly with the personal self. In these circumstances we are vulnerable to nihilistic thinking, because we may come to believe that the world has no real existence and hence conclude that there is no point in continuing to suffer. This may also lead to suicidal thoughts. Again there is logic in this thinking, but it arises in the personal ego mind. Such thinking comes from an intellectual grasp of non-duality without subsequent spiritual practice. The personal ego mind cannot understand, yet an unshakeable belief in personal identity can convince the assumed self that it does understand. There is no wisdom in nihilism. It is just another trap caused by an ego mind that does not want to give up the illusory right to self-governance. It may be informed ignorance, but it is still ignorance nonetheless.

The key to overcoming these pitfalls is the continuing practice of self-awareness, self-contemplation and self-forgetting. If we can be aware of how the conditioned ego mind is operating, and contemplate who it is that is having these nihilistic, self-destructive thoughts, then we gain the confidence to forget about our self-centered thinking and instead focus on allowing the Dark Night of the Soul to pass. The dawn of awakening will come soon enough as the balance of power shifts from human to Being.

26. The God Word

Having now referenced the four noble truths of Buddhism, the Advaita Vedanta of Hinduism, St. Francis of Assisi, St. John of the Cross and the biblical story of Jonah, it feels like the right time to tackle the vexed subject of religion. I could write a whole book on this topic alone. It would probably be called "The Folly of Religion", but for now we need to be brief and to the point. I am not a religious man, nor am I anti religion. All I can do is share my experience and understanding. My only suggestion would be to remain open-minded, because doctrine can very easily obscure wisdom.

The word *religion* is rooted in the Latin term *religio* which means to reconnect or bind back together. In early Roman times, religion was not based on faith but instead on knowledge and correct practice. Religion is really about reconnecting with Consciousness, Awareness, Knowingness, Mind, Spirit or Being.

The first thing to say is that the word *God* is just a word. It is a label or placeholder that references that which cannot be understood, explained or described. I have mentioned before the limitations of language when it comes to trying to use words to communicate such matters. Even Consciousness itself cannot understand that which gives rise to its very existence. Consciousness is, as it were, the first-born aspect of the Absolute, Ultimate Truth that is the Source. The Absolute is Pure Awareness, the Great Reality or Universal Emptiness. Source is neither male nor female, good nor evil, white nor black, straight nor gay, Christian nor Muslim. It is infinite nothingness, yet it gives rise to all of the beauty of finite manifest creation, which includes both visible and invisible phenomena. There are no objective qualities to describe, and it exists prior to words or language. For me, the closest that we can get is the analogy by Sri

Mooji of a lotus flower with the fragrances of unconditional love, peace, silence, joy, wisdom and bliss.

When a personal ego mind tries to perceive the nature of Source, its natural point of reference will be its own self-conception of a body and mind. This gives rise to a common belief in Ultimate Truth as some sort of deity. There are a great many to choose from, and we may even make up our own. Human beings are a manifestation of Consciousness, which itself arises from Source, yet we use our own limited minds to conceive of deities that equate to more powerful and perfect versions of ourselves. We also ascribe limited human attributes to these deities, such as anger and judgment. This is clearly all nonsense, yet such beliefs can be very convincing to a conditioned ego mind that is devoid of wisdom. The God word is problematic. Wisdom can have nothing to say about Ultimate Truth because the Absolute is the source of Mind. All personal opinion, belief and debate concerning the God word must be in the realm of personal ego mind. Wisdom knows that it does not know. Knowing knows everything other than its own Source. This is the end of the road. The only possible conclusion is that we do not know. This is the only valid place to stand. This is humility. To quote Shakespeare again, this time from As You Like It, Scene V Act 1 "The fool doth think he is wise, but the wise man knows himself to be a fool". In other words, the wise man knows that he does not know. The good news is that honest, open-minded, willing humility is the key to transformation. Admitting our own inadequacies opens to door to the experience of non-personal Consciousness, which in turn satisfies our inherent longing for happiness, peace, love and unity.

All religions, as we shall see later, are simply brands of the Consciousness Only model that I have been trying to explain. This may seem like a bold statement to make, but it comes from a position of non-personal wisdom rather than personal opinion or belief. There is only one Ultimate Truth; regardless of how many ways we may try to dress it up. All religions are founded on the teachings of various enlightened human beings who have existed throughout history. All of them were teaching the same non-dual philosophy. The teachings often used metaphors and parables relevant to the cultural setting at the time. The teachings were documented either contemporaneously or, more often, some time later. These scriptures then became the subject of translation, study, interpretation and debate. Doctrines and practices emerged and together these all formed the basis of a religion. Indoctrination then perpetuated these religions from generation to generation, often with splits and sub-branches due to disagreements or the influence of politics and socio-economic factors. Consciousness naturally produces diversity, so there is no surprise in the manifestation of large numbers of differing belief systems. The precise figures are difficult to pin down, but some estimates put the number of different religions in the world today at over four thousand.

The purpose of all mature religion is the metamorphosis that I have described. Whether this is called transformation, awakening, salvation, the second coming, the messiah, self-realisation, enlightenment, resurrection, nirvana, heaven or anything else makes no difference. These are all just words, or labels, that point to the same phenomenon. Each religion has the capacity to bring about varying degrees of spiritual development, or shifts in the balance between human and Being. When such a shift occurs, the personal self tends to equate the experience with their own particular belief system and hence is prone to believing that their specific religion is the only truth. The personal ego mind likes to be right, hence any religion that seems to propose an alternative truth must be wrong. This simple mistake has had catastrophic consequences over the centuries, with religious intolerance, conflict and persecution bringing out the very worst in human nature. Ironically such egocentric, arrogant behavior betrays the very spiritual principles on which each religion is founded. Humans have literally maimed, tortured and killed each other in the name of a word that conveys unconditional love, peace, silence, joy, wisdom and bliss.

The problem is self-righteousness rather than the diversity of religion. Each metamorphosis is inherently unique because each human being is unique. This is the whole point of life. The idea that all awakenings or transformations should follow the same pattern and be the same experience is simply an idea. It has no validity outside of the personal ego mind. There is scope for infinite diversity within the overall process, and hence we must be free to follow our own path. Each caterpillar and each butterfly is unique, and therefore so too is each metamorphosis. Religious doctrine restricts and constrains authenticity and is counterproductive. Religious beliefs can often keep the self-identified person trapped in personhood. The person simply adds a religious label to the long list of other labels than define them as a person.

Such attachment to personhood perpetuates the internal conflict between belief in the personal ego self and belief in the particular religious concept of Source. This sabotages the very transformation that the religious teaching is intended to bring about. Trying to live a life based on spiritual principles from the position of a personal self can be very disheartening. We aim for a moral code based on the qualities of Mind but we keep defaulting to the characteristics of our human nature. Without the persistent and consistent practice of self-awareness, self-contemplation and self-forgetting we will continue to experience the inherent suffering of the personal ego mind regardless of our religious or spiritual beliefs.

All of this confusion around religion is based on the single, fundamental misunderstanding of our own true nature. The personal ego mind does not want to give up its own identity nor can it grasp the concept that its own true nature is Mind. The idea seems too fantastic to be true. The inevitable consequence is that God is perceived as a third party object rather than the ultimate subject. The person cannot believe that it is ultimately the Source. The human cannot accept that it is the Being. This is where we need to be very precise. The person is not the Source. The Source is the illusory person. I am not God, but God creates

157

the apparent personal me out of Itself. God is not taking care of the person. God is the person. The separate person is a creation of ego mind, which is a limited version of God. There is nothing but God. Consciousness takes care of Consciousness. Life takes care of Life. The human is a creative and participative individual instrument of Source. The personal self is a misunderstanding born of the ego mind. The ego mind is a servant rather than the master. We live our lives in the light but are blinded by our own personal self-belief. The personal self is *the* problem and the non-personal Self is *the* solution. This only makes sense once the identity has shifted sufficiently from mind to Mind, and this can only come about by surrender of the personal self through regular spiritual practice.

If this understanding is valid, then we should find the same perennial, non-dual wisdom in all of the religions. This is indeed the case. Every religion that I have come across so far has the same non-dual teaching at its core. Once this is understood, it all becomes very obvious. To illustrate this, I will briefly cover each of the major religions, providing some basic information and focusing on the key non-dual message. I will start with the oldest, because each religion borrows from, and builds upon, previous versions. In truth, there is only one reality and there is only one religion. All of the paraphernalia of individual religions is just surface noise. It is simply Consciousness vibrating in a multitude of diverse ways.

The origins of Hinduism date back over 5,000 years and include a synthesis of cultural influences from the Bronze Age Indus Valley Civilisation and the Indo-Aryan Vedic religion based on the language of Sanskrit. Hinduism has around 1.15 billion followers today and is the third largest religion globally. Ancient oral traditions were eventually documented into the four Vedas, which each divide into Samhitas, Aranyakas, Brahmanas and Upanishads. Other notable scriptures are the Ramayana, the Yoga Sutras and the Mahabharata, which includes the Bhagavad Gita. The Vedas give rise to the six schools of Hindu philosophy, known as Vedanta. There is a wealth of wisdom contained in the

Hindu scriptures, including the origins of creation and the mechanics of mind. Much of it is considered to be revelations of Consciousness to mystics known as Rishis.

The concept of God in Hinduism is complex and varies enormously by tradition and philosophy. Overall God is perceived to be a supreme spirit called Brahman. This then gives rise to different words for different qualities of Brahman, such as Vishnu, Brahma, Shiva and many others. There is also Shakti, which is the cosmic, dynamic energy of Brahman. Next there is the concept of an individual, or condensed, version of Brahman known as Atman. There is then the idea of Paramatman, which is the universal version of Atman that also equates to Brahman. The Advaita Vedanta, or non-dual philosophy, collapses these distinctions so that Brahman, Paramatman and Atman are all aspects of a single supreme Source. This provides the understanding that all of these words are simply labeling differing vibrational 'layers' of a single Consciousness.

There is no single founding figure in Hinduism, but one notable individual was Krishna who is a mythical deity in scripture but also thought to be an historic figure, living from 3228 BCE to 3102 BCE. Interestingly there are many striking similarities between the stories of the life of Krishna and that of Jesus Christ some 3,000 years later. A key quote attributed to Krishna with respect to the true nature of reality is "Fear not what is not real, never was and never will be. What is real always was and cannot be destroyed." This is a reference to the transient nature of apparent material reality as opposed to the eternal essence of the underlying reality, which is Consciousness.

In terms of diversity, modern Hinduism is divided into four major devotional sects, namely Vaishnavism, Shaivism, Shaktism and Smartism, as well as the six schools of Vedantic philosophy and various other denominations.

The history of Judaism spans up to 4,000 years and originates from the time of Abraham, whose life is generally dated around

2000 BCE to 1800 BCE. With around 15 million followers, Judaism is relatively small as the tenth largest religion but is notable for the Hebrew Bible, or Tanakh, which also features in Christianity and Islam. Other scriptures include the Torah, which incorporates the first five books of the Tanakh together with supplemental oral tradition from later texts such as the Midrash and the Talmud. The scriptures are both allegorical and historical, and chart the experiences of the Jewish people and also set out religious practices and civil laws. The long exodus of the Israelites from the suffering in Egypt back to the Promised Land is, for example, a great metaphor for the spiritual journey from ego mind back to Mind.

There are seven main words for God in Judaism, namely YHWH, El, Eloah, Elohim, Shaddai, Ehyeh and Tzevaot. YHWH is also known as Yahweh or Jehovah. Other words for God include Adonai, which is the plural of Adon, meaning Lord, and Shalom, which means peace, harmony and wholeness, or unity. The traditional Jewish relationship to God is one of covenant, and God is understood to be absolute, indivisible, incomparable, the ultimate cause of creation and both personal and transcendent. Modern interpretations of Judaism place emphasis on God as a force rather than a being. All of these concepts fit easily into the non-dual model of Consciousness.

As well as Abraham, the other key figure in Judaism is Moses. It was Moses who received a revelation from within a burning bush on Mount Horeb. He also later led the Israelites from Egypt and across the Red Sea to Mount Sinai, where the Ten Commandments were revealed to him. Moses is also credited by some with writing part of the Torah. The most compelling quote from Moses comes from his experience with the burning bush, where it is revealed "Ehyeh Asher Ehyeh". This can be translated as "I am that I am" or "I am who I am " or "I am who am". All of these translations point to the originating nature of Consciousness as the non-personal Awareness of Being, which announces itself within each of us as "I am".

Judaism today mainly divides between Orthodox, Conservative, and Reform movements, but there are also others such as Hasidic, Karaite and Reconstructionist. In addition there are variations by geography.

The next oldest religion is Buddhism, which dates back 2,600 years to the time of Siddhartha Gautama, who became known as the Buddha. Buddhism currently has roughly 521 million followers and is the fourth largest religion. Key scriptures include the Tripitakas, Theravada texts and the Mahayana Sutras, although there are literally thousands of other ancient Buddhist manuscripts. Buddhism comprises the Four Truths, the Eightfold Path to Moksha and the Three Refuges, or Jewels, which cover firstly devotion to the Awakened One, secondly the Dharma, which are the various practices, and thirdly the Sangha or community of followers. Buddhism is all about escaping the cycle of inherent worldly suffering by following the path to personal liberation, and hence Nirvana. The word *nirvana* is Sanskrit and means blown out or extinguished. Nirvana is not a state to be achieved but is the natural state of Mind once identification with the personal ego self is blown out or extinguished.

The God word in Buddhism is Buddha Nature or Mind. There is no concept of a deity in Buddhism, but instead there is the understanding that Mind is the true nature of all beings and manifest creation. This means that God is not other, and that all human beings are therefore capable of enlightenment.

The key figure in Buddhism is of course Siddhartha Gautama, who is thought to have lived from 563 BCE to 483 BCE, although the precise dates are subject to debate. His spiritual journey included asceticism and studying with two different teachers of yogic meditation, but eventually he found enlightenment by sitting under a Bodhi tree and refusing to move until he found the Truth. He then spent the rest of his life travelling around and sharing his understanding. The teachings were not documented until several hundred years after his death. The most potent quote attributed to Buddha is, for me, "The root of suffering is attachment." This attachment to all aspects of the personal ego self is indeed the cause of all human troubles. Such suffering is inevitable given that the personal mind is a condensed, limited version of Mind and retains a deep longing to return to its natural state. We spend our lives trying to satisfy this deep longing by pursuing satisfaction in the material world, but this never provides a sustainable solution.

As with other religions, Buddhism has fractured into numerous denominations over the years. The three main schools are Theraveda, Mahayana and Vajrayana, but there are many others and they all subdivide yet further. Whatever the specific tradition, Buddhism retains the concept of Truth, the Middle Way, or Eightfold Path to liberation, and the Three Refuges of a teacher, the practices and a community. In this respect Buddhism is relatively simple and clear. It is also interesting to note that all of these ideas find their way into twelve-step recovery, as we shall see later.

Taoism is only slightly younger and dates back around 2,400 years. Together with Han Folk Religion, these Chinese traditions have a following of approximately 394 million, which ranks them as fifth largest. Taoism is based on the Tao, which is usually translated as the Way, and can be described as the ultimate creative principle in the universe where all things are unified and connected. Taoism includes the idea of Yin and Yang that represents opposing yet complementary forces within the unity. The religion promotes harmony with nature, self-development, good morals and the pursuit of spiritual immortality. Practices include meditation, energy flow, martial arts and the Three Treasures of compassion, frugality and humility. The primary text is the Tao Te Ching, which describes the nature of Tao as ineffable and accomplishing great things through small means. The text also offers guidance on how to attain Tao.

The God word in Taoism is Tao. As with Buddhism there is no overall concept of a deity, yet there is widespread use of symbolism and the worship of deities for certain aspects of Tao. As well as meaning the Way, Tao is also the One which is natural, spontaneous, eternal, nameless and indescribable. It is at once the beginning of all things and the way in which all things pursue their course. It is the ontological origin yet also something that individuals can find immanent in themselves. The concept of Tao maps perfectly onto Consciousness, Awareness, Knowingness, Mind, Spirit or Being.

The main individual in Taoism is Lao-Tzu, who is reputed to have written the Tao Te Ching. He lived in the fourth century BCE, or possibly earlier, and his name translates as Old Master. He is quoted as saying "There was something undifferentiated yet complete which existed before Heaven and Earth. Soundless and formless, it depends on nothing and does not change. It operates everywhere and is free from danger. It may be considered the mother of the universe. I do not know its name; I call it Tao." He called it Tao, but this is just yet another label for that which has no name and cannot be described with words.

The religion now divides mainly into Southern and Northern Taoism, but there are also other groups such as Chin tan, Ch'ing Wei, T'ien hsin, Shen hsiao and many others.

Next up is Christianity, which of course is just over 2,000 years old. Christianity currently has an estimated 2.4 billion followers and is the largest religion. The primary text in Christianity is the Bible, which comprises the Old Testament, from Hebrew scripture, and the New Testament, which is based on the life and teachings of Yeshua of Nazareth. Yeshua became known as Jesus Christ and this name in itself is a big clue. Jesus is the human and Christ is the Being, or Consciousness. The word *Christ* means anointed or messiah, and the term *Christ Consciousness* refers to the highest state of Mind. Jesus lived and taught from such a state and the word *Christ* was added to his name posthumously. Jesus taught by example and by using parables. He demonstrated how a human can live as non-personal Consciousness, yet he was still prone to aspects of the personal self. His teaching was entirely based on non-dual Consciousness, yet this has often been misunderstood and has led to him being deified himself.

The God word in Christianity is complex. As well as adopting God words from Judaism, the religion also uses Father, Son, Holy Spirit, Holy Ghost, Lord, Him, He, Thou and other capitalised words. There is also the concept of Trinity, which breaks out three separate aspects of God but then declares that they are all One. Sometimes God is deified, and others times not. Jesus as a human is mistakenly identified with this idea of the Son, distinct from the Father yet at one with Him. All of this is an attempt by the personal ego mind to rationalise the teachings, which are coming from Knowingness. The teachings are all non-dual Consciousness, and they all make sense once this is understood. Without such wisdom, the God word in Christianity can cause great confusion.

The main character in Christianity is obviously Jesus. Many of the recorded aspects of his life are suspiciously similar to pre-existing stories and beliefs, yet it is widely accepted that he did exist. He studied Hebrew scripture up until the age of around twelve but then mysteriously disappeared until the age of thirty or so when his ministry commenced. There is good evidence to suggest that he travelled to India during this time and studied Hinduism and Buddhism with various groups. This idea certainly validates his subsequent teaching, which is exactly in line with Eastern religion and was at odds with the prevailing Jewish beliefs. This conflict with the Jewish establishment meant that he only lasted a couple of years before he was condemned to die by crucifixion, which was a common form of execution at the time. Whether or not he did actually die at that time is also a matter of debate. His time on the cross was much shorter than usual, and the use of Aloe and Myrrh in the tomb indicate healing rather than preparation for burial. Jewish practices for burial did not include use of such herbs. Various people then saw him alive, and these sightings included eating, sleeping, walking and reports of his wounds. He then disappeared. There is good evidence that Yeshua reappeared in India after his crucifixion ordeal and traveled to Kashmir via Afghanistan, living into old age. There is even a tomb in Srinagar in Kashmir that is said to be his final resting place. There are many books and films available on this subject and the evidence seems fairly compelling. We will never know for sure what actually happened, but the resurrection story of Jesus Christ is fundamental to Christianity because it placed him in a category outside of regular human experience and led to his deification. Whether this misunderstanding was deliberate or accidental is a matter of conjecture, but the story of physical resurrection can only be a matter of belief rather than fact. The implications of this belief are unhelpful because the teachings of Jesus clearly point to the possibility of individual transformation for all of us. By making his apparent resurrection a special event, the opportunity for personal salvation or transformation seems out of reach. The idea that living a good Christian life will result in a heavenly experience after death is a complete misunderstanding of what Jesus actually taught. We are all both human and Being, as was Jesus, and the opportunity for metamorphosis is available to everyone in this lifetime. To quote the man himself "The kingdom of God is within you".

Jesus used many parables to try to explain non-dual Consciousness. The most relevant is perhaps the story of the prodigal son. This is the well-known story of two sons and the relationships with their father. The younger son takes his inheritance early and squanders it prodigally. He has many adventures and experiences, but ends up in a state of suffering and brokenness. At this point he decides to return home, and is eventually welcomed back with open arms by his father. The older son does not understand the celebration, because he has been there all along and has not experienced such a joyful reunion. It seems that "he was lost but now he is found" is preferable to not being lost in the first place. Interestingly there is a very similar story in the Mahayana Buddhist Lotus Sutra, which predates the biblical one. All of this is allegorical and points to Consciousness condensing into the personal ego mind and body, suffering the inevitable consequences and then returning to its original state. As this happens the identity moves from non-personal to personal and then back to non-personal. This is the whole point of life, and is why Source allows this journey to happen rather than just staying as it is. As well as being an excellent allegory for the spiritual journey, the parable of the prodigal son is also a brilliant metaphor for the experience of addiction. Addicts certainly behave in a prodigal way and eventually end up in a state of suffering and brokenness. The intention is that they return home, but many stay away and the suffering continues, even to the point of insanity or fatality.

The misunderstandings and mind-based debates about true meaning have caused great fractures in the Christian faith. Today there are numerous versions of Christianity. The main categories are Catholic, Eastern Orthodox, Oriental Orthodox, Anglican and Protestant, and each of these has a great many sub-divisions. If we define denomination as a separate church organisation within a specific country, then there are estimated to be over forty thousand Christian denominations in the world today. Given the potentially flawed historical basis of Christianity, and the history of borrowing and incorporating beliefs and metaphors from other religions, the idea that Christians should convert others to their way of thinking and believing is breathtakingly arrogant. Notwithstanding the undoubted good that committed Christians do in the world, history is littered with examples where Christianity has betrayed the very spiritual principles that Jesus taught. Belief is in the realm of personal ego mind. Consciousness simply is.

The youngest of the major religions is Islam. This religion is based on the revelations and teachings of the Prophet Muhammad some 1,400 years ago. There are roughly 1.8 billion followers of Islam in the world, making it the second largest. The main scriptures are the Quran and also the Sunnah, which contains accounts of the life of Muhammad called Hadith. Islam acknowledges the prophets Abraham, Moses and Jesus, but consider the Quran to be the verbatim and final word of God as revealed through the messenger Muhammad. The word *Islam* means to submit or surrender. This submission refers to the surrender of the personal ego self to non-personal Consciousness. The Five Pillars of Islam, as summarised in the Hadith of Gabriel, are the practices of faith, prayer, charity, fasting and pilgrimage. Followers of Islam are known as Muslims, and these mainly divide into the two denominations of Sunni and Shia.

The God word in Islam is Allah. In Islamic tradition there are then ninety-nine other names for God, each of which evoke a distinct characteristic of Allah. Examples of these aspects of Allah include lord, holy or whole, peaceful, omnipotent, creator, all aware, forgiving, witness, wise, life, eternal, absolute, indivisible, manifest, infinite and light. Basically the concept of Allah is non-dual. There is nothing but Allah.

Islam is all about the revelations of Muhammad, and he is considered to be the final prophet of God. He lived from 570 CE to 632 CE. He spend a lot of time secluded in a cave called Hira near Mecca and claimed to have been visited by the archangel Gabriel. His basic teaching was that "God is One" and that complete submission was the right course of action. He was persecuted in Mecca and eventually migrated to Medina in 622 CE. He continued to receive revelations up until his death and it is these insights that form the basis of Islamic scripture. Perhaps his most revealing quote is "Whoever knows their Self, knows their Lord". Here Muhammad is clearly pointing to the opportunity to 'know' though self-contemplation. He is saying that the true Self is Consciousness.

As well as Sunnis and Shias, there are many other branches and sub-branches of Islam. These include Karljite Islam and the various orders of Sufism.

Completing the top ten religions, we have Ethnic religions with 300 million followers, African traditional religions with 100 million, Sikhism with 30 million and Spiritism with 15 million.

The total number of religions including these top ten and all of the sub-divisions, but excluding the independent Christian churches, comes to over 4,000. The total number of followers is 6 billion, which is 84% of the global population at the time these estimates were made in 2012.

So with over 4,000 different religions there is certainly plenty of choice. The problem is that following a particular religion can close our minds to perennial wisdom elsewhere. The folly of religion is that specific beliefs and practices often keep an individual trapped in the identification of a personal ego self who is a follower of that religion. This prevents the non-dual transformational experience that lies at the heart of every religion. We have vast numbers of religious caterpillars but very few butterflies.

Krishna, Moses, Siddhartha Gautama, Lao-Tzu, Yeshua of Nazareth, Muhammad and many others were all human beings who realised their own true nature of non-personal Consciousness through self-contemplation and spiritual discipline. They tried to carry this message of salvation from the personal ego self through their teaching and by their own example, all of which was set in the particular culture at the time. Much of the teaching was initially passed on verbally and eventually documented in scripture. We have seen how difficult it is to communicate the nature of Consciousness using the limited tool of language. By the time the teachings were written down, translated and interpreted by personal ego minds, we can begin to see why so much original understanding has been lost. The purpose of mature religion is the metamorphosis of personal mind into Consciousness, Awareness, Knowingness, Mind, Spirit or Being. On this basis it seems that much of religion today is immature.

It is obviously not for me to question the religious beliefs of any individual. Each experience of life is purposefully unique, and such an experience can take place within or without religion. If we are going to follow a particular religion then we need to be wary of the folly of remaining a prodigal son who does not return home. The Roman poet Horace is quoted as saying that "Wisdom at times is found in folly" but we have to be aware and open-minded enough to see it.

My own preference is not to follow any particular religion. There is wisdom in all of them. The God word is just a word.

27. The Law of Three

According to the Vedas, the process of creation is very precise and measured. Creation is governed by simple mathematics that then build into complexity. The number three is fundamental to the Vedic system of knowledge, and crops up throughout religious scripture. It is worth reflecting on this briefly because the number three can give us a great deal of insight into the underlying nature of reality.

The ego mind tends to think in dualistic terms and hence experiences a dualistic world. Things are either right or wrong, good or bad, material or spiritual and so on. We often miss the third option, which is either the middle view or a paradox where two seeming opposites are both true. A simple example here would be to refer back to binary. On the face of it, binary is based on the number two. We either have zero or one. However binary originally related to a lamp being either off or on, hence zero or one. This means that there has to be a lamp, which is the 'hidden' third part of binary. There is something other than zero or one, and hence a triad is needed in order to produce duality.

The number three is relevant at all levels of Consciousness, and it seems is foundational. In Vedic terms, the relevance of three occurs right at the core of existence. The two eternal principles of Purusha and Prakiti together produce the whole Rta; the rhythmic order and regularity that gives rise to the experience of creation. Purusha and Prakiti may be perceived as male and female, with Rta being the offspring. Next we have the Trimurti which are the three aspects of Brahman, being Brahma the creator force, Vishnu the preserver and Shiva the destroyer. Then we have the three Gunas, with Rajas being the energy of activity, Sattva the blissful energy of being and Tamas as rest. The number three even finds it way into the primordial sound of AUM, or OM, where the three sound components represent the most profound concepts of universal creation, for example birth, life and death. All of this implies a triad of positive, negative and neutral, with neutral being the original state.

The Gospel of Thomas does not feature in the New Testament. It was discovered near Nag Hammadi in Egypt in December 1945. The manuscript is dated around 340 CE. There is speculation that it was buried because the teachings did not fit into the prevailing canon of Christian scripture. The Coptic text contains 114 sayings attributed to Jesus, known as logia. All of the logia refer in some way to non-dual Consciousness. Logion number 50 is particularly interesting in respect of the Law of Three. In response to the question "What is the sign of your father in you?", Jesus answers "It is movement and repose". This seemingly mysterious reply holds the key to understanding Consciousness, creation and life itself. We have a triad of father, movement and repose. Father is the Source, movement is the arising of Consciousness and repose is the subsiding of Consciousness. The whole of creation is the arising and subsiding of Consciousness. The manifest world is pulsing in and out of existence and experience, moment to moment, at such a rate that we cannot comprehend. Creation is not an event from the past that is gradually evolving, but is arising and subsiding continuously and evolving through its own experience. Life is just a temporary manifestation of Consciousness in an incredible diversity of forms. We are this Consciousness, and we arise and subside as it, moment to moment. All of this takes place in Source Awareness, and the movement and repose are vibrations of Source and perceived by Source. Whatever movements are taking place, the Source is silent and unmoving. This is the "peace that passeth all understanding" that Paul the Apostle mentions in his epistle to the Philippians. This peace is our own true nature. It is the foundational element of the triad. We can identify ourselves as the movement and repose, in the form of birth and death of the personal self, or we can identify as the underlying peace. All three components of the triad exist eternally, yet it is pretty obvious which part is Absolute Truth.

The Law of Three is always with us in practical terms in our breathing. There is the in-breath and the out-breath, which are the dualistic components. Then there is the pause between breaths, which is the third, and underlying, element. The unmoving position is no breath. From this position we breath in, which is movement, and then we breath out, which is repose. Without breathing in and out we would not be alive. Life only happens moment-by-moment, breath-by-breath, and meanwhile the underlying position of no breath remains peaceful and silent. This is why breathing is such an important part of spiritual practice. Pranayama, or breath control, features in both Hatha Yoga and Raja Yoga, and has ancient origins. The purpose is to abide as much as possible in the peaceful and silent underlying reality of no breath.

Trinity is derived from the Latin word *Trinitas* and means triad. The Christian version of Trinity is the three coeternal, consubstantial persons, or hypostases, of Father, Son and Holy Spirit. The idea is that God exists as three divine persons yet are one in substance or essence. The use of the word *person* in this context is very unhelpful, as it takes us back to deification rather than wisdom. A more mature understanding of Trinity would be Source Awareness as Father, Consciousness, Knowingness or Mind as Son, and whole Spirit or Being as Holy Spirit. In this understanding, Consciousness, Knowingness or Mind is, if you like, the first-born thought arising from Source Awareness in the form 'I Am', hence the idea of Son. The Holy Spirit is the movement and subsiding of Consciousness that gives rise to the experience of creation and life. This is the same Law of Three from the Vedas. If we align the Vedic model with the Christian version, then Father is Purusha, Son is Prakiti and Holy Spirit is Rta. Interestingly the Vedic version has Prakiti as female, hence it would be Mother or Daughter rather than Son. Consciousness is neither male nor female, but is the third part of the triad, so this divergence in terms of Son or Daughter is a mute point. It does however highlight the patriarchal attitude of Christianity, which is inherited from the Hebrew scripture. So Trinity is an attempt to capture the underlying reality that Awareness, or

Consciousness, is the originator of creation, that which perceives creation and the substance of creation. The idea that Father, Son and Holy Spirit are God, Jesus and some form of Holy Ghost is a literal and naïve interpretation of perennial wisdom born out of personal ego minds. Many do hold such a belief, but this simply adds weight to the assertion that much of religion is immature.

Discussion of the Law of Three is important because we tend to miss the significance of wisdom, both in the dualistic experience of the material world and in considering spiritual matters. Whenever we are faced with dualistic opposites, or choices, there is always a third option. It may not be obvious to the personal ego mind, but it is always there because the whole of creation is based on triads. When it comes to spirituality, the key understanding from the Law of Three is that peace and silence are the permanent screen on which the transient experience of life appears, moment to moment. We can get tangled up in the appearance on the screen, we can observe the screen or we can abide as the screen. The tangling up is the human experience. The abidance in silence and peace is the Being. The balance between human and Being is the third element that defines our experience of life. Whatever we experience as a human, it never changes the true nature of Being.

Bringing all of this wisdom to bear on the subject of addiction, we may perceive that the choice regarding active addiction is binary. Either we continue in active addiction, and suffer the inevitable consequences, or we stop using a particular substance or behavior. This choice may seem obvious, but it is not easy. The consequences of addiction get progressively worse, but so too does the fear of abstinence and change. Neither choice offers an attractive future. We cannot see a third option, and hence we do not believe that it exists. The good news is that it does exist. It must exist because there is always a third part of any triad. The unseen option is to disengage from the personal ego self where the addiction arises, and to abide in a deeper experience of Consciousness where addiction does not exist. It really is that simple. The core problem is the addiction to the personal self,

173

which gives rise to the use of substances and behaviours that ease the discomfort of human existence. The solution is to let go of the personal self and abide more and more as non-personal-Consciousness. The solution is spiritual. It has to be, because addiction is fundamentally a spiritual problem. Abstinence alone does not solve the problem of addiction. We have to go deeper than that.

Understanding the Law of Three gives us the opportunity to look past duality and see beyond the limitations of the personal ego mind. There is great wisdom contained in the number three. It is fundamental.

28. Aspects of Addiction

I do not claim to be an expert in addiction. What I can say is that, as Michael, I am an addict myself and that I have had long experience of working with others. This chapter is not intended to be scientific or academic. Such analysis is in the realm of personal ego mind. When it comes to addiction, there is perhaps too much mind and not enough Mind.

Addiction is necessarily part of the human condition. The condensed, limited form of Consciousness that manifests as a personal body and mind is inherently dissatisfied, because it generally lacks the experience of happiness, peace, love and unity from which it arises. As humans we spend our lives searching for these very things. Often we do this on a repetitive basis. We achieve them momentarily but never in a sustained way. This feeling of lack arises from personal identification as only human and overlooks our true nature of Being. This simple yet life changing mistake is made by all of us.

The word *sin* is translated from biblical Greek and Jewish language to mean the act or state of missing the mark, or miss take. The term arises from archery, where to miss the target was to *chait* in Hebrew, which then translates as sin. Basically then, a sin is a mistake. The whole idea of biblical original sin simply means the mistake in identity that humans make in believing themselves to be only personal. Each human is born with vulnerability to this original mistake and it quickly develops into the sense of personal self, as experienced by the individual body and ego mind. This is then reinforced by our family and cultural environment. There is no shame or guilt in original sin. It is simply a mistake.

Given that we all search for ways to ease our inherent dissatisfaction, it is fair to say that all humans are addicts to a greater or lesser extent. It is only ever a matter of degree and the specific nature of the addiction or addictions. Some may be offended by this suggestion, but we do have to admit that we are all driven by the search for happiness, peace, love and unity. This search means we are often addicted to our behaviours, to our personal thinking, or at least to our sense of personal self.

The question of degree relates to our particular psyche. I mentioned previously the concept of Samskara as an inherited psychic blueprint from previous experiences of Consciousness. This explanation, combined with childhood experiences of trauma, unworthiness, emotional or physical abuse or parental addiction, provide the ingredients for an infinite range of addictive tendencies of varying intensities. It is important to note that none of this is the personal responsibility of the individual. It is simply a feature of their human nature, as is any other natural feature. Those with strong addictive tendencies are destined to suffer the consequences of addiction. Sooner or later, this is likely to cause a great deal of suffering, both to themselves and to others. Addiction progresses at differing rates as well as intensities and hence there can be no standard experience or definition. What we do know is that the repeated use of substances and behaviours to satisfy our desires can eventually lead us to a state of powerlessness and desperation.

Whatever the differences in intensity, rate of progression, particular addiction or life circumstances, there are often strong similarities in thinking, feeling and behaviour. Most addicts report childhood feelings of self-centered fear, insecurity, anxiety, self-consciousness, inadequacy, low self-worth, isolation and wanting to be accepted. Sometimes these feelings develop into self-loathing and self-destructive tendencies. Everyone else seems to be fine but the addict feels himself or herself to be different. What we do not realise is that all humans have similar feelings and are wearing the mask of persona. The addict's basic feeling of personal discomfort, or dis-ease, is an accident waiting to happen. The addict will inevitably try to find the comfort and ease that is missing. As life progresses into teenage years, the addict finds his or her own way to cope. Peer pressure also often plays a part. We experiment with different substances and behaviours and find a combination that is effective for us. The solution seems to work. The crippling inhibition is relieved and we can participate in life, provided we can keep returning to our coping strategy. The stage is now set for addiction to take hold and progress.

The human body has an incredible ability to adapt to its particular environment. The term *homeostasis* is used to describe the dynamic process by which a living organism will always try to return to equilibrium. There are numerous functions of sensing, controlling and adapting going on within the body. Adjustments are continually being made to such things as core temperature, blood glucose levels, blood gases, blood pressure, levels of various minerals, fluid balance, pH levels, neurotransmission, the neuroendocrine system, organ function, gene regulation and energy balance. Basically the body gets used to the particular environment and adjusts itself to maintain equilibrium, or normality. So the body gets used to repeated use of a particular substance and regular usage becomes the new normal. The same is true for behaviours that produce chemical reactions in the nervous system, such as endorphins or dopamine release. The more we use these substances and behaviours, the more the body adjusts through homeostasis to normalise the effect. Once normalised, the sense of discomfort, or dis-ease, resurfaces. This inevitably leads to the desire to increase usage in order to once again obtain comfort and ease. As the body adjusts repeatedly, a dependency arises because the body wants normality. As the effects of previous usage wear off, the body naturally wants the chemical effects to be replenished. This explains the phenomenon of craving. The natural process of homeostasis has created a physical dependence on particular substances and behaviours in order for it to maintain equilibrium. Repeated usage becomes the new normal and the compulsion to use seems unstoppable.

The cycle progresses through homeostasis and can reach a point where the body constantly needs its fix. Despite increases in usage, the whole system keeps self-correcting and hence the desired sense of comfort and ease remains elusive. Eventually the body can become so dependent that sudden withdrawal causes symptoms of shock, such as delirium tremens or potentially fatal seizures. Even withdrawal during periods of sleep can produce such symptoms; hence the experience of morning shakes experienced by some addicts. Mitigating the effects of withdrawal is a medical matter, and hence medical treatment should be sought where necessary. Eventually the body will adjust to abstinence because homeostasis will gradually adjust the system back to equilibrium without the need for an external fix.

This is all bad enough, but it gets worse. Abstinence seems the obvious solution to addiction, but by now the sub-conscious mind is habitually programmed to continue unabated. Whatever psychic blueprint we may have inherited, our subsequent repetitive behaviour has habituated to the point that it is automatic. Neural pathways have formed at a level below conscious awareness and operate despite our best intentions. We are at a level that is similar to a knee-jerk reaction when a certain spot on the knee is tapped. We are powerless to stop the knee jerking, and likewise an addict is powerless to prevent a relapse when subjected to certain triggers, however hard he or she may try. Once a relapse occurs, then the previous addicted homeostatic state is rapidly reestablished and the phenomenon of craving is back with a vengeance. The cycle of stopping and restarting may repeat a great many times, and all the while the addiction is growing stronger and stronger. This is a hopeless state of body and mind, yet the suffering is far from over. Albert Einstein is credited with saying that "The definition of insanity is doing the same thing over and over again, but expecting different results." The repetitive cycle of relapse in addiction certainly seems to fit this definition.

The personal battle to control an addiction is utterly demoralising. Society values willpower and determination, and those who not understand addiction are baffled as to why an addict cannot simply stop their obviously self-destructive behaviour. The inability to stop, and stay stopped, becomes a source of failure, shame and guilt. This is made worse by anti-social, or even criminal, behaviour which takes place under the influence of mind-altering substances or behaviours. Failure to obtain the desperately needed fix can also lead to much other dysfunctional behaviour. All of this creates an intolerable burden of remorse and humiliation. The addict develops the ability to deny his or her own thoughts, feelings and actions. He or she tries to maintain some degree of normality despite the downward spiral. Family and friends who try to help are shunned in favour of isolation and freedom from restriction. The addict may move geographically in order to escape the consequences of addictive behaviour, but very quickly the same problems are recreated elsewhere.

As addiction progresses, the addict retreats more and more into a world of suffering and self-centeredness. All of the traits of the personal ego mind become amplified. I have mentioned these before, but they are worth repeating again. These attributes are all based on self-centered fear and include anger, criticism, dishonesty, disrespect, doubt, envy, gluttony, greed, hate, intolerance, impatience, jealousy, judgment, lust, pride, resentment, selfishness, self-condemnation, self-doubt, self-importance, self-justification, self-pity, self-righteousness, self-seeking, sloth, suspicion, thoughtlessness and worry. Those who have suffered with addiction will recognise many of these traits. Such self-centered thinking and action causes fractures in personal relationships, particularly with those closest to us. Problems may also arise in the workplace and in the ability to function effectively in society. Financial problems may also arise. Physical and mental health and wellbeing will suffer as the result of continuing self-abuse. The addict may seek out people and places where active addiction is acceptable, and this can lead to a dark and dangerous existence. Often there are brushes with the criminal justice system and sometimes these result in imprisonment.

The self-centered obsession with personal suffering also has another negative consequence. The ever-present qualities of pure Consciousness are blocked and inaccessible. As mentioned before, these qualities are based on selfless love and are the opposite of the traits of the personal ego mind. They include serenity, acceptance, honesty, respect, faith, gratitude, moderation, sharing, empathy, tolerance, patience, charity, compassion, purity, humility, forgiveness, selflessness, self-forgiveness, confidence, modesty, self-acceptance, self-love, humbleness, altruism, action, trust, consideration and courage. Such thoughts and feelings are distant memories for the addict. The personal ego mind is so agitated that the still, quiet voice of Consciousness is drowned out. The addict may wish for these positive qualities but they seem hopelessly out of reach. The selfish, self-centered mind is so full of fear and negativity that the idea of ever living in happiness, peace, love and unity seems utterly impossible.

Sooner or later the addict reaches a stage of desperation and brokenness. Everything worthwhile in life has either been lost or damaged beyond seeming repair. Each has their individual circumstances and pain threshold, but there comes a point where life becomes intolerable. We cannot live with addiction but also we cannot face the fear of living without it. This is a personal version of hell. Thoughts of suicide are not uncommon amongst addicts. We may make suicide attempts, and unfortunately some of these are fatal. Suicide is not the only risk. Other causes of death include heart attack, brain damage, organ failure, fatal seizure, choking on vomit, fatal accidents or fatal confrontations. Even if these risks do not prove fatal they can leave lasting physical and mental consequences.

Desperation and brokenness can however also be the turning point. Addicts reach a personal crisis and many reach out for help. Options may include doctors, medication, counselors, psychiatrists, rehab centers, fitness campaigns and self-help books. Most of these options focus on abstinence as the solution to addiction. Abstinence is certainly a prerequisite for recovery, but abstinence alone does not provide anything like an adequate solution. Addiction is a multi-layered condition and hence an effective solution needs to address each of the layers. The external compulsive addictive behaviour is really a symptom of the underlying inner problem. We need to deal with each layer in turn. First we have the physical addiction, which arises as the result of the natural process of homeostasis. Secondly we have the mental problem whereby neural pathways have established through repetition and keep taking the addict back to relapse. Thirdly we have the psychic blueprint with the original feelings of self-centered fear, insecurity and inadequacy that existed long before the specific addiction. Finally we have the misidentification with the personal ego self which ultimately is the root cause of addiction and all other human problems.

Available treatment options reflect an understanding of the depth of the problem of addiction. Inpatient and outpatient detoxification treatment focuses on the physical aspect of addiction and mainly uses medication to gradually allow the body to return a state of equilibrium that does not crave the chemical effect of addiction. There may also be a focus on relapse prevention. Such treatment works but it is not a solution to addiction. An addict who is abstinent is still an addict and prone to relapse at any time. The remaining three layers have not yet been addressed, and the underlying mental issues can continue to cause great distress. To compound the problem there can also be a feeling of grief in having to give up what was previously perhaps the most important thing in life. The Kubler-Ross model proposes five stages of grief whereas other models suggest seven. The stages include shock, denial, anger, bargaining, guilt, depression and finally acceptance. This may be an oversimplification but it does highlight the additional emotional pain that an addict may suffer during early abstinence. The addict may seek comfort and ease from other substances or behaviours, and this can create new addictions. Without additional help and support in can all be too much to bear. Suicidal tendencies are not unheard of even when an addict is abstinent.

Cognitive Behavioural Therapy (CBT) addresses the second layer of addiction through focusing on changes in thoughts, feelings and behaviours. This action-oriented form of therapy seeks to create new neural pathways that replace the old addictive patterns. The best known of these treatment options is SMART, which is an acronym for Self-Management and Recovery Training. SMART uses a combination of CBT and Motivational Enhancement Therapy in a four-point program that comprises building motivation, coping with urges, managing thoughts, feelings and behaviours, and lifestyle balance. Facilitated group meetings provide training and tools and also offer the benefit of mutual help, support and encouragement. A 2018 longitudinal study showed that SMART recovery has a comparable success rate to twelve-step recovery and does work in certain circumstances. The addict is however still left with two more layers of addiction yet to be resolved.

Psychiatric treatment options include psychotherapy and medication and are focused on the diagnosis, prevention and treatment of mental disorders. Addiction is itself a mental disorder, but there are often underlying issues which lead to addictive behaviour. Feelings of self-centered fear, insecurity, anxiety, depression, self-consciousness, inadequacy, low self-worth, self-loathing and self-destruction are sub-consciously rooted deep in the psyche. As discussed previously, some of these issues may be inherited and unfathomable. Psychiatric treatment can be a delicate and long-term process, and there is a risk of bringing up past trauma and trapped emotions that are difficult to deal with. This spells danger for an addict who may still remain vulnerable to relapse. If such a relapse does occur then all of the good work from previous treatment will quickly unravel. The whole cycle of addiction will recommence, often with even more devastating consequences. Even if psychiatric treatment is successful, we are still in jeopardy of addiction because the root cause of the problem in the final layer is still firmly in place.

Detoxification, relapse prevention, CBT, motivational enhancement therapy, psychotherapy and medication are all treatments focused on the body and mind. The sustainable long-term solution to addiction resides in Consciousness rather than the personal mind. The inevitable suffering of the self-identified personal ego mind is leading us to metamorphosis. A caterpillar addict who manages to stay sober through a combination of body and mind-based treatment is still a caterpillar. The opportunity to become a butterfly has been missed. Life will continue to desire a natural transformation and all continuing resistance will simply cause yet more suffering. This discomfort will arise with or without a relapse. An addict may be sober for months, years, or even decades, but it will make no difference. The measure of recovery is not the length of abstinence. Recovery is all about the shift in balance from human to Being through spiritual growth. Recovery is about letting go of the personal ego mind and embracing Consciousness, where all of the desired happiness, peace, love and unity reside. Recovery is spiritual growth. There is no true recovery without it.

I have known addicts who have faith, and engage in spiritual practices, but have still struggled to recover. These include Christians, Hindus and Buddhists. Spirituality on its own does not seem to provide the complete answer to addiction. An addict needs guidance and support from people who fully understand what suffering from addiction is really like. The opportunity to identify with, and relate to, other individuals with similar problems is crucial.

Twelve-step recovery addresses all four layers of addiction. Detoxification is obviously a medical matter, but advice on relapse prevention abounds in twelve-step fellowship. The program is action-based with a clear emphasis on changes in thinking, feeling and behaviour. The concept of sponsorship provides one-on-one support and guidance. The sponsor is not a psychiatrist but can draw upon their own experience to bring clarity to underlying issues. Help and unconditional love is also available at group meetings to support an addict through the various stages of recovery, some of which can be very emotionally challenging. Crucially the program also provides the spiritual disciplines necessary to bring about the shift from personal mind to non-personal Consciousness. As the shift takes place, the deep-rooted issues begin to surface and heal. Addicts already engaged in change selflessly provide guidance and inspiration to those who are beginning their own journey. All of this adds up to a powerful process of transformation which, if continued, will bring about the intended metamorphosis in identification and being. Addiction resides in the body and mind but not in Consciousness itself. The solution is spiritual because ultimately addiction is a spiritual problem.

The aspects of addiction are complex and multi-layered, but we have already seen that all complexity arises from simplicity. An effective solution needs to penetrate these layers and address the problem at the simplest level. Twelve-step recovery provides such a solution. This is why it works.

29. Origins of the Twelve Steps

Twelve-step fellowships are not religious in nature. This may seem a surprising statement to those who do not understand. It would be tempting to say that twelve-step recovery is secular, but the word *secular* unfortunately means 'not religious or spiritual'. Twelve-step recovery is not religious but it is spiritual. Religion is spiritual but spirituality is not necessarily religious. This distinction is very important. There is often understandable prejudice against religion, and such preconceptions can prove fatal if they prevent an addict from engaging in recovery. There need be no emphasis at all on religion in modern day twelve-step fellowship. Some members do have strong religious views, which is fine, but in my eight-year experience in the UK such views are the exception rather than the rule. Twelve-step recovery does not imply religion. I must place as much emphasis as possible on this point. Do not let the personal ego mind use the impression of religion as an excuse to avoid engaging in meaningful recovery.

Having made this clear, it is also important to acknowledge that twelve-step recovery does have its origins in Christianity. Echoes of these origins resonate loudly in the wording of twelve-step literature but, as we have seen, Christianity is just yet another brand of spirituality. It is the perennial wisdom of non-dual Consciousness that matters, rather than any particular doctrine.

The twelve steps originated from Alcoholics Anonymous (AA) in the 1930s. The co-founders of AA were Bill Wilson and Bob Smith who were both alcoholics and who separately became involved with a Christian organisation called the Oxford Group. This was an organisation founded by the American Lutheran Minister and Christian Missionary Frank Buchman. Originally called A First Century Christian Fellowship when founded in

1921 at Oxford University in the UK, it became known as the Oxford Group in 1928. By 1938 the name changed again to Moral Re-Armament (MRA) and Buchman continued to head the organisation until his death in 1961. MRA changed its name again in 2001 and became Initiatives of Change. The organisation has centres in numerous countries and continues to this day. Initiatives of Change has spiritual roots but no religious affiliation.

The Oxford Group philosophy was based on absolute honesty, absolute purity, absolute unselfishness and absolute love; known collectively as the Four Absolutes. These were recognised as not attainable, as this would imply 0/100 on our spectrum of balance between human and Being. They were used instead as ideals to be worked towards. The spiritual practices advocated by the group were the sharing of shortcomings with a fellow, the surrender of past, present and future life to God (or Consciousness), the restitution of harms done to others and the listening for guidance from God (or Consciousness) and then carrying it out. There was also an emphasis on carrying the message of "hope through change" by sharing experience with others. Those who are already familiar with the twelve steps will immediately recognise these practices.

Bob Smith first became involved with the Oxford Group in 1933 with his wife Anne, who had attended a lecture by Frank Buchman in Akron, Ohio. They attended meetings on a regular basis, but Bob did not get sober until 10th June 1935, shortly after having met Bill Wilson on 12th May 1935.

Bill Wilson's introduction to the Oxford Group was more convoluted. Roland Hazard was a prominent businessman and Rhode Island Senator who suffered from alcoholism. In 1926 he placed himself under the care of the Swiss psychologist Carl Jung. After some years of unsuccessful treatment Hazard was advised in 1931 by Jung that his only hope was a "vital spiritual experience". Hazard returned to America and began attending Oxford Group meetings. Although his sobriety was sporadic, he remained active in the Oxford Group and in the summer of 1934 he carried the message of hope to an acquaintance called Ebby Thatcher who was holidaying in Vermont at the same time. Thatcher was facing six months in prison for shooting pigeons with a shotgun and Hazard used his influence to have him released into his care. Thatcher sobered up, returned to New York and was lodged at the Calvary Rescue Mission, which was operated by the Calvary Episcopal Church. The minister at Calvary was Reverend Sam Shoemaker, who was also active in the Oxford Group. In November 1934, Ebby Thatcher visited his old drinking friend Bill Wilson and talked with him about the Oxford Group and his resulting sobriety. Wilson listened but continued to drink. He did however visit the Calvary Mission and engage in Oxford Group teachings. On 11th December 1934 Wilson was admitted to Town's Hospital for the fourth time and it was here, under the influence of the Belladonna Cure, that he had his spiritual experience. He credited this experience to his heartfelt appeal to God for help, and consequently he became very interested in the Oxford Group.

Wilson tried to carry the message to other alcoholics but was not successful. He did however stay sober himself. In May 1935 he travelled to Akron on a business trip and on Sunday 12th May he met with Bob Smith, having made numerous phone calls the previous evening when feeling vulnerable to a relapse. The connection was made with Smith via Oxford Group members. The impact of one alcoholic talking with another was not lost on either of them, and Smith became sober just four weeks later. Wilson remained in Akron for three months and the two co-founders began carrying the message of hope to other alcoholics.

Wilson finally returned to New York and continued carrying the message. The early approach was a bit evangelical and had limited success. He took alcoholics to Oxford Group meetings but they resisted what was perceived to be too much doctrine. Eventually Wilson decided to part with the Oxford Group in New York, and subsequently Smith did the same in Akron. They began holding meetings in each location specifically for alcoholics, but based on the same spiritual principles. Gradually others became sober and the groups began to expand. By 1938 there were around one hundred alcoholics in recovery and in May and June of that year Wilson began drafting chapters of a book intended to codify the approach. There was fierce debate within the fledgling fellowship as to whether the book should be religious or psychological in nature, and the result of this debate was the inclusion of the very important spiritual phrase "God, us we understand Him".

At this stage, the methodology being used was a six-step program that Wilson credited mainly to his Oxford Group talk with Ebby Thatcher back in 1934. He also gave credit to William James, who wrote the book 'Varieties of Religious Experience' in 1902, and to his doctor at Town's Hospital, Dr. William Silkworth. The six steps were 1) admitted hopeless 2) got honest with self 3) got honest with another 4) made amends 5) helped others without demands and 6) prayed to God as you understand him. One evening in December 1938 at home in his bed, Wilson subsequently expanded this six-step program to a twelve-step program, which was something that had been on his mind for a while.

The book gradually came together and comprised a contribution from Dr. Silkworth, eleven chapters drafted by Wilson and a number of personal stories from members of the fellowship. A lithograph draft was produced in mid-February 1939 and around four hundred copies were circulated to doctors, psychiatrists, ministers and members of AA for comment. A review of the changes made to that first draft provide some fascinating insights. Firstly, the whole tone of the book was changed from directive to descriptive. The words *must* and *should* were replaced by suggestions and descriptions of what had worked for others. Secondly the word *we* was included in multiple locations, most significantly at the beginning of step one. Thirdly, the words *on our knees* were removed from the beginning of step seven, and the words *holding nothing back* were deleted at the end of the same step. Fourthly, the word *conscious* was included in step eleven, along with the phrase *as we understood Him.* All of these changes, and many others, reflect the fine line between doctrine, which would most likely have been rejected by many alcoholics, and a program of actions and spiritual principles that would have wide appeal. This fine line was a compromise but it has opened the door of recovery for many more addicts than might otherwise have been the case, including myself.

The final result was publication of the book Alcoholics Anonymous on 10th April 1939. The book title also became the name of the fellowship. The book became known as the Big Book due to the thickness of the paper used in the original print run. There are books and articles that describe the history of AA in far more detail, but I have included this brief description in order to highlight two matters of fundamental importance.

Firstly, the twelve-step program is an expansion of the six-step program, which itself was based entirely on Oxford Group philosophy and spiritual practice. In turn, the Oxford Group ethos arose from first century Christianity, which closely followed the teachings of Jesus. We have seen that these teachings were totally based on non-dual Consciousness. Such teachings conflicted with the prevailing Jewish understanding at the time and are entirely consistent with the perennial wisdom that almost certainly came from India. Twelve-step recovery is therefore a process of transformation based on the same ancient Vedic wisdom that underpins the model of Consciousness that I have attempted to explain. This is no surprise. There is only one underlying reality, and all of the spiritual traditions and practices around the world are pointing at the same truth in a variety of different ways.

Secondly, Roland Hazard and Ebby Thatcher never became part of the AA fellowship. Both enjoyed periods of sobriety but neither of them experienced long-term recovery. Bill Wilson and Bob Smith remained sober for the rest of their lives and dedicated themselves to helping others. They maintained their own spiritual growth and supported the growth of AA over many years. They were not saints and neither of them claimed to be. They had inadvertently found a solution to alcoholism through serendipitous exposure to pre-existing wisdom. They did however make the crucial discovery that there is mutual benefit when one alcoholic helps another. The one who helps is practicing self-forgetting, which is an essential part of the transformation process. The one who is helped places trust in the experience, strength and hope of those who offer help. This is generally far more effective than any guidance provided by doctors, psychiatrists, ministers or others who have no personal experience of active addiction or the challenges and pitfalls of recovery. This mutual benefit is what forms the fellowship of the broken, and such fellowships have saved or improved the lives of many millions over the intervening years.

Bob Smith passed away on 16th November 1950. As well as carrying the message of recovery to countless others he is said to have also personally treated over 5,000 alcoholics in his clinic free of charge during his 15 years of sobriety. Bill Wilson was 36 years sober when he died on 24th January 1971. He remained active in AA throughout this time and wrote prodigiously. Although Wilson took most of the plaudits for the founding of AA, it was, for me, Bob Smith who epitomised and personified the spiritual principles of humility and altruism. In July of 1950, Smith gave his final public talk at the very first international convention of AA. In his speech he placed emphasis on the simplicity of the twelve-step program and said that, when simmered down, the twelve steps resolve themselves into the words *love* and *service*.

Humility, altruism, simplicity, love and service are key components of recovery. These principles remain embedded in the AA fellowship, and all subsequent twelve-step fellowships, to this day.

30. The Power of Fellowship

Following publication of the Big Book in 1939, the fellowship grew quickly with new meetings being started in towns across America. Given that these meetings were independent, and were comprised of alcoholics at various stages of recovery, it is not surprising that all sorts of issues arose. The problem was how to maintain a cohesive approach to recovery without creating a centralised bureaucracy. It took seven years of experience through problem solving and dispute resolution to arrive at a set of twelve traditions that would assure the future continuity of the fellowship. These twelve traditions were written by Bill Wilson and were first published in April 1946. They are based on spiritual principles and were molded in the fierce heat of AA experience. In many ways, they are a more important contribution to recovery than the twelve steps, because without an ongoing fellowship there would be no individual recovery.

The spiritual principles encapsulated in the twelve traditions are unity, group conscience, no discrimination, group autonomy, carrying the message of recovery, independence, financially self-supporting, non-professional, no formal organisation, no opinions on outside issues, attraction rather than promotion and anonymity. The emphasis on anonymity is often misunderstood. Anonymity is an expression of humility. It reflects non-personal Consciousness rather than personal ego. Anonymity is not about secrecy or shame, although it is easy to see how it could be perceived this way. Humility through anonymity is how Consciousness expresses itself through individuals and groups. The subsequent extraordinary growth in twelve-step fellowship is the natural result.

As the number of groups increased, they were coordinated through inter-group committees at the level of area, regional, national and international. The whole structure is an inverted pyramid, with the individual groups at the top level and the various levels of committee underneath in a supporting role. In modern-day management speak this is known as Servant Leadership and it is highly effective. There are no leaders in twelve-step fellowship. Everyone is in selfless service to the primary purpose, which is to carry the message of recovery to the addict who is still suffering.

Continuing participation in fellowship is an essential component in ongoing recovery. This is why addicts with decades of sobriety continue to attend meetings. It is all about being of service. Each group is autonomous yet ideally operates under the guidance of the twelve traditions. The meetings vary in terms of format and depth of spiritual understanding, but generally speaking they create a powerful effect because they work on multiple levels.

Firstly the meetings provide a safe place for addicts to spend time with others who understand and who are supportive. Addiction is a lonely, fear-based, shame-inducing condition and the power of fellowship with others who suffer should not be underestimated. Just as a caterpillar is cocooned in a chrysalis during metamorphosis, so the addict is cocooned in a loving fellowship whist he or she goes through their own individual transformation. Telephone numbers are exchanged and used. Social events and close friendships are not uncommon. Fellowship can be the beginning of reintegration into society.

Next there is identification with others who relate their individual stories. Most addicts are in denial as to the seriousness of their condition, and listening to others will help them to see many similarities in their own thoughts, feeling and behaviours. It is also an opportunity to learn about aspects of addiction and various helpful techniques for relapse prevention.

Thirdly, the very fact that the meetings are full of people who have found recovery through twelve-step fellowship provides inspiration and motivation for the addict who is still suffering. The attraction of those already in recovery produces a powerful incentive to follow the same path.

Once an addict has identified their own condition, it becomes apparent that a key part of the solution is to work through the twelve-step program. This requires a sponsor, whose task it is to provide guidance and understanding based upon their own experience, strength and hope. The meetings provide a reservoir of potential sponsors to suit all needs and preferences.

In addition, the sharing of problems can elicit specific help and advice from others who have had similar experiences. The general advice is to share problems with a sponsor and share the solution in meetings, but there are times when the sharing of problems in a group can be cathartic and beneficial. As recovery matures, it should be seen that all problems are personal in nature and that they provide an opportunity to further let go of the personal self rather than wallow in self-pity.

Importantly the fellowship also provides multiple opportunities to be of service to others, both at group and inter-group level. Self-forgetting is a key and necessary part of spiritual growth, and hence being of service is essential to healthy long-term recovery. It is not an optional extra. Also it is obvious that without service there would be no fellowship, and hence no recovery. If an addict claims to be in recovery but is not in service to others then he or she is fooling themselves. There are many ways to be of service in society, but an addict in recovery does have specific experience that is very valuable to the addict who still suffers. The experience of being in active addiction and then finding recovery is a priceless gift that can change or save the lives of others. It would be a betrayal of spiritual principles not to use this gift. Such withholding can only be the influence of a selfish, personal ego mind, and that in itself is an indication of the progress yet to be made.

Celebration is always good for motivation, and the meetings provide the platform for acknowledging progress. Cakes are a traditional way to celebrate, and some meetings provide embossed coins or chips to mark sobriety milestones. Whist these celebrations are all very positive, it is important to remember that length of sobriety is not the measure of recovery. The true measure is the shift in balance from human to Being, or mind to Mind.

Last but by no means least is the vibrational impact of attending meetings. Our cultures are generally based on the personal ego self. Without frequent exposure to humility and unconditional love, the individual vibration of Consciousness will quickly revert to resonance with the collective Consciousness of society. We are swimming in it every day and it can drag us down. In this respect, twelve-step meetings have similarities to the vibrational influence of satsang. When the ice-cube of personal ego self is repeatedly placed in the warm water of twelve-step fellowship then it gradually begins to melt with no effort. There is no need to understand or say anything at all. Just being in the presence of other human beings who are humble, honest, openhearted, compassionate and loving will naturally raise the vibration of an addict who is still firmly trapped in the limited, restricted bondage of the personal ego mind. Many who attend meetings find them to be an uplifting experience without really understanding why this happens. The experience though is beyond doubt. Given how powerful this vibrational influence can be, it is incumbent upon the regular group members to imbue the meeting with spiritual principles and appropriate words and actions. Given the potentially fatal nature of addiction, such words and actions can sometimes be a matter of life and death.

It is important to acknowledge that twelve-step fellowship meetings do vary in spiritual quality. Any meeting at any time will consist of a group of addicts from varying backgrounds and at various stages of recovery. The specific composition of any meeting, week to week, will influence the general tone. There can be unhelpful words and actions as well as good. There can be disruptions and disputes. We are dealing with brokenness, and sometimes brokenness can give rise to the negative aspects of the human ego. Generally speaking though, those members with longer-term recovery are able to handle such situations. Such occurrences are the exception rather than the rule and the vast majority of meetings are extremely positive and beneficial.

So twelve-step fellowship meetings are not a group of addicts getting together in a church hall to secretly brainwash others into some form of doctrine. Recovery is a serious matter and the combination of the twelve steps and twelve traditions is a tried and tested methodology that works. It is a shame that success rates are not higher, but the process does work if the program is followed effectively and the spiritual principles are practiced regularly. Failures arise mainly due to misunderstandings. Often an addict is not able to grasp quickly enough how and why the program works. Alternatively there is too much fear around the process of transformation or, having made a start, the experience of metamorphosis becomes too uncomfortable. There are many other traps, which I will cover in a later chapter, but overall it must be conceded that the success rates are low compared with the wisdom and efficacy of twelve-step recovery.

There is no humility without brokenness. There is no recovery without humility. Twelve-step meetings truly are a fellowship of the broken, and this turns out to be their greatest strength and source of power.

31. Cult Status

I attended just one AA meeting prior to going into rehab in the summer of 2010. We were then shipped out to three meetings per week whist in treatment over a four-week period, hence another twelve meetings. My early impressions were not favorable. My perception of twelve-step recovery was that of a pseudo-religious cult that was intent on brainwashing me into their way of thinking. The scrolls on the walls in each venue contained the God word, which had no appeal at all. The message that I heard loudest was that I should "keep coming back". This made me feel uncomfortable and further entrenched my suspicions. I could easily have walked away, but I didn't. As with many others, my life had fallen apart as a result of addiction. I was isolated, lonely and fearful of relapse. I had nowhere else to go, so when the time in treatment came to an end I started to attend meetings four or five times per week.

I was still firmly stuck in personal ego mind. I trusted my own thinking because that was all I had ever known. I was willing to give AA a try, but only up to a point and only on my terms. I did not feel that it was necessary to do the steps and I certainly did not want a sponsor offering me 'guidance'. I lasted five months and then relapsed badly. I went back to AA and asked how I should go about getting a sponsor. The person to whom I asked this question unexpectedly offered to sponsor me. We began to meet on a weekly basis but I procrastinated over doing the suggested work. After four months I relapsed again, and this time my drinking was the worst ever. My own behavior frightened me. The addiction was progressing and I knew for certain that there was only one direction that it was going to take me. The relapse lasted ten days but eventually I went back to the meetings and resumed work on the steps. My last drink was on 24th May 2011 and I have been sober ever since. The twelve-step program initiated a process of transformation that is still ongoing. The AA fellowship opened my eyes to a new perspective and my life today is enjoyable and purposeful.

Spiritual practice is the foundation upon which everything else depends. I take it seriously because I have seen what happens to friends and colleagues when we don't. As my recovery has progressed, so the experience and understanding has grown.

My early perception of twelve-step fellowship as a cult is not unusual, and it can be a big barrier to recovery. The definitions of the word *cult* in the Oxford English Dictionary are "a system of religious worship directed towards a particular person or object" or "a small religious group regarded by other people as strange or as having too greater control over its members".

There will always be people who take a disparaging view of anything wholesome and there is little point in debate. However, for the addict who is still suffering, I think it is very important to set out the facts, as I see them, so that an informed decision can be made.

Twelve-step recovery is not religious. There is no worship of any person. The word *God* is completely open to individual interpretation. Twelve-step fellowships comprise many millions of people and are therefore not small. There is nothing strange about human beings wanting a life based on happiness, peace, love and unity. It is what everyone naturally wants. Twelve-step fellowship has absolutely no control whatsoever over its members. There are no rules, regulations, requirements, fees or any other form of control or restriction. In fact twelve-step fellowship is a wonderful example of how human beings can come together for mutual benefit whist retaining freedom and individuality. Twelve-step fellowship does not come anywhere near meeting any aspect of either of the definitions of a cult. Any assertion to the contrary must have some hidden agenda, because it is simply not true.

Having said that, the mistaken perception of a cult does nevertheless exist. I am not aware of all of the reasons for this, but I can offer some suggestions as to why this might be the case.

As mentioned previously, anonymity is an expression of humility. It is intended to keep the personal ego mind right-sized. Unfortunately in more general understanding, anonymity is perceived as secrecy. This is reinforced by the idea that an addict may wish to keep his presence at recovery meetings confidential. This perception of secrecy adds weight to the misconception that twelve-step fellowships have something to hide.

We have seen that the personal ego mind needs repeated exposure to spiritual principles in order begin the process of change. This can be perceived as brainwashing. What is perhaps not realised is that the individual personal mind is already the result of conditioning, or brainwashing. Parental influences, environment, education, peer groups, media and culture all play a part in creating the seemingly independent thinking of a personal ego mind. Rather than being authentic, it is the result of conditioning. The process of recovery disempowers the personal ego mind and allows Consciousness itself to surface. This in turn cleanses the lens of perception which, if you like, can be interpreted as brainwashing. The brain of an addict needs washing in this respect, otherwise there will be no recovery. The negative connotations around this term arise from misunderstanding and from the unscrupulous use of brainwashing techniques elsewhere. These impressions can unfortunately increase the impression of cult status.

The idea of attraction rather than promotion is spiritually sound but this lack of publicity also can imply that twelve-step fellowships want to remain unknown. Again this raises a general suspicion that visibility is unwanted.

The use of the word *God* clearly implies religion to those who do not understand.

The practices of prayer, meditation and selfless service also have strong religious connotations, but again this is a misperception.

There is a fine line between evangelism and trying to be helpful. Sometimes our attempts to carry the message of hope and recovery can be misconstrued.

Many twelve-step fellowship meetings are held in churches or church halls. These venues are typically low cost, and churches tend to support altruistic initiatives to be of service. However many meetings have their own clubhouses, and many others use community halls or other venues. The association of twelve-step recovery with churches is understandable but can lead to misleading conclusions.

Finally the symbolic logo of a triangle within a circle, adopted by AA in 1955, is perhaps another factor that gives the misleading impression of a cult. Interestingly this symbol is not original to twelve-step recovery. In AA, the circle stands for the whole world of AA and the three sides of the triangle represent the Three Legacies; namely Recovery, Unity and Service. The same symbol is used by a wisdom-based organisation called The Universal Order that was established in 1923. In their case the circle is symbolic of the One Principle and the three sides of the triangle represent the fundamental predicates of Truth, Beauty and Goodness. The same symbol is said to have ancient spiritual significance, with the three components of mind, body and spirit together as one. There are also obvious similarities with the concept of trinity. Whatever the origins, in the early 1990s AA World Services decided to phase out use of the symbol on its literature, letterhead and other material. In 1994 the AA General Service Conference resolved that the logo be discontinued on all conference-approved literature. Despite these decisions, the logo remains in widespread use today. There is an understandable attachment to the logo as a symbol of recovery, unity and service, but it is also fair to say that such symbolism does add to the myth of cult.

The combination of these eight factors, and perhaps more, provide enough ammunition to brand twelve-step fellowship with aspects of cult status. For those of us already in recovery, this is of no great importance because we know that it is not true. However the primary purpose of twelve-step fellowship is to carry the message of hope and recovery to the addict who still suffers. There are many of us in recovery, but there are a great many more who are not. If the general perception of cult status prevents an addict from engaging in meaningful recovery, as it nearly did for me, then leaving this issue unaddressed undermines the whole purpose of twelve-step fellowship.

The cult status of twelve-step fellowship is an urban myth. Anything that we can do to gently debunk this myth would be consistent with the primary purpose of helping others into recovery.

32. The Four Triads

Having explained the model of Consciousness, reviewed aspects of addiction, covered the origins of the twelve steps and highlighted the importance of fellowship, it is now finally time to take an in-depth look at the twelve-step program of recovery. Rather than being a set of instructions, the style of wording in the twelve steps deliberately describes what the early founders of AA did themselves in order to recover. This sharing of experience is obviously far more palatable than any amount of evangelical doctrine. The tone of the twelve steps is therefore more suggestive than instructional, but we should not make the mistake of thinking that individual steps are optional. We need to practice all of the steps if we want to engage in effective recovery. We should also understand what is really meant by a suggestion in this context. The often-quoted metaphor is that of a parachutist jumping out of an airplane. It is suggested that the ripcord is pulled in order to activate the parachute. The suggestion is really a conditional instruction. If the parachutist wishes to survive the fall then he needs to pull the ripcord. The choice is still optional, but the repercussions of the choice are severe. If the parachutist chooses not to pull the ripcord than he will almost certainly fall to his death. If he chooses to follow the suggestion then he will almost certainly survive. This metaphor may seem a bit extreme, but addiction heads in only one direction and will continue ever-downwards towards fatality unless we engage in recovery.

Before exploring each of the steps in detail, it is worth reflecting on the overall structure of the process. The twelve steps can be neatly broken down into four sets of three. These triads address each of the four layers of addiction. This may, or may not, have been the original intention but it does make sense to look at the steps in this way.

The first triad deals with the first layer of addiction. Steps one, two and three are all about surrender. The physical addiction reaches a stage where life becomes intolerable. The addict wants to stop and eventually realises, through repeated failed attempts, that help is needed. This form of surrender is not failure. In fact, surrender to personal powerlessness over addiction is the gateway to recovery. Surrender is simply an acknowledgement that some form of assistance is necessary in order to experience recovery. It later becomes apparent that this assistance comes from Consciousness itself.

The second and third triads address the second layer of addiction, which is the mental vulnerability. Steps four, five and six are concerned with humility. Denial of selfish and self-centered thinking, feeling and behaviour is a key feature of addiction. It takes courage to look at our own dysfunctional traits, but it is comforting to know that such attributes are simply aspects of the personal ego mind rather than individual blemishes. Humility is the admission of our brokenness and hence comes the willingness to change. Humility is a priceless gift, and it only comes through brokenness. The arrogant, self-confident, self-contained human has no chance of ever receiving this gift. In this respect, addicts are fortunate although, admittedly, this may not yet be apparent at this stage of recovery. Without humility, there will be ongoing resistance to change.

Steps seven, eight and nine are all about change and forgiveness. This requires thinking, feeling and behaving in ways that the personal ego mind will find uncomfortable. Change does not take place within our comfort zone. If we are not experiencing discomfort then we are not changing. New neural pathways will only develop through the repetition of new behaviours. These new behaviours will bring surprisingly positive results, which in turn provide more motivation for change.

The fourth triad gets to the root of the problem of addiction in layers three and four which cover the psychic blueprint and the misidentification with personal ego self. Steps ten, eleven and twelve provide, in turn, the spiritual practices of self-awareness, self-contemplation and self-forgetting. These practices form the basis for a new way of being which is free from the burden of addiction. The process can take time, but gradually there is a shift in the balance of power between mind and Mind. The self-centered aspects of personal ego mind give way to the selfless qualities of non-personal Consciousness. This results in a natural cleansing of the lens of perception, and hence the individual becomes aware of a completely different experience of life. The previously elusive feelings of happiness, peace, love and unity begin to come naturally. It all seems miraculous, but actually it makes complete sense. We just have to keep up the spiritual practices.

It is said that scripture and authentic spiritual writing can be understood at four different levels. These levels of understanding have nothing to do with individual intelligence, but rather relate to the level of Consciousness from which the words are being read and absorbed. The four levels can be described as literal meaning, implied or allegorical meaning, deeper meaning and hidden or mystical meaning. These levels relate to the Consciousness Only model as personal body and mind, personal Consciousness or Soul, pure non-personal Consciousness and Ultimate Truth. We have seen that the twelve steps originate from perennial spiritual wisdom, hence we ought to be able to discern the four layers of understanding in each of them.

It has taken many chapters to reach this point, but we can now turn our attention to each step in turn. The purpose is to uncover all levels of meaning in the steps and hence hopefully make sense of twelve-step recovery. There is real depth in this program and we can each progress as far as we wish. The prize on offer is freedom in the form of happiness, peace, love and unity.

33. Step One

"We admitted we were powerless over addiction - that our lives had become unmanageable."

As with all of the steps, the precise wording of step one is very important. I will take time to dissect the wording of the steps in order to extract maximum understanding. This may seem a bit pedantic, but the wisdom is in the detail.

The first word to focus on is *we.* As noted in the chapter on the origins of the twelve steps, this small word was added as part of the consultation on the original draft. It is the first word in the whole twelve-step program and encapsulates the crucial importance of fellowship. Addiction is a lonely, bewildering and potentially fatal condition. It is difficult enough to recover, let alone try to do it on our own. We need each other. We need unity.

The word *admitted* also needs attention. The word means "confessed to be true". The word *confess* implies reluctant acknowledgement. An addict in active addiction will be reluctant to accept that the problem is out of control, because such an admission will mean that they have to stop doing the very thing that their body and mind seems to depend upon. Unless and until this admission is made there is no real prospect of recovery. We may realise that we have a problem but we will be unlikely to engage in a solution unless we fully admit that we have it, and that it is serious.

The personal ego mind will resist the word *powerless*. Hitherto it has been personal thinking that has determined our actions. The idea that the personal self has reached a point of powerlessness over addiction is not welcome, despite plenty of evidence to prove it. The word *powerless* implies that the personal self has no power, ability or influence over its own actions. This despairing loss of hope is brokenness, and the personal ego mind is naturally unwilling to accept that it has lost power and control.

Each of the different fellowships replace the word *addiction* in step one with the relevant addictive substance or behavior. It is the only time in the twelve steps where there is mention of the specific problem. We have already covered aspects of addiction in a previous chapter, and all of it applies whatever the particular issue. When it comes to step one, the more complete the understanding of addiction the better. It is a multi-layered condition and it progresses to the point of potential fatality.

The word *lives* refers both to our individual existence and to our personal concept of what our life is all about. We all have differing ideas about the purpose of life, and it is these ideas that are being referenced.

Finally the word *unmanageable* is used to indicate a lack of ability to manage or control our lives. The use of the words *had become* suggests that we previously had this ability but have now lost it due to our powerlessness over addiction.

Step one may seem pretty obvious if an addict has reached a hopeless state of body and mind and is suffering all sorts of consequences. Experience shows however that there can still be reluctance to fully admit the seriousness of the problem. Denial can be even more of an issue if the addiction has not yet reached a critical stage. When it comes to the carrot or the stick, step one is most definitely the stick. Addiction progresses relentlessly so, however bad it may or may not be at the moment, it is only going to get worse. There is no going back to recreational use of particular addictive substances or behaviours. Step one requires an acceptance that complete abstinence is the only realistic option. This abstinence does not need to be projected into the future, but can simply be practiced one day at a time, or in even smaller chunks of time in early sobriety.

So a literal understanding of step one would be that a particular addiction has run out of control and that it is causing our lives to be chaotic and unmanageable. There is acceptance that this is the case and that help is required to recover. By engaging in the steps, there is an appreciation that abstinence is necessary and that personal willpower is not sufficient to maintain such abstinence.

A deeper understanding of step one would include a more comprehensive identification with all of the aspects of addiction. This would incorporate an acceptance of the multiple layers of addiction that give rise to our behaviours and also the undoubted progressive nature of the condition. This level of understanding would validate the need for the solution to penetrate the deeper layers and would thereby encourage the honesty, open-mindedness and willingness needed to work through the rest of the steps effectively.

The next level of understanding would be that powerlessness and unmanageability apply not only to addiction but to all facets of life. The illusion of personal control over life circumstances is seen through. Our previous belief that our limited influence over certain aspects of our lives extended to the whole experience is undermined by the realisation that anything could happen at any time to bring about complete change. It becomes apparent that we are powerless over the weather, other people, health issues, local, national or international events or indeed almost any aspect of our lives that we care to consider. The personal ego mind thought it was in control but actually it was just a thought. We have allowed our state of happiness, peace, love and unity to become dependent on external factors, and all of these are ultimately out of our control. We have been trying to manage something that is unmanageable. No wonder life has been full of suffering and struggle. We become very keen to find a different way of being.

The deepest level of understanding of step one relates to the process of metamorphosis. The caterpillar has reached the end

206

of its phase of life and is now ready to undergo the necessary transformation into the intended life of a butterfly. This was always the intention so there is nothing wrong. The admission of powerlessness and unmanageability is simply a recognition that the time has come for change. The caterpillar, in the form of the personal ego self, can enter into the cocoon of fellowship and safely undergo the metamorphosis into non-personal Consciousness. Few caterpillars make it to the butterfly stage, but every human has the chance to emerge into Being. In this respect, step one is a tremendous opportunity rather than a personal failure. The prospect of a period of discomfort may not be appealing, but it will be temporary and will lead to liberation. The prodigal son admits that he has exhausted his inheritance and begins to think that life at home was not so bad after all.

Whichever level of understanding of step one we may relate to, they all require surrender. It is either surrender to the consequences of addiction, surrender to addiction as a condition, surrender to life itself or surrender of the personal self to the intended process of transformation. This surrender is not failure. It is the gateway to a far more enjoyable life and the attainment of the desired state of happiness, peace, love and unity.

My own experience of step one has naturally deepened as my recovery has progressed. It is still important however to be continually reminded of the suffering that preceded my surrender. The impact of the personal state of desperation and brokenness will fade over time and hence the stick of step one will gradually become less influential. Listening to the experiences of others, when they share at meetings, provides a constant and necessary reminder.

Each step builds upon, and hence depends upon, the previous one. Step one is therefore the foundational step of recovery. The stronger the step one, the more effective the subsequent recovery. It might be tempting to move through step one very quickly because it all seems fairly obvious at the literal level of understanding. Taking time to fully appreciate the depth of the problem will pay long-term dividends.

34. Step Two

"Came to believe that a Power greater than ourselves could restore us to sanity."

Step one is all about admitting personal powerlessness. Step two introduces the idea of a replacement Power that is not personal. Nearly all of the words in this step are worthy of detailed investigation.

Use of the words *came to* can imply a sudden change, or they can allude to a gradual change over time. There is no right or wrong interpretation here. Change takes place in the moment, so in this respect it is always sudden, but equally a big change can take place through a series of smaller changes. It is worth noting that resistance to change can slow down, or even stop, the natural process. If we want to recover from addiction then change is necessary. This is why a good understanding of step one is so important. The personal mind tends to avoid change if it can, but step one makes it very clear that recovery is not possible by maintaining the status quo.

The word *believe* obviously refers to belief. We tend to think that our beliefs are fixed. Belief exists in the realm of the personal ego mind, but beliefs are just thoughts that come and go. It is the idea of a personal self that gives power to these thoughts. The fact that our thinking has led us into the nightmare of addiction can sometimes be conveniently overlooked in favour of holding onto our entrenched beliefs. It is all a function of the personal ego mind, and ultimately it is the personal ego mind that is causing all of the suffering. If a belief is not working for us, then we are perfectly entitled to change it. It takes humility, through brokenness, to accept that our personal thinking is not reliable. Being willing to allow our beliefs to change is an early indication of humility.

The words *Power greater than ourselves* are clearly open to widespread interpretation. The word *ourselves* is referring to the personal self, which comprises the body and personal ego mind. It is this personal self that has admitted powerlessness and unmanageability in step one. The words *greater than* imply a higher degree of strength, extent, ability, quality or importance. The word *power* means the ability to do or the ability to influence, and also means strength, force or energy. The use of a capital P in the word *Power* indicates spiritual terminology. Bill Wilson uses capitalisation throughout the Big Book when referring to that which cannot be described. So the implication here is an ability, strength, force or energy beyond the capability of the personal self. This Power is also sometimes referred to as a Higher Power, with the word *Higher* having the same meaning as *greater than* as opposed to any concept of height or distance.

The word *could* indicates a possibility. There is no requirement for certainty. The new belief is simply asking for the willingness to entertain a possibility.

The word *restore* means to bring back or re-establish. This does not imply something new, but rather a return to a previous state.

We do not need to be Einstein to recognise the insanity of repetitive addictive behaviour. The word *sanity* means the ability to think and behave in a reasonable and rational manner. It is tempting to refer to sanity as being normal, but in my experience and understanding there is no such thing as normal when it comes to each unique individual human mind. Normal is the antithesis of diversity, and diversity is so clearly and undeniably evident in the multitudinous aspects of the world of manifest creation. We can be sane without having to defer to the uninspiring and soulless societal expectations of being normal. Such expressions of normality are constantly changing anyway, so surely it is preferable to be authentic rather than normal.

So step two is all about coming to believe in a Power greater than ourselves that can relieve our suffering. My very strong suggestion is that this Power is what I have referred to as Consciousness. I have devoted many chapters of this book to an explanation as to why this model of Consciousness not only makes sense but is the perennial wisdom that underpins a true understanding of life. If our concept of this Power is third party and separate from ourselves then we are going to remain disempowered. Consciousness is a Power greater than our personal selves but Consciousness is also our true nature once the limited personal ego mind is transcended. I accept that there will be those who will resolutely hold onto their existing beliefs, and I have no issue with that. I am offering a broader perspective with the sole purpose of trying to be helpful.

It may seem that this model of Consciousness conflicts with the Big Book and twelve-step literature in general. In this respect I would like to include a quote from the Big Book. This is one of the few times that I will do so, but for me this understanding is pivotal to recovery. The wording appears on page fifty-five of the fourth edition and reads "Sometimes we had to search fearlessly, but He was there. He was as much a fact as we were. We found the Great Reality deep down within ourselves. In the last analysis it is only there that He may be found. It was so with us." These sentences appear at the end of a long chapter and are easily overlooked. Once understood, the words are deeply profound. Bill Wilson is using the words *Great Reality* and *He* as substitutes for the God word. The clear inference is that the only place that we are going to find the Power necessary to overcome addiction is within ourselves. Twelve-step recovery is about moving from personal powerlessness to non-personal empowerment. It is all about shifting the balance of identification from human to Being.

A literal understanding of step two then is that we become willing to believe that there might be a force or energy beyond our personal capability that could relieve us from specific addictive behaviour. If we are not yet willing, then we can at

211

least have the willingness to become willing. This is all that is needed in order to pass through the gate of step two.

A deeper understanding would be that there is a Power greater than the personal self, and that this Power has the ability to remove our addictive compulsions through gradually restoring the layers of our psyche that are giving rise to the addictions.

The next level of understanding would be that this greater Power is not external or separate from us, but is internal. The solution is now seen as an inner journey of discovery rather than reliance upon some concept of a third party Power that we struggle to place our faith in. This belief arises from our own self-contemplation, whereby we come to see that there is an Awareness of thoughts, images, feelings, sensations and perceptions. This Awareness does not move or change, whereas all of the objects of perception are constantly moving, including our own idea of who we are. There is an understanding that this position of Awareness allows us to witness the personal ego mind and hence begin to detach from it. There is a sense of being restored to authentic Consciousness rather than being at the mercy of a conditioned personal mind.

The deepest understanding of step two is that Consciousness is the one and only Power. This is no longer a question of personal belief, but a matter of absolute certainty based on experience. The personal self that believes in this Power is seen to be an expression of the very thing that it had previously been reluctant to believe in. Consciousness is the Power that exists at all levels of manifestation, and the spiritual journey becomes a gradual shift towards abiding at ever-deeper levels. The result is an increasing experience of the state of Being that the personal ego self had been searching for all along. The caterpillar realises that the process of metamorphosis is natural and necessary. He comes to believe that he does not have to make the changes himself, but simply has to surrender to the process. The prodigal son comes to believe that the only way to relieve his suffering is to return home.

As with step one, my understanding of step two has gradually evolved over time. When I worked through the steps with my sponsor, I had no belief in any sort of greater Power, but I did have the open-mindedness and willingness to accept that I had more to learn. This willingness was sufficient for me to progress to step three, because I was prepared to believe in something, even if it was only the fellowship itself. In the meetings there were many addicts in recovery that said they had started with no belief at all but had subsequently found faith in their own concept of a greater Power. This opportunity for belief by proxy is another important aspect of fellowship.

Before we can proceed to step three, we need to believe, or be willing to believe, that there is a restorative Power beyond the capability of the personal ego self. The fact that we have admitted personal powerlessness and are seeking recovery must surely mean that we believe that there is some help available. If we want to avail ourselves of such help then we need to be willing to allow it. This again implies surrender, even if we do not understand what we are surrendering to. The understanding will come soon enough if we continue with our commitment to recovery.

35. Step Three

"Made a decision to turn our will and our lives over to the care of God as we understood Him."

Step three is the final part of the first triad. The precise wording is again crucial. There is much more to this step than we may realise.

The word *decision* simply means a conclusion or choice reached after consideration. Often a decision will result in a specific course of action.

The use of the words *turn* and *over* in the context of this sentence means to transfer control or management.

The word *will* refers to the faculty or power by which a person makes decisions and initiates action. This then is the power of the personal ego self, which we have already admitted is powerless in step one.

The word *and* means in addition or as well.

The word *lives* has the same meaning as in step one, which is our personal existence and concepts of what our lives are all about.

The word *care* means the provision of what is necessary for the health, welfare, maintenance and protection of someone or something.

The words *God as we understood Him* are open to widespread interpretation, and hence misinterpretation. We have covered the true meaning of the word *understanding* and have also investigated the God word at length. We have then briefly looked at the historical context and debate that led to the use of this particular phrase in the twelve steps. It is worth emphasising that the personal ego mind cannot understand Consciousness, or whichever God word we choose to use. Just as the eye cannot see itself, so Knowingness cannot know itself. Consciousness can only be itself and know that it is. Whatever concept of God we may hold, it is just a thought. Our concepts may be very different, but we are all conceptualising the same Ultimate Truth from an individual perspective. Everyone is entitled to his or her own perspective, but we should be clear that all perspectives are personal, and therefore not absolutely true. There is only Consciousness, and Consciousness does not, and cannot, understand itself.

Step three requires a decision about handing over our assumed right of self-determination to whatever concept of a Power greater than ourselves that we may currently have. Having admitted that the personal self is powerless over addiction, and come to believe that there is some form of greater Power, this next step seems pretty obvious. Without placing ourselves in the care of a Power greater than ourselves we are never going to recover from addiction. However, although this handing over of the problem does requires surrender, it does not imply inactivity. This surrender is all about initiating a change in the balance of power from personal self to the greater Power. We are making a decision to stop taking actions based on the personal agenda of ego self and start taking actions in accordance with the guidance of a Power greater than our personal selves. At the very least this means making a decision to continue with the rest of the steps, but actually the implications run far deeper than this.

The Big Book suggests that we make this surrender through prayer. The wording of the proposed prayer has a strong religious flavour but this is of no real consequence. The important thing is to understand the intention. The prayer reads "God, I offer myself to Thee – to build with me and do with me as Thou wilt. Relieve me of the bondage of self, that I may better do Thy will. Take away my difficulties, that victory over them may bear witness to those I would help of Thy Power, Thy Love, and

Thy Way of Life. May I do Thy will always". This is the surrender of the personal ego self to Consciousness. The prayer is therefore selfless. Notice that we praying for relief from the bondage of our own ego minds. This is not so that we can feel better and have a better life, but so that we can be of service. Notice also that we are asking for our difficulties to be taken away, again not for our personal sake but so that we can help others. There are those who believe that recovery is selfish. This is a fundamental misunderstanding. Recovery is selfless.

A literal understanding of step three would be that we make a one-off decision to hand over the problem of addiction to whatever conception of the God word we may have at the time. The practical implication of this decision is that we are willing to continue with the rest of the steps, even if we find the prospect uncomfortable and unappealing. This can feel much more like acquiescence than liberation. The personal ego self feels that it is making this decision reluctantly.

A deeper understanding of step three would be that the problem of addition is more than just the physical and mental compulsion. It is rooted right down at the level of identification with the personal ego self. If we are going to recover effectively then we need to make a decision to hand over not just the addiction but also our personal agendas and hence the future course of our lives. It becomes apparent that this is not a one-off decision, but a decision that needs to be made and renewed every single day.

The next level of understanding would be that the Power greater than our personal self is the Consciousness, or Mind, that gives rise to the personal ego mind in the first place. Consciousness has been here all along but we have been overriding its guidance by insisting that the personal ego mind knows best. Most of our thinking and behaviour has been based on the assumption that the body and mind is personal rather than individual. No wonder that our search to find happiness, peace, love and unity for the personal self has always resulted in struggle and suffering. Consciousness is ever present and ready to express itself through each body and mind. All we have to do is make a decision to let that happen and then act in accordance with the guidance received. Such a decision will need to be made throughout each day otherwise we will quickly forget and return to identification with the personal self.

The deepest understanding of step three is totally life changing. The whole manifest world is Consciousness only. There is nothing but Consciousness, including the previously imagined personal self. Our will and our lives never were under the control or management of the personal self because the personal self was only ever a thought that was given power through belief. The personal self that makes the decision to hand over power eventually fades away as a result of the transformation that then takes place. The decision to allow Consciousness to determine our thoughts and actions, and hence the course of our lives, is made moment-to-moment until there is no longer a decision to be made. There comes a point when the balance of power between human and Being shifts sufficiently that the Being is simply expressing itself through the human. In order for this to happen we have to start the process of transformation, and step three is the starting point. The caterpillar makes a decision to build its own cocoon and enter into metamorphosis. The prodigal son makes a decision to give up his old life and begin the journey back home.

When I did step three with my sponsor, we knelt down together and read the step three prayer from the Big Book. I had no idea who or what I was praying to. My overriding thought was embarrassment that someone might look through the window and see what we were doing. It has taken many years of practice before the profound importance and significance of step three began to sink in. They say that more will be revealed as recovery progresses, and this has certainly been the case for me. I also realise that there is yet more to come, and today I find this exciting rather than daunting.

I was told in early recovery that if we were able to fully grasp and implement the full implications of step three then there would be no need for the rest of the steps. I can see that the solution to addiction is the surrender of the personal self, because this is from where addiction arises. However it has not been possible, in my experience, to jump from personal ego self to Consciousness as the result of a single decision and stay there. We may get sudden glimpses of Consciousness but we always return habitually to the personal ego mind. There is some sort of pull towards the duality of the material world that is automatic and uncontrollable. The only way to progress is through the process of transformation, or transcendence, and this requires consistent, persistent spiritual practice. The remainder of the steps introduce these practices and then consolidate them into daily rituals that keep up moving forwards. The original problem of addiction gradually melts away in the process.

36. Step Four

"Made a searching and fearless moral inventory of ourselves."

Now we get down to action. If things are going to change then we need to change. Nothing will change if we remain inactive and hope for the best. The proposed actions are uncomfortable, but they are necessarily uncomfortable because if we remain within our comfort zone then we will remain where we are. We have made a decision to hand over our personal will, and that includes our will to remain personally comfortable. Step four is one of the more uncomfortable steps but it is actually no big deal when fully understood. In order to get to the true meaning we once again need to look at the wording in detail.

The word *searching* means thoroughly investigating, especially in a disconcerting way.

The word *fearless* simply means lacking fear. This is easier said than done, because fear is a natural instinct of the personal ego self.

The word *moral* is concerned with the principles of right and wrong behaviour, with right and wrong referring to what is acceptable and unacceptable in society.

An *inventory* is a complete list of items.

The word *ourselves* is again referring to the personal self, which comprises the body and personal ego mind.

On the face of it then, step four seems pretty straightforward. What we are doing is taking an inventory of the personal ego mind. The trouble is that, at this stage, the personal ego mind is who we think we are. Our inventory is to be searching, which implies that it will be unsettling and uncomfortable. The primary reason for addictive behaviour is to escape discomfort, hence the idea of a searching personal inventory is understandably not appealing. The inventory is also to be fearless, which again raises a problem because we are fearful. The word *courage* means the ability to do something that is frightening. Courage does not imply a lack of fear, but instead requires us to push through fear. This idea is nicely summed up in the title of Susan Jeffers' best-selling book "Feel the fear and do it anyway".

We do need courage to do step four, but we should take great comfort from those in the fellowship who have already been through it. Fear does have a purpose in the right context, but the fear of step four turns out to be irrational and self-serving. In truth there is nothing to fear in having the humility to admit that we are human. Accepting that we are broken turns out to be the best thing possible. Brokenness has already caused us to seek help, come to believe in a Power greater than ourselves and make a decision to relinquish our personal self-will in favour of this Power. The fact that the personal self does not want to do step four is irrelevant. We have handed over the personal will and it is no longer in charge. The personal ego mind will obviously put up some resistance, but such resistance is to be ignored. If we find that the resistance is too strong, then we obviously need to go back to step three because by now we are supposed to have made a decision to surrender self-will.

Addicts tend to be very ashamed of their past behaviour, so it is very important to comprehend that the traits of an addict are no different from any other human. I have already mentioned these attributes twice before, but we need to look at them again here because this list is really what step four is all about. The attributes will vary in intensity from one individual to the next, but they are all present in each of us. They are present even if we do not want to admit it to ourselves. They are present because they are the natural consequence of Consciousness limiting itself and condensing into an individual human mind and body. It does not matter who we think we are, or what we may have done. When we do step four we will all end up revealing exactly the same list of traits. I try to reassure those who I am sponsoring that step four is not intended to be a humiliation or a groveling admission that we are bad people. Step four is just an honest self-appraisal that highlights the attributes of the personal ego mind. The good news is that the personal ego mind is not who we are. The process itself will reveal the original mistake in identity, and subsequently the aspects of personal self will gradually lose their intensity and fade away.

If we honestly look at our past thinking and behaviour then this will reveal the same list of traits for each of us. These attributes of the personal ego mind, in alphabetical order, include anger, criticism, dishonesty, disrespect, doubt, envy, gluttony, greed, hate, intolerance, impatience, jealousy, judgment, lust, pride, resentment, selfishness, self-condemnation, self-doubt, self-importance, self-justification, self-pity, self-righteousness, self-seeking, sloth, suspicion, thoughtlessness and worry. All of these arise from self-centered fear, which in turn is caused by the belief that we are only the personal self. It really is that simple. The belief in the personal self is the root cause of all suffering, including addiction. If we cut this root, then the whole self-constructed clump of stinging nettles will slowly wither away. We will no longer be stinging others, or ourselves. Something far more beautiful will emerge in its place.

The process of undertaking personal inventory, as suggested in the Big Book, is relatively straightforward. The primary focus of our attention is to be on four key areas, although other areas may also be explored if helpful. The four suggested areas are resentments, fears, intimate relationships and harms done to others. The methodology for each of the areas is broadly the same. Taking resentments as an example, first we compile a list of all people, institutions or principles against which we have a resentment. Secondly we specify what the exact resentment or resentments are that we have against each item on the list. Thirdly we look at the actual cause of the resentment by identifying which part of personal self is being impacted. Finally we set aside what actually may have happened, and focus instead on how our human characteristics may have aggravated the situation, and how our reaction could have been different. What emerges in practical terms is equivalent to a spreadsheet with four columns and as many rows as are required. This is repeated for each of the four areas. In addition to the Big Book guidance, there are resources available online that provide the documents to complete and also lists of suggested items to look at.

Some sponsors prefer the format of a life story in order to identify the traits. Most prefer the Big Book method. Others do both. The important thing in all of this is to identify the list of human attributes that are causing all of the trouble, and to realise that all of this is happening due to the strong attachment to personal identity. It is the human part of the human being that is problematic, but we are not just human. The solution is to increasingly become the Being.

These aspects of human nature are sometimes referred to as our shadow self. The idea is that Consciousness casts a shadow into the world through the individual Soul, and then identifies itself with the shadow rather than as itself. The shadow contains all of the negative traits listed above, and the shadow identity behaves in accordance with its own nature. It tries to deny its own thinking and behaviour and creates a mask of persona to hide behind. This identity will persist until the shadow is acknowledged and embraced. Once this happens then the shadow is not only seen to be the problem, it is also finally perceived to be just a shadow. We know that shadows are not real. Shadows arise when light is blocked by an object. The shape of the shadow will be influenced by the object, but will also vary according to the direction and intensity of the light. The shadow is illusory and is dependent upon the light. This shadow metaphor is useful up to a point. The shadow is the human ego mind, or the Subtle level of the Antahkarana. The object is the Soul or the Causal level. The light is Consciousness. The light of Consciousness shines through the lens of Antahkarana and produces a shadow human, which is assumed to be the personal self. This personal identity is reinforced by the resulting personal experiences and by the fact that all humans make the same assumption. This is the mistake in identity that causes personal suffering. In truth, as we have seen, it is differing vibrations of Consciousness that play all of these parts, yet the metaphor does provide good insight into why we need to take an inventory of the shadow self.

A literal understanding of step four would be that the personal self needs to do this personal inventory even though it doesn't want to. In many cases this will be first time for such an undertaking. The idea of the inventory being searching and fearless is heard but we are nevertheless uncomfortable and fearful. Procrastination is not unusual with step four, but sooner or later the fear of relapse outweighs the fear of looking at ourselves and we get on with the work. We may experience emotional pain as we go through the process, but it gets a bit easier as the repeated patterns of thinking and behaviour begin to emerge.

A deeper understanding would be that step four is the beginning of the spiritual practice of self-awareness. The practice of writing down our past thoughts and actions, and then reviewing them, creates a small space between what is being seen and the observer who is seeing it. This is the first little detachment from the personal ego mind and it means that we have to abide at a slightly deeper level of Consciousness in order to do the work. The change may be subtle, but it is the beginning of the process of transformation. Self-awareness is one of the three primary components of spiritual practice, and we cannot become self-aware until we are willing to honestly look at ourselves.

The next level of understanding would be that step four is just a process for identifying and relating to the egocentric nature of a human who is fully identified only as a personal self. The particular attributes are no different from any other human, but they have been amplified by the downward spiral of addiction.

The traits are all based on self-centered fear and obviously result in selfishness and self-centeredness. This has been the cause of our addiction and all other problems. The humility to see and accept this brokenness provides the willingness for further action and change. We may even begin to have some compassion for ourselves, because we didn't know then what we know now. We may start to see that being engaged in this process of recovery is a tremendously positive thing to do rather than a necessary burden.

The deepest level of understanding of step four is that the process is really just Consciousness looking at its own shadow. The Mind sees how the thinking and behaviour of the personal ego mind has literally cast a shadow over this particular experience of life. Consciousness has somehow believed its own shadow into existence, and the idea of a personal self has then suffered the inevitable consequences. The attributes of ego are not seen to be wrong, but rather that they have a purpose in respect of survival of the individual body and mind. It has been the identification as a personal self, and the resulting dominance of the negative attributes, that has been the mistake. It has all been the play of Consciousness, and perhaps the purpose has always been to bring about the awakening of non-personal Consciousness that is now beginning to take place.

My own experience of step four was more difficult than it needed to be. I had just got to step four when I had my second relapse, which is probably not a coincidence. Once I sobered up my sponsor encouraged me to get on with the work. It still took me another five months. It could have been even longer, but I was eventually asked to set my own deadline, and that gave me the incentive to finish by the target date. I had spent my whole life in denial of my own thinking and behaviour, so it is no surprise that I struggled to take inventory. Having progressed in recovery, I now see that step four was a crucial and very necessary step along the way. As well as allowing me to clearly see the extent of my identification with personal ego self, it has also given me a powerful tool to use whenever something new comes along that causes personal disturbance. The truth is that any disturbance can only ever be personal, so a quick inventory and look across the columns will immediately show me what the problem is.

Step four brings humility. It helps us to see how the personal ego mind operates in our particular case. Humility is essential to progress, and hence the more humility we have the better. Having made our inventory, it now makes sense to increase our humility by sharing our findings with someone else.

37. Step Five

"Admitted to God, to ourselves, and to another human being the exact nature of our wrongs."

Step five is where we share our inventory. Prior to this our self-analysis has been a private matter, but now we need the courage to reveal ourselves to someone else. We will have to have complete trust in this individual and in the confidentiality of the process, otherwise we are prone to hold back. The wording of the step seems fairly obvious, but it is worth reviewing in detail in order to extract maximum understanding.

The word *admitted* was used in step one and the meaning here is the same. The meaning is "confessed to be true" and the implication is one of reluctant acknowledgement.

The God word is used, but this time it is not qualified by the words *as we understood Him.* This is as per the original drafting of the steps, although the words *as we understood Him* were handwritten in for this step but then crossed out again. The fact these words were excluded is very probably a matter of Bill Wilson's writing style, which tried to avoid too much repetition. Whatever the reason, the word *God* is just a word and is therefore always a placeholder for individual interpretation.

The word *ourselves* has the same meaning as in step four, which is the personal self of body and ego mind.

The words *another human being* obviously imply someone else. It is interesting for me that these specific words were used rather than simply using the words *another person.* I may be reading too much into this, but using the words *human being* can be seen to suggest that the chosen individual should at least have some awareness of *being* as opposed to an exclusive identification with *human.* The reason for highlighting this is that the choice of individual will have an impact on the effectiveness of step five, and hence we should ideally be choosing someone who is spiritually aware.

The word *exact* means precise. Our inventory is not intended to be rough, approximate, indefinite or vague. We are looking at specific thoughts, feelings and behaviours and we are admitting specified human traits.

The word *wrongs* refers to our thoughts and behaviours, and the singular word *wrong* means not correct, not true, mistaken, in error, unsuitable, bad, abnormal, unjust, dishonest or immoral. Some of these meanings have a stronger flavour than others. My understanding is that the focus should be on admitting the mistakes we have made due to over-identification with the personal self, rather than going down the road of labeling ourselves as bad, abnormal or immoral.

Step five then is a courageous act of opening ourselves up to another human being. It involves revealing specific details about ourselves in a way that perhaps we have never done before. The objective is to be analytical rather than judgmental. This is not intended to be an exercise in humiliation, nor does it need to be. Our confidant should ideally be spiritually aware and have experience of addiction. This is important because part of the purpose of step five is for our spiritual advisor to help us see aspects of the personal ego mind that we may have missed or overlooked. The tendency of an addict is to be in denial of his or her own thoughts, feelings and behaviours, and an element of this denial may deliberately or inadvertently spill over into our personal inventory. An experienced adviser will be able to see hidden causes or motives that perhaps the addict cannot see. He or she is also likely to admit the same traits in themselves. A guide who is spiritually aware will be compassionate and non-judgmental. They will also understand the paramount importance of confidentiality.

The other main purpose of step five is to begin the process of self-healing. Many addicts have carried a heavy burden of guilt and shame for years prior to coming into recovery. This burden has literally dragged them down. The simple act of sharing this burden with a sympathetic and like-minded colleague can have a powerfully liberating effect. In this respect, the more revealing we can be the greater the effect. It is said that "our secrets keep us sick" and this is certainly true for addicts. Step five is an opportunity for us to share our secrets and thereby experience cleansing and healing. It is well worth taking this risk to be vulnerable because the humility that results is priceless. If we are willing to put our refuse out for collection then it will certainly be taken away.

A literal understanding of step five would be that we share our step four with our sponsor and thereby somehow also share it with ourselves and with the God word, as we may or may not understand it. This may be a relatively quick process, or it may take several sessions, depending on the size of the step four inventory. Our sponsor may point out some additional traits that might be uncomfortable to hear. We should experience some relief from having shared our brokenness, but this will depend upon the depth of our revelations.

A deeper understanding of step five would be that this is a life-changing opportunity to be totally honest about the inherently flawed nature of identifying only as the personal ego self. An honest self-appraisal will reveal all of the traits that are listed above. If we are in denial about any of them then we are fooling ourselves. There will also be a recognition that the process of inventory must mean that there is a deeper sense of self that is able to observe the workings of the personal ego mind. This small detachment is the beginning of the journey towards abiding as Consciousness and also changes our self-perception. Once the self-centered nature of the personal mind is witnessed then there is an increased willingness for change. The feedback from our sponsor will add to our understanding. The feeling of relief and cleansing will be tangible. By completing this step diligently we may feel that we have reached a milestone and are firmly on the path to recovery. We may also find that we become more open and honest in our sharing at fellowship meetings.

The next level of understanding involves including the God word in our step five. Revealing our innermost selves to a trusted sponsor or spiritual advisor is one thing but the step also requires us to admit these things to ourselves and to God, as we understand Him. Once it is understood that Consciousness is the creator, the substance and the witness of all visible and non-visible manifestation then this all becomes much clearer. Consciousness is not only the true nature of the apparent personal self, but it is everything and everywhere at every moment. The air that we breathe is Consciousness. The chair that we are sitting on is Consciousness. Our sponsor or spiritual advisor is Consciousness. By sitting down and honestly revealing our thoughts, feelings and behaviours we are literally sharing our inventory with Consciousness, with ourselves and with another human being. Consciousness, in the form of the personal self, is revealing itself to Consciousness in the form of universal non-personal Consciousness. It is also revealing itself to personal Consciousness as itself and finally to Consciousness as expressed in the individual sponsor or spiritual advisor. The single revelation addresses the three apparently separate targets, which actually are one.

The deepest level of understanding is that Consciousness is revealing itself to itself in an act of self-recognition or self-realisation. The shadow is seen to be just a shadow and hence ultimately unreal. Once a shadow is understood to be a shadow then it loses its previous power and influence. It will still be there of course, but it is seen to be an individual expression of Consciousness created by the act of Consciousness shining itself through a lens of Consciousness. The effect is liberation from the bondage of the personal self and it is the ultimate freedom. It is the true meaning of revelation. These understandings of non-duality will almost certainly only arise much later in recovery, but they are worth mentioning again here because this does give significant credence to the wisdom contained in step five.

At the end of the section in the Big Book that covers step five there is a paragraph that suggests that we pause at this point and reflect. We should review the work that we have done over the first five steps and satisfy ourselves that we have been honest and thorough. The implication here is that step five is a turning point. However tempting it may be to cut corners, or leave out particular issues, it is far better to leave no stone unturned. Our work on the steps does not have to be perfect, but it must be honest. If we cheat ourselves at this stage then we will compromise the future quality of our recovery.

As with the first four steps, my experience of step five, at the time that I did it, was in line with the first level of understanding, if that. I sat with my sponsor over two long sessions and read out my step four. Sometimes he would identify or offer some insight, but other times he would remain silent. Surprisingly some of what I perceived to be the bigger items were met with silence, whereas some of the smaller, trivial issues caused comment. I remember being tempted to skip over some of the more embarrassing parts, knowing that he could not see what I had written. Thankfully I avoided this temptation. When we had finished, we read the final paragraph noted above and he suggested that I take a week to reflect and make sure that I felt ready to proceed. This turned out to be the most important moment in my recovery.

I knew that there were some shameful issues concerning my past behaviour that I had vowed would never see the light of day. The delay of a week gave me time to see the choice that I faced. I could either confess, and hence be totally sure that I had been honest and thorough, or I could say that there was nothing else to reveal. My sponsor did not know what was in my mind so I could easily have chosen to keep it to myself. My fear was that I might relapse again if I did not reveal everything. Thankfully the fear of relapse outweighed the fear of confession, so I updated my step four and went through it with my sponsor the following week. The revelations were a non-event in the sense that my sponsor dismissed them as nothing. The secrets that I had buried for so long simply vanished. It was analogous to air bubbles being trapped in water that then rise to the surface and disappear. As I drove home that evening, I experienced a sense of relief and exhilaration that I will never forget. I was just six months sober, and for the first time I really started to believe that the steps might actually work.

My understanding has grown significantly since that step five moment, and I certainly recommend taking a pause at this stage to reflect. The personal ego mind will try to protect itself by resisting scrupulous honesty. The personal mind is the problem. We made a decision at step three to surrender the personal agenda in favour of recovery. This is the moment to override personal discomfort and be honest. It will turn out to be the best thing that we ever do.

Once we are satisfied with the work so far then we can proceed to step six. If there is uncertainty then we should backtrack and run through the steps again. Remember that each step builds upon the previous one. We may need to go back to the powerlessness of step one in order to find the willingness. The twelve steps are not a tick-box exercise to complete as quickly a possible. Unnecessary delay is obviously to be avoided but it is far better to be honest and thorough than quick.

38. Step Six

"Were entirely ready to have God remove all these defects of character."

If we have been honest and thorough so far then it will have become fairly obvious that we need to change. The dysfunction of over-identification with the personal ego mind will have been revealed. We have been fighting with life rather than being an expression of life. Step six is all about the willingness to change. The wording is straightforward, but worth a quick look.

The word *entirely* means wholly, completely or totally.

The word *ready* means willing or eager and also means a suitable state for action.

The God word has the same meaning as in previous steps.

The word *remove* means to take off, take away, dismiss or abolish.

The word *all* means the whole extent or quantity.

The word *defects* means faults, shortcomings or imperfections.

The word *character* means the mental and moral qualities distinctive to an individual.

So step six means that we are totally willing to have our understanding of the God word take away the whole extent of the faults or imperfections in our personal mental and moral qualities. This is not about tinkering with certain aspects of our personal behaviour or toning down certain troublesome characteristics. This is about being completely ready for wholesale change and a total willingness to let this happen. This may seem drastic, but addiction cannot be removed from the personal ego self. The whole problem with addiction is over-identification with the personal self, so the solution has to be detachment from it. This means letting go of the entire idea of who we think we are, and that takes time and practice.

Before anything can happen, we need to be ready and willing to let it happen. If we are not willing then nothing much will occur. Willingness to attend twelve-step recovery meetings is one thing, but willingness to undergo a complete transformation is another matter entirely. The personal ego mind will find all sorts of clever ways to compromise or postpone, and thereby retain its identity. A caterpillar cannot begin the process of metamorphosis yet still hold on to being a caterpillar. If we try to do this then any changes will be prolonged and painful. We will either need to 1) move forwards without reservation 2) edge forwards slowly and painfully or 3) stay stuck where we are and continue to suffer. These are the only choices available.

There are only a handful of sentences in the Big Book covering step six. We should not draw conclusions from this brevity. If we do not have sufficient willingness to allow personal change, then the wording in the Big Book on step six suggests that we should pray for such willingness. The limited wording on step six, and also step seven, has led to these steps sometimes being referred to as the forgotten steps. This is unfortunate because these steps in reality are essential. The degree to which we are willing to change our identity will directly impact the quality of our recovery. If we have limited willingness then we may remain abstinent, but we will just be an abstinent caterpillar and continue to suffer. If we forget about these steps then we can forget about becoming a butterfly.

The book "Twelve Steps and Twelve Traditions" was published in 1952, thirteen years after the Big Book. In this later book, Bill Wilson places great emphasis on step six. He suggests that this step differentiates quality of recovery between those who allow change in accordance with their own self-determined idea of how they should be, and those who surrender self-will completely and allow change to take its own course. Clearly the latter approach is in line with step three, whereas the former is not.

Another useful reference is a book called "Drop the Rock" first published independently in 1993 and then republished by Hazelden in 1999. This book specifically cover steps six and seven, and identifies the "Rock" as the personal ego mind. The simple metaphor is that if we do not drop the rock of our personal thoughts, feelings and behaviours then we will always struggle to swim. There is little point in loosening our grip of the rock slightly because it will still drag us down. Either we let go or we don't. The book goes on to explain that change is a cooperative process rather than an abdication of responsibility to our understanding of the God word. Such cooperation requires willingness on our part. We will cover more of "Drop the Rock" in step seven.

A literal understanding of step six would be that we are ready to have our understanding of a third party God remove from us those troublesome aspects of character that were identified in our step four inventory. This understanding would imply little action on our part and an expectation that change will take place on its own. I have heard many shares from addicts who have been abstinent for years who say that God has not yet removed all of their defects of character. This expectation that God will do the work is a misunderstanding.

A deeper understanding would be that these defects of character are aspects of the personal ego mind, which in turn is a limited form of Consciousness. In order to be entirely ready to change we need to be willing to let go of our defects. The positive qualities of Consciousness will then emerge in their place, and it will seem as though the personal self is changing. If we are not prepared to let go of our old behaviours then obviously nothing much will happen. Nothing changes if nothing changes. If we find ourselves resistant to change, then we should use prayer to petition for willingness.

The next level of understanding would be that our readiness to change needs to include not only a willingness to let go of our defects of character but also a willingness to put in the effort to behave differently. Consciousness is not solely external to us, nor is it merely within us, but it actually is us. The desired qualities are the inherent nature of Consciousness but we are not yet abiding as Consciousness. We therefore need to align the personal ego mind with the qualities of Consciousness and act accordingly. This means an entire readiness to override the self-centered, selfish instincts of the personal ego mind and act in accordance with the attributes of Consciousness. These attributes are the opposite of the personal ego traits identified in step four. As mentioned previously, these qualities are based on selfless love and include serenity, acceptance, honesty, respect, faith, gratitude, moderation, sharing, empathy, tolerance, patience, charity, compassion, purity, humility, forgiveness, selflessness, self-forgiveness, confidence, modesty, self-acceptance, self-love, humbleness, altruism, action, trust, consideration and courage. Step six is saying that we need to be entirely ready to allow these qualities to determine our behaviour. We need to be willing to act in this manner even if the personal ego mind does not want to. This will not happen unless we are totally willing to try.

The deepest level of understanding of step six is that transformation is not really about changing the characteristics of the personal self. We have seen that the personal ego mind is a condensed, limited form of Mind. Transformation is not about changing our personal minds but rather about becoming Mind. Metamorphosis is not about producing an upgraded version of the caterpillar but is instead about creating a butterfly out of the caterpillar. The spiritual journey is not about the prodigal son reading self-help books and seeking to improve himself. The journey is all about giving up the old life and returning to the happiness, peace, love and unity of home. Step six means that we are entirely ready to begin the detailed process of transformation. Having made the decision to surrender the personal self in step three, and having taken and shared our personal inventory in steps four and five, we are now in a position where we can see in detail what needs to change and we are entirely ready to begin.

At the time that I worked through the steps with my sponsor, my experience of step six was non-existent. I did not even understand it at the first level because I had no concept of what the God word might mean, let alone any belief that it could somehow remove my obvious faults. Step six was certainly a forgotten step in my experience, and it was only when I discovered "Drop the Rock" some years later that I began to see what I had missed. The wonderful thing about the twelve steps is that there is always more to learn and understand. It is never too late to begin the process of transformation. I may have misunderstood step six at the time but I understand it better now.

The distinction made in "Twelve Steps and Twelve Traditions" between changing the personal self and surrendering self-will completely is of fundamental importance to recovery. The personal self is the addict. Consciousness is not an addict. The personal self is powerless. Consciousness is powerful. This is the solution. This is why it works. If we really want the solution then we need to be entirely ready to die to the personal self and become non-personal Consciousness. This will take time and practice, so meanwhile we must be willing to act in accordance with the qualities of Consciousness rather than against them.

39. Step Seven

"Humbly asked Him to remove our shortcomings."

Step seven is the shortest of the twelve steps. There are just seven words, yet these few words have far reaching implications.

The word *humbly* means meekly or with humility.

The word *asked* means requested, petitioned, implored or prayed.

The word *Him* is one of the many God words.

The word *remove* is the same as in step six and means to take off, take away, dismiss or abolish.

The word *shortcomings* is a substitute for *defects of character* in step six and means faults, shortcomings or imperfections in the mental and moral qualities distinctive to an individual.

Once we are entirely ready in step six, we now petition or pray with humility for the whole extent of the faults in our personal mental and moral qualities to be taken away or abolished. We now see why the willingness required in step six is so necessary. We also see why the humility arising from steps four and five is crucial. Without willingness and humility, step seven is unlikely to have much impact.

The wording in the Big Book suggests that we again use prayer to make this petition. The religiosity of the wording is once more irrelevant, but the words do provide significant insight. The step seven prayer reads " My Creator, I am now willing that you should have all of me, good and bad. I pray that you now remove from me every single defect of character which stands in the way of my usefulness to you and my fellows. Grant me strength, as I go out from here, to do your bidding. Amen." This prayer is step seven. Notice that the wording mentions all of me, good and bad. The clear implication here is that we are willing to surrender the whole personal ego self, including those parts of us that we may consider to be good. Notice also that the removal of the defects of character is not offered for personal gain, but so that we can be useful to Consciousness and hence to our fellow human beings. This prayer is again selfless rather than selfish. Such selflessness is a true expression of humility.

Referring to the original drafting of the twelve steps, I previously mentioned that the words *on our knees* and *holding nothing back* were deleted. Presumably these changes were made to tone down the overly religious nature of the original wording. Nevertheless they are worth considering. The idea of being on our knees does evoke an image of earnest prayer, but it can also just imply genuine humility. Being *on our knees* is a popular turn of phrase that is used to indicate brokenness. Exhaustion brings us to our knees and so too does suffering. The idea of *holding nothing back* indicates complete surrender and literally suggests that nothing is held back. This would include those parts of ourselves that we consider good, as well as the more obvious shortcomings. The deletion of these two phrases may have inadvertently softened the seriousness of step seven, but hopefully the wording of the prayer makes the intention very clear.

The main message of step seven in the book "Drop the Rock" is that we cannot expect God, as we may understand the word, to remove our shortcomings without our cooperation and active participation. We have the inventory of negative attributes of the human ego mind and we have the list of the spiritual qualities of Consciousness that are the polar opposite. Our job is to act "as if" we are living the spiritual qualities until such time as they become habitual and automatic. It is worth remembering that these attributes of Consciousness are already present as the Being, but to date have been largely overshadowed by the self-centered traits of the human ego mind. It is practically impossible to surrender the entire personal self in one go, so the suggestion is that we work towards this state by acting as if we are already there. This is the process by which the balance of identity gradually shifts from human to Being. This is a key part of the practice of self-awareness.

This is best demonstrated by using an example. If one of our recognised defects of character is dishonesty then the obvious solution is to be honest. If we cease to be dishonest then we automatically become honest. We naturally become the spiritual quality by dropping the ego trait. The problem is that dishonesty has become so much a part of the personal ego mind that it is almost impossible to drop it in isolation. The solution would be to drop the entire personal ego mind but this is also nearly impossible. The way to move forwards is to act as if we are honest. This will involve being self-aware enough to notice when we are tempted to be dishonest, and then choosing to behave honestly. In this way we assist the process of surrendering the personal ego self by continually changing our behaviours to those of non-personal Consciousness. Given the long list of ego traits that we have seen, this will require an ongoing commitment to recognising and changing our habitual behaviour. Sometimes we will succeed, and other times we will have reacted and behaved from ego self before we even notice. This is all ok. The purpose is gradual improvement rather than perfection.

You may have noticed that this suggestion of acting "as if" sounds very similar to Cognitive Behavioural Therapy (CBT). In fact step seven can be seen as CBT in a different guise. CBT is a combination of the basic principles of behaviorism and cognitive psychology. It focuses on challenging and changing distortions in thoughts, beliefs, attitudes and behaviours and improving emotional regulation through coping strategies that address specific problems. The basic idea is that a repetitive action-oriented form of therapy will replace old neural pathways with more beneficial new ones, and that the resulting new thoughts and behaviours will improve emotional and mental health. In this respect, it can be seen that the practice of step seven as detailed in "Drop the Rock" is pure CBT. The repetitive use of spiritual qualities instead of personal ego traits will replace old negative habits with new neural pathways in the brain. These new neural pathways will process Consciousness differently than before. It is therefore not true to say that CBT is an alternative to twelve-step recovery. The principles of CBT are embedded in the twelve steps. This is most noticeable in step seven, but the same principle of repetitive practice also applies to all of the steps. This is particularly true for steps ten, eleven and twelve, as we shall see later. It is fair to say that CBT is a useful tool, but is not true to say that CBT is the whole toolbox. There is more to recovery than simply changing some of the negative habits of the personal self.

A literal understanding of step seven would be that we hand over our identified defects of character to whatever convenient third party understanding of the God word we may have. This is effectively an abdication of the problem to someone or something else, and hence avoids personal responsibility for change. All we have to do is say the prayer, and then hope that God will take away all of our difficulties. This is obviously rather naïve, although unsurprising given the wording of the step. The personal ego mind can be very subtle in interpreting words to satisfy its own agenda.

A deeper understanding would be in line with "Drop the Rock" and would mean acting as if we have already undergone a psychic change. Every time a defect of character arises, we would firstly need to recognise it as such, and then choose to react or behave in accordance with spiritual qualities. This will be far from easy because we will be acting against our basic ego instincts. We will naturally make mistakes, and will need to persist in trying to behave differently. We will also need to keep learning from these mistakes so that we become more self-aware. This will be like a caterpillar choosing to react and behave like a butterfly. It will feel inauthentic and incongruous for a while, but at least it will be an improvement on the old ways and it will be aiding the process of transformation. The practice of spiritual qualities in this manner gives rise to the idea of always doing the next right thing. The word *right* in this context means selfless rather than selfish. This use of self-will to bring about change may have to continue for the rest of our lives unless and until the balance of identity finally shifts from personal self to non-personal Consciousness.

The next level of understanding would be that all of the traits of the human ego mind dominate instinctively only because we identify ourselves solely as the personal self. It is this identification with the personal self that is the root of all the problems. These ego traits are not mistakes, or sins, but they are instead the inevitable implication of the original sin of misidentification. The purpose of step seven is intended to be the gradual realisation of this core mistake. We keep acting as if we are grounded in spiritual qualities until such time as we completely surrender the personal self and abide as non-personal Consciousness. When this happens, the spiritual qualities then become natural rather than the result of effort. The individual self will still be present, and so too will all of the ego traits, but the personal ego self will have been right-sized and no longer dominate the individual thoughts, feelings and behaviour. There will be times when the ego self provides useful thoughts and reactions, but the power of discernment will reside at a much deeper level of Consciousness. This abiding in non-personal Consciousness will allow the Being to determine which course of action to take in any given circumstance, and Knowingness will naturally become spontaneous.

The deepest level of understanding of step seven would be that we became entirely ready in step six to surrender the personal ego mind in favour of the Mind of non-personal Consciousness. The implementation of this surrender is to act in accordance with spiritual qualities at all times. There is Awareness of how the individual ego mind continues to operate, but we remain grounded in Consciousness. As we abide as Mind, the light of Consciousness shines through the lens of Antahkarana and this gradually purifies the Subtle and Causal levels of ego and soul. Eventually the guna of Sattva becomes dominant and the Ahamkara identifies more and more as pure non-personal Consciousness. The qualities of non-personal Consciousness rise to the surface and are expressed through the individual body and mind. The butterfly emerges from the chrysalis. The prodigal son makes his way home.

My own original experience of step seven was the same as for step six. Both of these steps were forgotten because I had no concept of the God word to which I could petition. Thankfully this changed once I read "Drop the Rock" and I began to see that the greater power from step two was internal rather than third party. Step seven is now part of my daily prayers and also increasingly part of my moment-to-moment self-awareness. My inherent brokenness as a human means that I can never practice step seven perfectly, but my experience has been that consistent, persistent practice does move us in that direction. Setbacks and mistakes are inevitable and forgivable. Indeed it can be seen that mistakes are necessary in order to continue the process of refinement and growth. The important thing is to keep moving forwards.

40. Step Eight

"Made a list of all persons we had harmed, and became willing to make amends to them all."

Step eight seems very simple, but as usual there is more to it than meets the eye. We tend to focus on making the list but the real importance of step eight is in the willingness. We should again take a look at some of the words.

The word *all* means the whole extent or quantity.

The word *harmed* means injured, damaged or caused ill effects.

The word *willing* means ready, eager or prepared to do something.

The words *make amends* mean to compensate or make up for a wrongdoing.

So step eight is saying that we should compile a list of every single person to whom we have caused damage or ill effects, and that we should be ready and eager to make up for our wrongdoings and compensate them all in some way.

The wording in the Big Book on step eight assumes that the list of persons whom we have harmed has already been made as part of step four. The fourth part of step four is to look at harms done to others, so we should have this list readily available. We may wish, upon further reflection, to add to the list at this stage, but we should not be removing anyone. Addicts cause harm to others not only physically or financially but often also emotionally. We greatly disturb the peace of mind of those who love and care about us, and we also have a tendency to let people down when we give priority to addictive behaviour. We may be tempted to believe that we have not caused much harm to anyone but ourselves. An honest look at our selfish and self-centered behaviour in the past will however almost certainly highlight many people who have been damaged in some way. A good suggestion here is to set aside our own thoughts and feelings and try to understand from the perspective of the other person. As the saying goes, we cannot really understand anyone else until we walk a mile in their shoes. If we do this honestly then we will begin to see how harmful our past behavior has been.

In the absence of willingness to make amends, the Big Book suggests that we should ask until such willingness comes. This asking implies prayer. There will probably be cases where the personal self does not want to make amends, hence the need for prayer to override the personal agenda and act in accordance with non-personal Consciousness. Even if a situation in the past has only been partly down to our behaviour, we should nevertheless be prepared to make amends for our part. There is no time period specified, and some situations will be more problematic than others, but the implication here is that we should continue to pray for willingness until we become willing.

The main block to willingness in respect of step eight is the fear of how our amends may be received, or the fear of even putting ourselves in danger by confronting old issues that may be dormant. Self-centered fear is the core driver of the personal ego self. Such fear is understandable from this perspective. However we are now in the business of acting in accordance with the qualities of non-personal Consciousness. Recognition of self-centered fear is itself a very useful practice of self-awareness. The noticing of such fear will highlight how the personal ego mind still dominates. The solution is the renewed surrender of the personal ego self through prayer.

Ultimately, step eight is all about forgiveness. The word *forgive* means to cease feeling angry or resentful towards someone for an offence, flaw or mistake. Often forgiveness is seen as transactional in the sense that one person will forgive another only if the other person offers forgiveness first. This is a clash of personal ego minds and neither is comfortable with being the first to concede. This logjam of forgiveness can leave resentments festering for many years, and even to the end of our lives. Step eight is encouraging us to acknowledge our part in emotional harms done to others and to be the first to act with forgiveness. If there are people that we think we can never forgive then we should pray for specific willingness.

A literal understanding of step eight would be that we already have our list of people who we have harmed from step four and we should now be willing to go out and make amends to them.

A deeper understanding would be that we should take time to consider how much emotional harm we have caused to others through our active addiction and also through our selfish and self-centered behavior in the past. This is likely to be a longer list than the one that we made when we did step four. This is because we now have the benefit of having worked through steps five, six and seven and consequently have a better understanding of how the human ego inevitably creates conflict with other human egos. There can be no happiness, peace, love or unity in life if we continue to take everything personally. We cannot change other people but we can begin to change ourselves. This should increase our willingness to make amends to those who have been impacted by our behavior.

The next level of understanding is that all-round forgiveness is highly desirable. Guilt, shame and bitterness are all obstacles to spiritual progress because they keep us stuck in identification with the personal ego self. We have made the decision to surrender our personal agenda in favour of Consciousness. We have seen how the exaggerated traits of the human ego mind have negatively impacted our experience of life. He have been honest enough to expose and release our hidden selves. We have become willing to change and we are choosing to act in accordance with qualities of Consciousness. Steps four, five, six and seven have now led us to having to swallow our pride and make amends to everyone in the spirit of forgiveness, however much we may feel that they have harmed us. We do not become willing to make amends so that we can feel better. This would be a selfish motive. We see that everyone makes mistakes and behaves selfishly. We see that everyone is identified as the personal ego self and therefore thinks, feels and behaves accordingly. We have been making the same mistake. We now see it all through the eyes of forgiveness. We forgive ourselves and we forgive others. It does not matter what they may or may not have done. We become ready and eager to make up for our wrongdoings in the past. It is a movement of identity in the direction of non-personal Consciousness. It is the right thing to do. We become willing to make amends so that others may be healed. This is a selfless motive. This is progress.

The deepest understanding of step eight would be that our willingness to make amends is an expression of the qualities of Consciousness. This willingness on its own will raise the vibration of the individual body-mind and aid the process of transformation from personal mind to the non-personal Mind of Consciousness. The nature of Consciousness is happiness, peace, love and unity. The qualities of Consciousness are all expressions of this nature. Forgiveness is one of these expressions and is obviously a higher vibration than fear, bitterness or resentment. As our own vibration increases, so resonance attracts more of the same. Our attitude of forgiveness towards others will invariably produce a similar reaction from them. This may not always be the case, and it will depend on how dark the shadow may be in the other person. This however is not important. Our task is simply to shine the light of forgiveness into all of our relationships. We do not need to explain why we are doing it. Every expression of higher Consciousness adds to the collective vibration. Consciousness is unity itself, and always seeks harmony. This harmony will significantly enhance our experience of life but this is not the motive. Our purpose is to be an expression of Consciousness. Improved relationships are not the reason for making amends, but are the inevitable by-product of living by spiritual principles. Our willingness to forgive and make amends is a selfless expression of non-personal Consciousness, even if we may not realise it at the time. The metamorphosis is taking place.

Step eight for me was a complete non-event. I had my list of people from step four and I was anxious about making amends to any of them. I certainly did not consider adding to the list, nor did I pray for willingness. I just moved straight onto step nine and conferred with my sponsor about which amends I should make first. I was keen to proceed, but my motives were selfish.

It is only through experience and the blessing of wisdom that this understanding of step eight has emerged. I can see that there are still people to whom I owe amends. There remains some personal anxiety, but this is swamped by a willingness to do the next right thing. I have learned to trust that life will present me with these opportunities to make amends when the time is right. It is not for me to force the issue. If I try to act too quickly then my motives are unsound. Meanwhile there is a strong sense of forgiveness for everything that has happened in this life, including my own thoughts, feelings and behaviours. We do what we do in accordance with the level of Consciousness that dominates at the time. It has only ever been a matter of over-identification with the personal self. Once the personal self begins to fade, then the true light of Consciousness emerges. Forgiveness then becomes natural.

41. Step Nine

"Made direct amends to such people wherever possible, except when to do so would injure them or others."

Having made our list and become willing in step eight, it is now time to begin making our amends. The objective may seem to be a clearing away of the wreckage of our past, but the real purpose is to become instruments of forgiveness. Most of the words are fairly clear but a few of them are worth exploring.

The word *direct* in this context means frank, straight to the point, explicit and without intermediaries or intervening factors.

The word *amends* is the same as in step eight and means compensation or making up for wrongdoing.

The words *wherever possible* mean in every case that is achievable or can be done.

The word *except* means other than or not including.

The word *injure* in this respect means to do physical or emotional harm.

The words *them or others* refer to the potential recipient of the amend and to any other individual.

Step nine is therefore about making amends to those we have harmed, but being careful not to cause more harm in the process. If it is felt that attempting to make an amend will result in emotional, physical or financial harm to other people, then such amends should not be made. The willingness expressed in step eight will be sufficient. We should always be mindful of others when making amends. Indeed we should now ideally be selfless and mindful of others at all times. Amends should therefore acknowledge the emotional, physical or financial harms done to others without reference to any harm that we may feel they have done to us. This is about clearing away our side of the street without any expectations as to what the other person may do or say. Reparation of this sort is not transactional. We take the initiative without any anticipation of reward.

The Big Book wording on step nine offers great insight. Suggestions are made regarding certain types of amends and examples are also given. The point is made that although we are, at this stage, attempting to put our own lives in order, the real purpose is to be an instrument of Consciousness. The point is also made that a one-off apology is often insufficient and that compensation should really be in the form of living amends on an ongoing basis. Emphasis is made that a life based on spiritual principles is not theoretical or abstract but practical and actionable. Evangelism should be avoided and instead we should concentrate on our own behavior. We can be a humble expression of Consciousness without demeaning or devaluing ourselves. The essay on step nine in "Twelve Steps and Twelve Traditions" also provides useful guidance and in particular offers advice on the prioritisation and timing of our amends. Whatever the form of an amend, or the timing, the motive should always be selfless and the emphasis should be on forgiveness.

Step nine is also the part of the Big Book that contains the promises of recovery. These promises are often read out at the end of meetings in the UK. They offer a vision of what life in recovery can look like. The promises appear on pages 83 and 84 of the fourth edition and read "If we are painstaking about this phase of our development, we will be amazed before we are half way through. We are going to know a new freedom and a new happiness. We will not regret the past nor wish to shut the door on it. We will comprehend the word serenity and we will know peace. No matter how far down the scale we have gone, we will see how our experience can benefit others. That feeling of uselessness and self-pity will disappear. We will lose interest in selfish things and gain interest in our fellows. Self-seeking will slip away. Our whole attitude and outlook upon life will change.

Fear of people and of economic insecurity will leave us. We will intuitively know how to handle situations that used to baffle us. We will suddenly realise that God is doing for us what he could not do for ourselves. Are these extravagant promises? We think not. They are being fulfilled among us – sometimes quickly, sometimes slowly. They will always materialize if we work for them."

The wording of these promises is very important and there is a great deal that we can glean from them. The promises relate to the phase of recovery that is roughly half way through making our amends. They do not arise half way through the twelve steps, nor do they happen half way through any other time period that we might imagine. Some of them may come true earlier to some extent but we should not let this lull us into a false sense of security. If we have a mistaken belief that the promises will come true simply by going to twelve-step meetings, and remaining abstinent, then we are setting ourselves up for disappointment and frustration. Likewise if we work through the steps in a half-hearted way then the promises will not fully result. Perhaps the most important yet overlooked word in the promises is "if". This word appears right at the beginning and also in the last sentence. The promises are contingent on being painstaking and on putting in the work. The promises are not theoretical. They are promises. The word *promise* means assurance or guarantee. These things are guaranteed to happen if we work through the steps diligently.

Notice that the promises include things that we will lose and also experiences that we will gain. We are promised to lose regret, uselessness, self-pity, selfishness, fear of people, fear of economic insecurity, bafflement and failure. All of these things are aspects of the personal ego self. It is clear that if we let go of identification with the personal ego self then we will lose these undesirable human aspects. It is also this change in identity that gives rise to the gains. We are promised to gain freedom, happiness, understanding, peace, usefulness, altruism, selflessness, changed attitude, intuition and certainty. These gains are obviously desirable. They arise from the qualities of non-personal Consciousness. This is why the promises are guaranteed. All human beings are expressions of Consciousness. There are no exclusions. Existence depends upon Consciousness. Existence is Consciousness. If we relinquish our personal ego selves then pure Consciousness will emerge. It really is that simple. The rate at which this happens will vary. Sometimes it will be quick. Other times it will be slow. The variation in speed will depend entirely on the diligence and persistence with which the steps are practiced. There are no shortcuts. If we want the promises to come true for us then we need to put in the committed action. It is our decision. We are already supposed to have made this decision in step three, but experience shows that step three nearly always needs to be reaffirmed and deepened. The step nine promises are the carrot that works in tandem with the stick of step one. Together they can bring about forward movement in even the most challenging of cases.

A literal understanding of step nine would be that we work through our list over time and make amends to those people who we think are worthy of our remorse. Amends typically take the form of one-off apologies or financial compensation. Other amends will be more specific. Sometimes letters are written, especially when people have passed away and are no longer with us. We will avoid amends if we feel that the raising of old issues may cause emotional harm to others. Sometimes we use this as an excuse to delay amends indefinitely, when really a gesture of forgiveness might be extremely beneficial.

A deeper level of understanding would be that true amends require more than a one-off apology or other gestures of compensation. Twelve-step recovery is about living life on an entirely different basis. Our amends should be living amends in the sense that our ongoing attitude and behavior should be based on spiritual principles rather than our personal agenda. This will be particularly true in our intimate relationships and general family conduct. Our behavior in active addiction has undoubtedly caused great emotional harm to those who are closest to us and care about us. Our amends should be in the form of an ongoing commitment to think, feel and behave in accordance with the qualities of Consciousness. Repeated behavior in line with step seven will naturally feed into living amends. This is primarily for the benefit of others, but it will also help to move us further along the spectrum of balance between human and Being.

The next level of understanding is that step nine is really all about the act of forgiveness. I covered this in step eight in respect of the willingness to forgive, but now we put this willingness into action. Amends are approached with care, compassion and sincerity. The focus is on emotional healing and reconciliation in the spirit of forgiveness. If our approach is not well received then we do not react or respond unkindly to anything that may arise in the other person. It may well be that the other person really needs to vent their anger or frustration with our past behavior. This can be a necessary part of their healing. We respond in line with the qualities of Consciousness and resist taking their response personally, even if the ego mind tries to pull us back into a defensive mode. Just observing our own reactions will provide more impetus for step seven. On the other hand, the amend may be well received and lead to mutual forgiveness and emotional healing. It will literally lift the spirits of both parties. Consciousness will be connecting with itself through the interactions between the one making amends and those who receive them. Step nine can be a very powerful shift away from the personal ego self towards non-personal Consciousness. It feels good because we are acting in line with the harmonious nature of Spirit. We are becoming increasingly selfless. This is why the promises start to come true during this phase of the transformation.

The deepest understanding of step nine would be that the making of amends through the expression of forgiveness is the unifying movement of Consciousness itself. Again I have already covered this in step eight. The effect of actually making amends will be even more impactful than our willingness to do so. This should be true regardless of how the other person reacts. Every amend will have some benefit. The underlying truth is that the individual who is making the amend and the individual who is receiving it are both expressions of the same Consciousness. All human beings long for a return to happiness, peace, love and unity in the same way as our metaphorical bath sponge. It is a natural desire, but we generally prevent it because we insist on taking life personally. The making and receiving of amends is a vibrational exchange at a level of Consciousness higher than the condensed, limited human ego mind. It is Consciousness resonating with Consciousness at a higher vibration. It feels good because the natural state of pure Consciousness is unity. The prodigal son wants to return home, and the making of amends is a big part of the journey in this direction. With this understanding, we should be motivated to make amends to as many people as possible rather than trying to do the minimum. The more we do, the more the promises will come true.

My own experience of step nine has been very mixed. As before, my understanding at the outset was very limited and hence my early amends were clumsy. I took the personal view that all of my past harmful behavior had been the result of addiction, and hence I tried to use addiction as an excuse. This was not well received, and rightly so. My amends lacked the essential ingredient of humility. As understanding matured, I began to see that addiction is not just part of a personal self that is otherwise without fault. The whole personal ego self is the problem, and addiction has simply amplified and highlighted all of the ego traits. Amends need to arise from the qualities of Consciousness rather than from a personal self that tries to justify and excuse its harmful behavior. I learned from this early experience and hence my subsequent amends have had more positive outcomes. My most recent amend has been the most meaningful so far in terms of forgiveness and emotional healing. I still have some amends to make but feel uncertain about timing. I am willing and eager to proceed but this is tempered by a feeling of not wanting to do more harm than good. The solution to this conundrum is prayer. I am confident that the multitudinous expressions of Consciousness throughout life itself will conspire to provide the right opportunities at the right time. There is, in my experience, no rush to complete step nine, but equally it would be unwise to delay unnecessarily.

It is also my experience that the step nine promises do come true. It has taken some time but I can now confirm and relate to every statement made. The promises may seem extravagant from the point of view of a personal self, but they undoubtedly do come true as identification with the personal ego self fades. These promises are what we have been seeking as the personal self. We personally pursue these things in countless different ways without ever realising that it is over-identification with the personal ego self that has prevented us from experiencing what we desire on any sustainable basis. This is the ultimate irony of life. We already are that which we seek, but we have been completely unaware of this truth due to the original mistake of overlooking our own true nature as Consciousness. We no longer regret the past. We remain aware of our former mistakes. We see that twelve-step recovery is the gateway to transformation. We become deeply grateful for this opportunity to experience the beauty and wonder of life. We express this gratitude through fully embracing the remaining steps.

The butterfly is emerging from the chrysalis and discovers that it now has wings. These wings will be of no use unless they are put into action. If we want to fly then we have use our wings, and we have to keep using them. If we stop using them then we will fall back to the ground. It is time to practice self-awareness, self-contemplation and self-forgetting on a continuous basis.

42. Step Ten

"Continued to take personal inventory and when we were wrong promptly admitted it."

Step ten is all about self-awareness. It is effectively the regular repetition of steps four, five, six, seven, eight and nine. Before we look at the application of step ten, we should take a look at the key words.

The word *continued* in this context means to persist with an activity or process.

The words *personal inventory* have the same meaning as in step four, which is a complete list of items referring to the personal ego self.

The word *and* means in addition or as well.

The word *when* in this step means whenever or at any time.

The word *wrong* has the same meaning as in step five and means not correct, not true, mistaken, in error, unsuitable, bad, abnormal, unjust, dishonest or immoral.

The word *promptly* means with little or no delay or, in other words, immediately.

The word *admitted* has the same meaning as in step one, which is confessed to be true, and implies reluctant acknowledgement.

So step ten says that we should persist in the activity of taking personal inventory. In addition we should confess our mistakes immediately. Notice that the step uses the word *when* rather than *if.* The implication here is that we will continue to make mistakes based on identification with the personal ego self. It is always going to be a matter of when rather than if. The Big Book wording for step ten also suggests making amends for such mistakes. This is therefore a continuous repetition of steps four through nine. This requires constant self-awareness.

The Big Book wording goes on to describe the experience of being placed in a position of neutrality regarding addiction, provided we remain in fit spiritual condition. The initial motivation for engaging in the steps was to recover from addiction. Remaining abstinent in the early days required relapse prevention techniques and short-term targets. We tried to stay sober one day at a time whilst making progress on the steps. By the time we reach step ten, this phase of recovery should have passed. Addiction should now largely be a non-issue. Thoughts of acting out may arise from time to time, but these thoughts have no power or personal hold. This is because we have now detached from, or given up, our over-identification with the personal self. Such personal thoughts are seen to be just thoughts, and hence can be acted upon or ignored depending on the guidance of non-personal Consciousness. This is the spiritual solution to addiction. Rather than trying to fix the personal mind, we move identity gradually to the Mind of Consciousness. When seen in the this way, the solution is actually pretty obvious. It is also clear that the new spiritual condition needs to be maintained, otherwise we will slip back into the personal ego self and addiction will regain its hold.

This idea of maintenance of our spiritual condition can be very misleading and problematic. Our understandable tendency can be to think that maintenance implies staying where we are. Indeed the word *maintenance* means the process of preserving a condition, situation or state. The problem is that these differing states of Consciousness that I have been describing are not static points that can be reached and maintained. Consciousness is in a constant state of vibration and movement. There is no static place to stand or state to preserve. Our identity is constantly moving within the spectrum of balance between human and Being. The experience of day-to-day life seems to pull us back in the direction of the personal ego self. The more we practice spiritual principles, the less powerful this ego pull will be, but it will always be there. It is supposed to be there to ensure survival and to facilitate a unique experience of life. We need to stay grounded in our newfound identity as Consciousness and this requires the maintenance of our spiritual condition. It is the practice that needs to be maintained. The spiritual condition depends upon the practice. This is why recovery is contingent upon continuing our spiritual practices. Self-awareness is one such practice.

The wording on step ten in "Twelve Steps and Twelve Traditions" focuses on the different frequencies of practice. There is the periodic step ten that is effectively a step four conducted from time to time, perhaps annually or semi-annually. There is the daily step ten that is suggested as an evening routine where we review our thoughts, feelings and behaviours during that day and notice where our self-centered human traits have surfaced. This can be balanced by acknowledging when we have acted in accordance with the qualities of Consciousness. This daily balance between ego traits and expression of Consciousness will give a good indication of where we are in terms of progress. Finally there is the moment-to-moment step ten where we remain constantly aware of how we are thinking and reacting, and hence how identified we still are with the personal ego self. There is also mention of the spiritual truth that whenever we are disturbed there is inevitably some aspect of our personal ego self that is causing the disturbance. It is always tempting to blame someone or something else, but the truth is always much closer to home. This is why Mooji points out that all problems are personal. It is over-identification with the personal self that causes our thinking, feeling and behaviour to arise from the human ego. The more we practice the more we notice, and hence the more often we can choose the qualities of Consciousness instead. Gradually these spiritual qualities become the natural reaction and hence the dominance of the ego self recedes.

A literal understanding of step ten would be that we continue to undertake a step four process from time to time, and make amends in accordance with step nine when we think that we have done something wrong.

A deeper understanding would be that we work through steps four, five, six, seven, eight and nine on a daily basis. This seems a tall order but it should not be overly time-consuming. First we should do a quick inventory of any resentments, fears, relationship issues or harms done that have occurred during the day. Next we should share key issues with our sponsor or spiritual advisor. We should then pray for willingness to change and also commit to acting more in line with the qualities of Consciousness in future. We should also pray for willingness to make amends where necessary and then we should make such amends immediately. All of this becomes routine with persistent practice.

The next level of understanding would be that step ten is really about continuous self-awareness. The daily practice noted above will naturally lead to us becoming increasingly aware of our thoughts, feelings and behaviours as they happen. This will enable us to override the personal ego in real time and act in accordance with spiritual principles. This will not happen all of the time but will progressively become natural and normal. This will be aided by the gradual realisation that it is better to avoid getting resentful in the moment rather than have to do a step four about it later in the evening, share it, pray about it and apologise. If we are not practicing step ten on a daily basis then of course these real time changes in our thoughts, feelings and behaviours are less likely to occur, or at least will take much longer to develop.

The deepest level of understanding of step ten is that the qualities of Consciousness are ever present in all human beings. These qualities are largely overridden by the traits of the human ego because this is who we think we are. If we are convinced that we are only a personal self then the majority of our thoughts, feeling and behaviours are obviously going to the based on this belief. There will still be expressions of the qualities of Consciousness from time to time but these will be the exception rather than the rule. For those suffering from addiction, these positive moments will become increasingly rare as the condition progresses. Our thoughts, feelings are behaviours become progressively selfish and self-centered. It takes time and practice for this to change. Progress through the steps has a cumulative effect and is driven by both the stick and the carrot. From the perspective of the personal self, steps four through nine require effort and action. As the identity shifts increasingly away from the ego mind towards the Mind of Consciousness, so step ten becomes easier and more natural. As we practice abiding in non-personal Consciousness, we are naturally able to witness and observe the workings of the personal ego mind. This then leads to more abidance in Consciousness, which in turn increases awareness of the personal self. In this way, self-awareness builds upon itself and produces the desired transformation. A snowball grows in size as it rolls down a hill, but we need to get the snowball moving in the first place. We need to practice self-awareness until self-awareness practices itself. This is the true purpose of step ten, and it is an essential component of effective recovery.

Step ten was again a bit of a non-event for me at the time that I worked through the steps. My understanding was that I should make more amends if I did anything else wrong, but according to my personal mind I was no longer doing anything wrong. I felt that sobriety was enough and that I had already done my inventory in step four. Step ten did not really seem necessary. I quickly moved onto steps eleven and twelve and overlooked step ten completely. Fortunately, part of my weekly routine was to attend a Big Book Study meeting. The format was to read a step each week and then people shared their experience. Each time we got to step ten, my conscience would be pricked. I heard others share about how they practiced step ten and I began to see that I was missing something of vital importance. Also my eventual sponsoring of others helped me to realise that step ten was missing from my practice. It was several years before an understanding began to emerge. Today self-awareness is part of an integrated daily practice and way of life. I am far from perfect, but I continue to make progress. The more self-awareness I have, the more motivation I have for change. This humility to remain willing and open to change keeps me in fit spiritual condition.

Self-awareness goes hand-in-hand with self-contemplation. The two practices work together and reinforce each other. Moment to moment self-awareness will cause us to question where our identity sits on the spectrum of balance between personal ego mind and the Mind of Consciousness. Prayer, meditation and self-inquiry deepen our abidance in Consciousness and hence lead to enhanced self-awareness. It makes sense therefore that the next step should focus on the practice of self-contemplation.

43. Step Eleven

"Sought through prayer and meditation to improve our conscious contact with God as we understood Him, praying only for knowledge of His will for us and the power to carry that out."

Step eleven is the daily practice of self-contemplation. We have covered prayer, meditation and self-inquiry in previous chapters. It is now time to put these rituals into practice. The words of step eleven contain all of the detailed insight that we need. It will be helpful to go through them very carefully.

The word *sought* means asked, attempted or desired to find, obtain, bring about or achieve something.

The word *through* in this context indicates by means of.

We have covered prayer and meditation previously, but *and* is the key word. It is not sufficient to just pray. There also needs to be a daily meditation practice, otherwise spiritual progress will be painfully slow, or non-existent.

The word *improve* means to make or become better. This is not about just staying sober. This is about continuous improvement.

I mentioned before that the word *conscious* was added to step eleven as part of the final drafting of the Big Book. This addition is not without meaning. The word *conscious* variously means aware of, having knowledge of, deliberate or intentional. The word *conscious* is also obviously closely connected with *consciousness*. In fact *Consciousness* is a noun that means the state of Awareness or Knowingness, whilst *conscious* is an adjective that describes this state. The implication of including the word *conscious* is that we should be improving our Awareness or Knowingness. In other words we should be increasingly abiding as Consciousness.

The word *contact* means to communicate with.

The words *God as we understood Him* are as previously described.

The word *only* is often overlooked in this step and means solely, no more than or nothing more besides. This is arguably the most important word in step eleven.

The word *knowledge* in this context means Awareness or Knowingness.

The word *His* is yet another God word.

The word *will* means desire, intention or wish.

The word *power* means the ability or capacity to do something or act in a particular way. It also means the capability to influence the behavior of others or the course of events.

The words *carry that out* relate to the performance of specific tasks.

The analysis of this wording provides us with a very clear picture of what step eleven is saying. We are to practice prayer and meditation on a regular basis in order to bring about continuous improvement in awareness and knowledge of our deepest sense of intuition and guidance. The only purpose for doing this is to be aware of how Consciousness wishes to express itself through our individual body and mind, and to gain the power needed to act in accordance with these wishes and perform specific tasks as guided. In other words, we are seeking Consciousness in order to become our true selves, which is Consciousness. We start by praying to Consciousness from the position of the personal ego self and we end up as Consciousness itself. This gradual change in identity disempowers the personal human self and empowers the Being. This is the transformation that we are seeking. The person that starts the journey of recovery gradually disappears as we get closer and closer to home.

The relevant passage in the Big Book highlights the interrelation between steps ten and eleven. Self-awareness leads to sincere prayer and meditation, which in turn produces more self-awareness. There is also emphasis placed on the need to avoid selfish, self-centered prayer. There is an admission that a lot of time has been wasted on this. In fact, it can be seen that selfish, self-centered prayer is not only a waste of time but is actually counter productive.

The process of recovery is about letting go of the personal ego self. If we pray for our own wellbeing, or for outcomes in line with our own personal ideas about how things should be, then we are reinforcing our sense of personal self. We can spend time making progress on other spiritual practices but then undo this progress through selfish prayer. We should not underestimate the power of prayer. Consciousness is all-powerful. Consciousness is all there is. We start our prayer life with the self-identified person petitioning Consciousness for surrender and guidance, and offering gratitude. We pray in the morning for a sober day and we give thanks at the end of the day. Somewhere along the journey, the balance of identity between human and Being needs to shift towards Consciousness. This is the transformation that brings about recovery. If we continue to pray for our own selfish ends then we will remain identified as the personal ego self. Prayer always works. It is not a mystery. Prayer is only ever one aspect of Consciousness communicating with another. It is all about identity and the vibration of Consciousness. The misuse of prayer can inadvertently reinforce the belief in the personal ego self and hence thwart the desired recovery. This is a common mistake. The whole purpose of prayer is selfless surrender and the seeking of guidance. This will lead to abidance in, and as, Consciousness. This is why the word *only* is so important in step eleven.

In his essay on step eleven in "Twelve Steps and Twelve Traditions", Bill Wilson quotes the words attributed to St. Francis of Assisi as a really good example of prayer. I would certainly concur. We covered this prayer in the chapter on self-forgetting, but the key messages are worth repeating. The wording used by Wilson is slightly different and reads "Lord, make me a channel of thy peace – that where there is hatred, I may bring love - that where there is wrong, I may bring the spirit of forgiveness – that where there is discord, I may bring harmony - that where there is error, I may bring truth – that where there is doubt, I may bring faith – that where there is despair, I may bring hope – that where there are shadows, I may bring light – that where there is sadness, I may bring joy. Lord, grant that I may seek rather to comfort than to be comforted – to understand, than to be understood – to love, than to be loved. For it is by self-forgetting that one finds. It is by forgiving that one is forgiven. It is by dying that one awakens to eternal life. Amen."

There are several important points to note. This prayer is not selfish. It is completely selfless. The petition is to be a channel of peace, or an instrument in the original version. This idea of being a channel or instrument of peace is the same idea as the individual body and mind becoming a channel or instrument of Consciousness. The various related opposites mentioned are directly related to the list of human ego traits as opposed to the qualities of Consciousness. The personal ego mind is the source of hatred, wrong, error, doubt, despair, shadows and sadness. The personal self wants to be comforted, understood, loved, self-obsessed, forgiven and to live forever. Consciousness is the source of love, forgiveness, harmony, truth, faith, hope, light, joy, comfort, understanding, self-forgetting and eternal life. These qualities emerge when the personal ego self is surrendered in favour of being a channel or instrument of Consciousness. This prayer is all about the shift in balance of identity from human to

Being. This is step eleven. This is transformation. This is recovery.

The book "Twelve Steps and Twelve Traditions" also uses the words "self-examination" in step eleven and mentions "the good that is in all of us". Self-examination is typically understood to mean taking inventory of the self-centered human ego traits. It is a detached observation of the ego mind from a deeper level of personal Consciousness, or Soul level. However self-examination can also be an even deeper practice where we observe, or witness, personal Consciousness from the position of non-personal Consciousness. This is the practice of self-inquiry that I covered in detail in the chapter on self-contemplation. Self-inquiry is the exploration of the True Self. This practice reveals the good that is within all of us, which is non-personal Consciousness. Persistent practice of self-inquiry shifts the balance of identity even further from human to Being.

A literal understanding of step eleven would be that we use prayer and meditation to deepen our conscious contact with our understanding of a third party God. We seek guidance in our lives and we pray for strength. In some cases, even this literal reading of the words is not practiced effectively. A typical mistake is to use only prayer and overlook meditation. Another mistake is to ignore the word *only* and continue with selfish, self-centered prayer indefinitely. Sometimes we ignore the word *improve* and simply try to maintain whatever connection we have. These simple misunderstandings can bring recovery to a standstill and hence perpetuate the struggle to stay sober one day at a time.

A deeper understanding would be that step eleven is just a more detailed version of step three. It is all about having the humility to concede our personal will and the course of our lives to our individual concept of a higher power. The purpose of improving conscious contact is to deepen this connection and hence enhance the surrender. The more we surrender, the more clear the guidance will become and the more strength we will have to follow this guidance. It is tempting to think that our external higher power is taking care of us and keeping us sober, but in reality it is the guidance and strength of Consciousness that is keeping us safe.

The next level of understanding would be that step eleven is ultimately about abiding in, and as, non-personal Consciousness. The practice of prayer, meditation and self-inquiry gradually loosens the identity of a personal ego self and brings about a realisation that, in truth, we are non-personal Consciousness. This self-realisation or self-revelation is what is referred to as a spiritual awakening, vital spiritual experience or psychic change. We literally wake up from the mistaken personal identity and realise who we truly are. This realisation will take time to become established, but once it starts there is no doubt at all about its authenticity. The whole world is increasingly seen and experienced differently. This is the beginning of a new phase of life. This is the butterfly stage that was intended all along.

The deepest level of understanding of step eleven is that this is the step that takes us all the way home. Consciousness condenses itself into a finite personal mind and body in order to experience the finite world that it has created out of itself. In order to survive and thrive, this limited form of Consciousness has a vibration of self-centered fear and overlooks its own original nature. This naturally leads to identification as a personal self that lacks the sense of happiness, peace, love and unity that gives rise to its apparent existence. So begins the journey of life to find the things that we lack. Our motives are driven by self-centered fear and desire. Our identification as a personal self inevitably causes suffering for ourselves and other personal selves. As we try harder, so the suffering intensifies and we end up in a state of brokenness. As with the prodigal son, this brokenness causes us to turn around and head back home. The personal ego self is surrendered and the identity gradually returns to non-personal Consciousness which, in reality, is what it was all along. Consciousness now shines through the individual body and mind in a unique and beautiful expression.

The ego mind still operates to perform basic functions, but it is no longer the identity of the Being. The spiritual journey is complete and life can now be experienced on the intended individual and unique basis. The human is reborn into its second stage of life as Being.

Step eleven has been a key part of my recovery. This step, together with step twelve, has transformed my life. I have explored prayer, meditation and self-inquiry with various teachers from various faiths. It is out of these practices that the understanding of perennial wisdom has emerged. This wisdom underpins all spiritual teaching, including the twelve steps. My own experience has therefore been that spiritual practice both inside and outside of twelve-step fellowship is necessary in order to really make progress. This understanding is also found in the final step of the twelve-step program.

44. Step Twelve

"Having had a spiritual awakening as the result of these steps, we tried to carry this message to addicts, and to practice these principles in all our affairs."

Step twelve is the spiritual practice of self-forgetting. The step is in two distinct but related parts. The first part concerns carrying the message of recovery to other addicts. The second part relates to practicing spiritual principles in our daily lives outside of twelve-step fellowship. Both of these elements are important and necessary for effective recovery. We should take one final look at the precise wording of the steps in order to draw out the exact meaning.

The words *having had* are past tense and imply that something has already happened.

The words *spiritual awakening* specifically describe the awakening of Consciousness, Awareness, Knowingness, Mind, Spirit or Being in the individual. The term *spiritual awakening* has the same meaning as other phrases such as self-realisation, self-revelation, unveiling, vital spiritual experience, psychic change, shift, transcendence, ascension, transformation, metamorphosis, resurrection, rebirth, second coming or salvation.

The words *the result* imply a specific outcome or consequence.

The words *these steps* obviously apply to the previous eleven steps.

The word *tried* means made an attempt or effort to do something.

The words *this message* unquestionably refer to the earlier part of the sentence, which clearly states that a spiritual awakening has taken place as a consequence of these eleven steps.

The word *and* means in addition or as well.

The word *practice* in this context means the actual application of ideas and methods as opposed to theoretical understanding.

The words *these principles* relate to the behaviours and attitudes that are fundamental to the first eleven steps.

The word *all* means the whole extent or quantity and without exception.

The word *affairs* relates to the various activities that comprise our day-to-day lives.

As with all of the steps, the wording of step twelve is in the style of describing what others have done in order to bring about recovery from addiction. This is what they did after having had a spiritual awakening. It is included as a twelfth step precisely because self-forgetting is an essential practice in becoming yet more established in, and as, non-personal Consciousness.

The wording of step twelve is very clear. We will have had some sort of spiritual awakening as *the* result of the first eleven steps. We are to make an effort to carry this message of spiritual awakening to other addicts. We do this because we now know that it works and, as addicts ourselves, we are in a unique position to share our individual experience, strength and hope. In addition, we are to apply the behaviours and attitudes contained in the steps to every single aspect of our daily lives, without exception.

Spiritual awakening is a unique individual experience. There is no standard against which we should be seeking to measure ourselves. Some do have a sudden, dramatic revelation that instantly changes the course of their lives. Descriptions sometimes include bright lights or a tremendous feeling of serenity and presence. For the rest of us, it is more often the case of a gradual awakening, punctuated by moments of understanding and clarity that are sometimes followed by periods of doubt or depression. This is all par for the course. Even for those who do have a sudden awakening there is still the necessity for continuing self-awareness, self-contemplation and self-forgetting, otherwise there is the inevitable return to identification with the personal ego self. There is also the risk that such a dramatic happening will be perceived as a personal experience and hence reinforce the sense of personal self. Spiritual awakening is not a personal experience. It is the temporary absence of the personal ego self that allows the revelation of non-personal Consciousness. There can be no pride in a spiritual awakening because pride only exists as an aspect of the personal self that is now absent. This is all rather ironic and easily misunderstood.

Whether a spiritual awakening is sudden or gradual makes no difference to the overall process. A caterpillar may get a temporary glimpse of the potential life as a butterfly but it still needs to go through the process of metamorphosis. There are no short cuts, and all attempts to artificially speed up the process will be futile. All we can do is remain focused on the suggested actions and allow the process to unfold in its own time. The eventual transformation is inevitable because non-personal Consciousness has been our underlying true nature all along. It may not happen until physical death, but it will happen. Our opportunity is to wake up to our true nature whilst we are still alive. We all have the chance to die to the personal ego self before we die physically.

Carrying the message of spiritual awakening, and hence recovery, to other addicts is an act of self-forgetting. Our own previous burden of suffering in active addiction now turns into treasure to be shared with others. We do not do this selfishly in order to protect our own recovery. We do this selflessly, and often with a degree of personal inconvenience, precisely because this is the most effective way to practice self-forgetting. It is most effective because an addict in recovery is best placed to carry the message. Experience is far more valuable than any amount of instruction, advice or doctrine. An addict in recovery is the most potent channel or instrument for the revelation of Consciousness in other addicts. The fact that this further enhances the shift in identity for the one practicing step twelve is a by-product of this activity rather than the purpose. If we are helping others in order to help ourselves then we have fundamentally missed the whole point of recovery. The personal self who is trying to help their own recovery by doing this is supposed to have been surrendered by this stage. Step twelve is about self-forgetting, not self-development.

We can be at our most useful when helping other addicts, but we also have an important role to play outside of twelve-step fellowship. Simply being an expression of non-personal Consciousness in our day-to-day lives will have a vibrational impact on all those with whom we come into contact. It is not so much about what we say but the whole manner of how we react and behave. The qualities of Consciousness expressed through us will resonate with the same qualities of Consciousness that are the underlying reality of all humans and other sentient beings. All that is needed is to be present and to be our authentic, individual, non-personal selves. To be or not to be. To be an authentic expression of Consciousness or to be the inauthentic, limited, self-centered, fearful personal ego self. Self-forgetting is about being the Being.

There is another important aspect to this second part of step twelve. I mentioned in step eleven that selfish prayer can actually be counterproductive and keep us identified as a personal self. Likewise if we practice spiritual principles within twelve-step fellowship but then return to being a personal ego self in our daily lives then we are actually undermining our spiritual progress, and hence our recovery. We are also

271

preventing the individual body and mind from being an effective instrument of Consciousness. We will constantly yo-yo between feeling the positive qualities of Consciousness within twelve-step meetings and suffering the traits of the personal ego mind in all other areas of our lives. This understanding explains why we often continue to struggle in our lives despite being sober and in long-term recovery. We can very easily undo all of our spiritual progress by behaving selfishly in our careers, our families or in our lives in general. The whole point of self-forgetting is to forget about the personal self. This is not a part-time activity. We may think that we have pulled the ripcord but actually we have only pulled it part way out. The parachute is not yet deployed.

The Big Book devotes an entire chapter to step twelve and offers detailed suggestions on how best to carry the message of recovery to those who still suffer from addiction. The practical experience of the early pioneers of twelve-step recovery was that this focus on helping others worked even when other spiritual practices did not. Self-forgetting is a powerful spiritual practice. We have seen that the spiritual journey is all about surrendering the personal ego self in favour of non-personal Consciousness. All spiritual practices work to achieve this transformation. Self-forgetting is perhaps the most practical and effective practice because we literally forget about ourselves. The more we do this the better.

There are many ways in which we can be of service in helping to carry the message of recovery. We can honestly share our experience in twelve-step meetings. We can offer practical help to those in early recovery. We can speak at other groups and share our story. We can volunteer for the various service positions within the individual groups, or at inter-group, regional or national levels. We can volunteer for telephone service. We can sponsor others through the twelve-step program. We can advise friends or family members who are struggling with addiction. We can do all of these things, some of these things or anything else to be of service. The important thing is to forget about ourselves.

The essay on step twelve in "Twelve Steps and Twelve Traditions" is by far the longest chapter in the book. As well as covering various ways in which we can help to carry the message of recovery within twelve-step fellowship, there is also discussion of how spiritual principles can be beneficial and helpful in the many different aspects of our lives. The third paragraph in the chapter describes some common factors of individual spiritual awakenings. Included in this paragraph is a sentence that reads "He has been granted a gift which amounts to a new state of consciousness and being". This state of Consciousness and Being may seem to be a gift from the perspective of the personal ego self, but in reality it is not new. This state of Consciousness, Awareness, Knowingness, Mind, Spirit or Being is our true nature, and always has been. It is over-identification with the personal ego self that has obscured our underlying true nature all along. The real gift has been the circumstances of our lives that have brought us to the point of personal surrender. The word *grace* means favour, kindness, benefaction or beneficence. In this respect addiction can be seen as grace. It may seem strange to be grateful for addiction, but there is no doubt that addiction can lead us from hell to heaven.

A literal understanding of step twelve would be that we are sober, and in recovery, and that we try to help other addicts do the same. We also try to take the principles of recovery into other aspects of our lives. My observation is that even this rudimentary understanding of step twelve is often not always followed.

A deeper understanding would be that we have indeed had some sort of psychic change as the result of staying sober and working through the steps with a sponsor. There is gratitude for recovery and a feeling that we should give something back by being of service in some way. We also listen and learn in twelve-step meetings and combine this understanding with advice from our sponsor and the principles of the steps to live our lives on a different basis.

The next level of understanding would be that spiritual awakening is an ongoing process of transformation. Working though the first eleven steps has been a good grounding but there is no end to the possibilities. The stick of addiction is still present but it is now the carrot of purpose and usefulness that dominates our motivation. We feel that we are now in the flow of life rather than fighting against it. Wherever we may be in our recovery, we remain committed to self-awareness, self-contemplation and particularly to self-forgetting. The qualities of Consciousness become a way of life, both within twelve-step fellowship and in all other areas of our lives. Recovery is no longer a separate activity but increasingly becomes integral.

The deepest understanding of step twelve is in line with the St. Francis of Assisi prayer. The personal ego self is still present but the true self is recognised as non-personal Consciousness. There is a constant focus on the individual behaving as an instrument of Consciousness rather than as a self-centered person. The more this is practiced the more deeply we naturally abide in Consciousness and the more authentic we become as an expression of Consciousness. The underlying state of Consciousness is eternal happiness, peace, love and unity. This increasingly becomes the state that we experience. The parachute is now fully open and we can enjoy the ride. The butterfly is experiencing the same world in a completely different way and is blessed with freedom. The prodigal son has returned home and finds all that he ever desired. The previous experience of hell is seen as an illusion and a necessary part of the journey. The kingdom of heaven is found within. All that remains is to be who we truly are and to move in accordance with the will of Consciousness.

Steps eleven and twelve have been the core of my recovery. Step eleven continues to enhance my understanding and experience. Step twelve has become increasingly meaningful as time has gone on. I have been in service within twelve-step fellowship right from the start and feel a keen sense of purpose and usefulness. I have had the privilege of sponsoring others through the twelve-step program and have witnessed wonderful transformations in life circumstances and experiences. The qualities of Consciousness have risen to the surface and generally express themselves freely, except when I make the mistake of taking things personally. There is no end to the depth of Consciousness and hence there is no limit to the potential for this life. I have recovered from the hopeless state of body and mind that was active addiction, yet at the same time I will be forever recovering. Twelve-step recovery is literally taking me from beer to eternity. My predominant feeling is one of gratitude, whatever the circumstances of my life may be in any given moment.

45. Twelve-Step Slogans

As well as the twelve steps, there are a number of slogans and sayings within twelve-step fellowship that can be helpful in understanding the process of recovery. These common clichés can lose their impact through familiarity but there is great wisdom within each of them, both at a literal level and also in the deeper meanings. There is also unfortunately the potential for misunderstanding. This is not indented to be an exhaustive list, but it is worth looking at some of the better-known ones.

One day at a time (ODAAT) – the simple idea of recovering one day at a time is very helpful and also true. We can only ever recover in this moment. It is often impossible in early recovery to contemplate being abstinent for the long-term, but the idea of just one day is much more manageable. Sometimes we can go for one hour at a time if need be, or even shorter time periods. We postpone the temptation to relapse until the following day, by which time the compulsion will most likely have diminished. The same can also be true for attending meetings and practicing the twelve-step program. It only ever has to be done today. There is no need to project into the future. Later in recovery it becomes clear that life can only ever be lived moment-to-moment. Thoughts of the past and future exist only in the realm of the personal ego mind. As non-personal Consciousness, there is only ever the eternal moment of now.

Honesty, open-mindedness and willingness (HOW) - we have covered each of these key ingredients for recovery in previous chapters. Honesty is really about self-honesty. Open-mindedness means having the humility to accept that our personal beliefs and opinions are barriers to wisdom. Willingness is all about accepting our brokenness and committing to an ongoing process of transformation. Without these three ingredients there will be no recovery. This is HOW it works.

Keep coming back – regular attendance at meetings is important at all stages of recovery. There is no official membership of twelve-step fellowship. The only requirement for attending meetings is a desire to become abstinent. There is also no cost other than a small voluntary contribution to cover the cost of room hire and refreshments. Meetings provide all of the benefits previously described and the primary motivation for attending will change as recovery progresses. The meetings are as valuable to those in long-term recovery as they are for those in the early days. The early benefit is in receiving help whereas the later value is in selfless service.

Keep it simple – addiction is a complex condition but the solution is simple. There is a tendency to over-complicate recovery but this is not necessary. In fact, the simpler we keep it the better the result. Attend meetings, get a sponsor, follow the guidance, work through the steps, practice the spiritual principles and help others. This is all we need to do. At a deeper level, we have seen that all complexity arises from simplicity. Recovery is about dealing with the problem of addiction at the deepest level, and the root problem is simple misidentification. Keeping it simple means keeping focused on the core problem.

It works if you work it – this saying is often followed by "it won't if you don't" or "so work it, you're worth it". There is great wisdom in all of this. Twelve-step recovery definitely works, but we have to actually do it rather than just talk about it. If we do not put in the action then it will not work. Spiritual progress requires action. It really is that simple. It is also true to say that we are worth it. Often an addict will feel so broken and worthless that they find it difficult to believe that they are worthy of recovery. All human beings are worthy of recovery because transformation into the second half of life is the natural cycle of Consciousness. There is no such thing as being too broken. It is the personal ego self that is broken rather than the true self or Being. Every human being is equally worthy because we are all expressions of the one Consciousness.

Surrender to win – admitting our brokenness and powerlessness is the first step in recovery, and we cannot recover without this surrender. It is also important to remain surrendered throughout recovery otherwise the personal ego self will take credit for the progress that we have made and the identity will remain as personal. The whole point of recovery is to finally surrender the personal ego self, and so we need to be wary of going backwards. Brokenness leads to surrender and humility. There can be no ongoing spiritual progress without continuing humility. We need to remain a fellowship of the broken so that Consciousness can reveal itself through each of us.

Let go, let God – this is the same idea as above but we need to be careful not to abdicate responsibility for recovery. If the God word is conceived as third party then this slogan can be very misleading. It is abiding in, and as, Consciousness that provides the solution to addiction, and Consciousness is our true nature. We are letting go in favour of non-personal Consciousness and we need to take action in order to bring this about. Letting go in isolation is highly unlikely to result in sustainable surrender of the personal self. We need to act as if we truly are Consciousness until such time as this new identity becomes established. Having faith in the God word without taking any action is a naïve misunderstanding.

Hand it over – this is often said in the context of handing problems over to a Higher Power. The potential for misunderstanding here is again that a third party Higher Power will solve all of our issues, including our addiction. We tend to hand over problems only when we can't solve them as our personal selves. This can be useful in early recovery because the personal self does need help, but this is not the eventual solution. Without understanding the purpose of the steps, we will hold onto problems that we think we can solve and hence remain identified as the personal self. Whatever our individual conception may be, the Higher Power is non-personal Consciousness. What we really need to be handing over is the personal ego self who thinks that it has problems. The subsequent emergence of identity as non-personal Consciousness will obviously not perceive any personal problems.

Fake it to make it – there is more wisdom in this slogan than first appears. It is usually used in early recovery to indicate that we may not really understand what we are doing but we do it anyway. It is also used in respect of trying to conceive of a Higher Power. The idea is to believe in something or anything until our own conception gradually emerges. Often we use the fellowship itself as a Higher Power, which of course it is in the sense that it is a more genuine expression of Consciousness than we might find elsewhere. The real wisdom in this slogan relates to step seven. We act as if we already are non-personal Consciousness until such time as our sense of identity shifts. The truth is that the qualities of Consciousness that we are faking are actually far more authentic than the fake mask of personal self that we have hitherto been taking ourselves to be. We need to be wary of the idea of reaching a stage where we 'make it'. There is no end to the shift in balance of identity between human and Being whist we still exist as human. We can however continually move closer to Being without ever actually 'making it'.

Progress not perfection – this slogan can easily be misunderstood and cause stagnation in recovery. As just covered, there is no end to the progress that we can make and we can never reach perfection. This is the intended meaning of this saying. We will continue to make mistakes in identity and hopefully learn from them, hence we make further progress. The problem arises if we use this slogan as an excuse for not making progress. The personal self will be tempted to make excuses for itself. Imperfection is inevitable, but it is not without purpose. If we learn from imperfection then we can make progress towards perfection. If we settle for imperfection and lose our willingness for more change then we stagnate. Using this slogan as an excuse for continuing selfish and self-centered behavior is willful ignorance of the whole concept of recovery.

279

Yet – this tiny word is intended to capture the progressive nature of addiction. We may hear others share their consequences of addiction and conclude that we are not that bad. We are told that addiction progresses but somehow the personal ego self is able to make itself an exception. This terminal uniqueness will prevent an addict from engaging fully in recovery, and hence the probability of relapse remains. When a relapse occurs, the consequences are generally worse than before. This cycle may be repeated many times. The consequences that had previously seemed unimaginable now happen, and cause suffering to us and to our loved ones. It had always been a case of when rather than if, yet we had been unable to believe it or accept it. If we are addicts then we are all suffering from a similar condition, even if the inevitable consequences have not happened yet.

Similarities not differences – this suggestion is all about identifying with the aspects and levels of addiction. Each human being is unique and hence each addict has an individual story and experience. It is very easy to find differences in our particular circumstances, but all this does is reinforce personal uniqueness and keep us in denial of addiction. If we are going to recover then we need to rule ourselves into twelve-step fellowship rather than rule ourselves out. There are many similarities in the way that addicts think, feel and behave, and these outweigh the differences. The personal self will hear what it wants to hear, and use this to justify its own imagined existence. If we focus on similarities then we will come to see that the deeper we go the more alike we are. Ultimately we are all expressions of the same Consciousness and hence, at that level, we are not only similar but identical. Individual differences are then seen as expressions of diversity rather than proof of separation. Wholeness and individuality co-exist once it is seen that Consciousness is all there is.

Easy does it – we need to be careful about the true meaning of this slogan. Recovery can be easy if we can grasp the idea of living one day at a time and relax into the process of transformation. However, we have seen that recovery requires consistent, persistent action on our part. This is not easy, particularly in the early stages. Taking it easy does not mean taking no action. We need to practice the steps until they become easy. We need to put in the effort until it becomes effortless. It is an effort for the personal self to act as non-personal Consciousness, but once the balance of identity shifts to Consciousness then it becomes easy. It is no effort for Consciousness to be itself. Once we are identified as Consciousness then we can take it easy because life is taking care of life.

A bridge to normal living – this is another slogan that requires care. The idea of a bridge implies a one-off crossing from one place to another. The concept of normal living can be interpreted to mean living as others do in society. If this slogan is understood in this way then we are heading for disappointment. Recovery does lead us to cross from personal identity to Consciousness, but this is an ongoing journey rather than a one-off event. Living as non-personal Consciousness is far from normal in today's selfish, self-centered world. The context of this slogan is all about not having to spend our whole lives in twelve-step fellowship. Normal living is about family, career and all other aspects of life. Our opportunity is to participate in life as an expression of Consciousness rather than as a personal ego self. The bridge to normal living is really an ongoing journey of living an extraordinary life. There is no such thing as normal.

Give it away to keep it – this slogan is technically correct but is open to a fundamental misunderstanding of recovery. We have seen that self-forgetting is one of the key spiritual practices, and forms the basis of step twelve. It is therefore true to say that giving recovery away to others is beneficial to our own progress. There is a sense of flow, whereby selfless giving creates a surge of the qualities of Consciousness through us that cleanses the lens of perception. There is also the idea of resonance whereby we attract experiences that match our own vibration of

Consciousness. There is a sense of purpose and usefulness that feels good. This is, however, all from the perspective of the personal self. Sooner or later the purpose of recovery is to identify as Consciousness. From this perspective, Consciousness is a constant flow of its own qualities that are based on love. When the human becomes Being, there is a natural tendency to give because the nature of Being is unconditional love. For those in recovery, this giving is most effective in helping other addicts. As this happens, we abide more and more in Consciousness and this takes us ever closer to home. The wisdom in this slogan is therefore all about motive. If we are giving recovery away in order to keep it for ourselves, then our motive is still personal and selfish. If we are living in a natural state of giving then our motive is selfless. As we cross the bridge, we should find that our motives change. A human being is always part selfish and part selfless, but it is a question of balance. If we are still giving it away in order to keep it then we have further to go. Self-honesty will reveal the truth.

More will be revealed – this slogan states that there is no end to revelation. As we progress in recovery, by practicing spiritual principles in all of our affairs, then we gradually come to understand. We learn more about ourselves and we begin to see wisdom where previously it had escaped us. As we abide more deeply in Consciousness then this wisdom and understanding will emerge naturally. It is not the personal ego self that becomes wise. Consciousness is wisdom, and this is what we become. This is what we are. The further we go, the more will inevitably be revealed.

Stick with the winners – the idea behind this slogan is well intentioned, although it can be seen as rather disparaging. Twelve-step fellowship is full of addicts at various stages of recovery. Length of sobriety is one indication of progress, although this is not always a reliable measure of recovery. The idea then is to follow the advice and mimic the behavior of those with good recovery rather than gravitating towards those who are struggling. The idea of winners obviously implies that some of us are losers, but this is not the intended meaning. We are all winners to some extent if we are in recovery, whatever stage we may be at. We also ebb and flow in recovery, so in effect we take it in turns to be winners depending on how we are doing at any given moment. Sometimes we are able to offer support and at other times we need support. Fellowship is mutually supportive.

Attraction not promotion – this saying comes from Tradition Eleven, which concerns public relations policy. The principle is valid at both individual and fellowship level. Humility is a key feature of Consciousness, and one important expression of humility is anonymity. The best way to encourage spiritual principles in others is not through evangelism or promotion but by living as non-personal Consciousness in our daily lives. Not every caterpillar is yet ready for metamorphosis. There is little point in promoting recovery to those who are not really interested. There is also the matter of vibrational resonance and the law of attraction. All of this underpins the concept of attraction rather than promotion. Our task is simply to live the principles rather than preach them. We will naturally attract those who are ready to open up to perennial wisdom.

Yellow card – this is often a physical yellow card with the words "who you see here, what you hear here, when you leave here, let it stay here". It is usually read out during a meeting to remind us that confidentiality is of vital importance. This confidentiality should not be confused with secrecy. Anonymity is all about humility, and confidentiality is about the safety of individual openness. Those who attend meetings need to feel safe that they can share openly without fear of gossip or other repercussions. Some will also want their attendance at meetings to remain confidential for personal reasons. The principle of the yellow card provides these reassurances and it operates very effectively for the majority of the time. Occasional breaches of the principle do occur, but these are by far the exception rather than the rule.

Serenity prayer - this short prayer is well known throughout twelve-step fellowship. It originates from a longer prayer attributed to Reinhold Niebuhr and dates from the early 1930s. The wording used in twelve-step fellowship reads "God grant me the serenity to accept the things I cannot change, courage to change the things I can, and wisdom to know the difference". This is a petition by the personal self for serenity, acceptance, courage, change, wisdom and knowledge. These are qualities of Consciousness, and the prayer can be understood at different levels. In early recovery, it can be used to accept addiction as something that cannot be changed by the personal self. Later it can be understood to mean that we cannot change anything about our lives other than ourselves. It can be used to pray for acceptance in challenging circumstances. A deeper understanding would be that the "I" that is praying for serenity and courage is the personal self, and that it is only the identity of the "I" that can really be changed. The deepest understanding would be that the condensed, limited form of Consciousness that is the personal ego self is turning towards its own true nature and seeking revelation as non-personal Consciousness. This is the wisdom of the serenity prayer that comes through praying for wisdom. This prayer can take us all the way to Consciousness, Awareness, Knowingness, Mind, Spirit or Being revealing itself to itself.

All of these slogans, and many others, work through repetition. The important thing is to remain open-minded about what they actually mean. If we hold onto an early understanding of a slogan then repetition can simply entrench a particular interpretation and we can miss the deeper meaning. These slogans have developed over time and each one of them can provide us with an instant reminder of the actions needed for effective recovery.

There is one particular slogan that I have omitted from this list because it deserves an entire chapter on its own.

46. Just For Today

The Just For Today Card is a little piece of twelve-step literature that can be very useful at all stages of recovery. The wording originates from a newspaper column from 1921 written by Frank Crane in the Boston Globe. The wording used in twelve-step recovery is only slightly different from the original and reads as follows:

"Just for today I will try to live through this day only, and not tackle my whole life problem at once. I can do something for twelve hours that would appall me if I felt that I had to keep it up for a lifetime.

"Just for today I will be happy. Most folks are as happy as they make up their minds to be.

"Just for today I will adjust myself to what is, and not try to adjust everything to my own desires. I will take my luck as it comes, and fit myself to it.

"Just for today I will try to strengthen my mind. I will study. I will learn something useful. I will not be a mental loafer. I will read something that requires effort, thought and concentration.

"Just for today I will exercise my soul in three ways: I will do somebody a good turn, and not get found out; if anybody knows of it, it will not count. I will do at least two things that I do not want to do - just for exercise. I will not show anyone that my feelings are hurt; they may be hurt, but today I will not show it.

"Just for today I will be agreeable. I will look as well as I can, dress becomingly, talk low, act courteously, criticise not one bit, not find fault with anything and not try to improve or regulate anybody except myself.

"Just for today I will have a programme. I may not follow it exactly, but I will have it. I will save myself from two pests: hurry and indecision.

"Just for today I will have a quiet half hour all by myself, and relax. During this half hour, sometime, I will try to get a better perspective of my life.

"Just for today I will be unafraid. Especially I will not be afraid to enjoy what is beautiful, and to believe that as I give to the world, so the world will give to me."

These words provide a succinct summary of a daily life based on spiritual principles. The nine ideas presented do not cover the whole twelve-step program but they do provide a useful guide. Some of them seem challenging because they highlight the difference between self-centered thinking and an attitude of selflessness, between mind and Mind, between human and Being, between personal ego self and non-personal Consciousness. This is the whole point of the Just For Today Card.

Sometimes, in early recovery, a sponsor will suggest picking one of these items at random each day in order to provide some short-term focus. Others suggest reading the card every day and using it to consciously try to think and behave differently. Many use it as part of their daily spiritual practice in order to prepare for the day ahead. Whatever use we may put it to, there is no doubt that the Just For Today Card contains helpful daily guidance and also deep spiritual wisdom. It is worth investigating each of the nine suggestions so that we can understand them literally and also spiritually.

The overall concept of *just for today* is of course identical to the idea of *one day at a time* that we covered in the previous chapter. The first of the nine suggestions can be applied simply to abstinence or to any aspect of our lives. By focusing just on the present day we can cope with whatever challenges life may bring. It also means that we can more readily engage in daily spiritual practices without having to worry about future commitment. As recovery progresses we become more present to life as it unfolds in the moment. We can only ever act in the moment. It may seem irresponsible to only live for the moment, but this is the truth of life. We may make plans for the future, but even then such plans can only be made in the present moment. Future moments will come, and we can act then rather than worry about them now. There is tremendous opportunity for peace of mind once it becomes clear that Consciousness is only ever vibrating right now. The past does not actually exist, even though it may seem to have reality due to memories stored in the mind and body. The future cannot possibly exist because Consciousness only ever arises and falls in the present moment. There is no time in the realm of non-personal Consciousness. The whole world of creation flashes in and out of existence at speeds beyond comprehension and there is only ever the eternal moment of now. Given this understanding, it makes complete sense that we can only experience life in the present moment. The personal ego mind is always stuck in the past or projecting into the future. We miss the content of our own lives because the mind is forever elsewhere. We need to be fully present in order to experience the richness of life, and the only way to do this is to step back from the personal ego mind. Just for today. Just for now.

The original wording of Just For Today referenced Abraham Lincoln as quoting that "folks are usually about as happy as they make up their minds to be". There is great truth in this saying. There is no doubt that our personal attitudes and perspectives do make a difference to personal happiness. A good example is an attitude of gratitude that leaves us grateful for what we have rather than unhappy at what is missing. At a deeper level, given that Consciousness exists as it is from moment to moment, it can only be our personal opinions that determine whether or not we can find any happiness in a given circumstance. Such happiness can only be fleeting in any case because circumstances are constantly changing. The only reliable source of happiness is

Consciousness itself. We can make up our minds to abide as Consciousness, or at least we can decide to engage in spiritual practices that will lead us in this direction. In this respect, we do have the ability to experience happiness regardless of circumstances.

The third suggestion is all about acceptance and going with the flow of life rather than fighting against it. The self-centered person will always want life to go in accordance with their own thinking and feeling. This is obviously a recipe for disappointment and frustration because life is only ever an expression of Consciousness. Life will do what life wants to do, moment-to-moment. The purpose of life is for Consciousness to experience and participate in its own creation. It is the personal ego self that causes all of the friction by insisting that the purpose of life is to satisfy its own agenda. This mistake in identity is the cause of all internal and external conflict. The personal ego self is at odds with its own source and true nature. The wise advice is therefore to adjust ourselves to what is rather than continuing to fight an unnecessary and pointless battle.

The next idea is about remaining teachable and open-minded. There is little point in reading and studying materials that reinforce our existing thinking and beliefs. It is our current conditioned thinking and belief system that is causing suffering to ourselves and others. The suggestion is to challenge the status quo by reading something different. This means letting go of self-righteousness, which in itself is an exercise in acting as if we are not closed-minded. The deepest wisdom is that there is only one ultimate truth. All religions and spiritual traditions point to this one truth in a multitude of different ways. Doctrine restricts this wisdom. We need to take off the blinkers and see the bigger picture.

The idea of exercising our soul is really about letting go of the personal ego self. Doing things that we do not want to do is precisely the point. The human mind is selfish and necessarily driven by self-centered fear. If this is all that we think we are then this will be the dominant motivation. Doing a good turn for someone else is a selfless act. Doing such a thing without recognition removes any possibility of personal motive. It is an act of unconditional love, which arises from non-personal Consciousness. Overcoming self-centered fear and doing things that feel uncomfortable is also a useful exercise. There can be no change inside of our comfort zone. The outcome is never as bad as we fear. The suggestion here is to do two things that feel uncomfortable rather than just one. The more we do this the better. The final suggestion relates to overcoming hurt feelings. We tend to think that hurt feelings are valid because they certainly feel real. What we overlook is the fact that we experience hurt feelings only because we take things personally. It is the constant personal self-reference that causes these emotions. By allowing them to pass without reaction we are practicing letting go of the personal ego self. We have seen that self-forgetting is one of the key spiritual practices and is the basis of step twelve. All three of these soul exercises fall into this category.

Suggestion number six is all about humility. We have admitted our brokenness and are willing to let go of the personal self in favour of Consciousness. The behaviours suggested are all expressions of humility; agreeable, presentable, humble, courteous, non-critical, non-interfering and focused only on self-regulation. This is not just intended to be about self-improvement but also about self-awareness leading to self-forgetting.

The use of the word *programme* in the next item does not mean the twelve-step program but instead references a daily schedule. This may seem inconsistent with the idea of living in the moment, but the two are not incompatible. It is a matter of practicalities to have some sort of schedule for the day. It may change as the day progresses but some structure is helpful. The key is not to over-commit and spend our time rushing from one thing to the next. It makes sense to build in some contingency and some down time. We often create our own stresses by trying to do too much in a given day. If we do this then our minds are constantly on the go and we miss the present moment. Unnecessary hurry is certainly a pest. So too is indecision, but decisions are easy if we are abiding more in Consciousness. Life always knows what it wants to do next.

Item number eight is simply the suggestion of meditation. We covered the significance of meditation in an earlier chapter, and also the numerous forms that it can take. The important thing is not so much how we practice but rather that we do meditate on a daily basis. The suggestion here is for half an hour of quiet time and the practice of self-reflection or self-contemplation. We gain perspective by stepping back and observing from a deeper place within ourselves.

The final suggestion comprises three important elements. The first suggestion is that we be unafraid. This is not easy for the personal ego self, but it is easy from the perspective of non-personal Consciousness. The emphasis should be on Being. In order to be unafraid we simply have to be. The second idea is that we enjoy what is beautiful. The whole of creation is beautiful, and temporary, and we can only enjoy it in the moment. Our experience is coloured by our unique lens of perception. In order to really enjoy beauty we need to be present with a clear lens. This implies abiding more deeply in non-personal Consciousness so that the lens can be unveiled. Finally we have the idea of selfless giving and the flow of Consciousness. As we abide more deeply as the True Self so the flow of loving qualities becomes increasingly natural. Vibrational resonance attracts more of the same and the world seems to freely give the very things that we had previously spent our whole lives chasing. We do indeed reap what we sow.

The various suggestions of the Just For Today Card are really just different flavours of the same fundamental idea. Each of them is intended to reduce the dominance of the personal ego self and move the identity increasingly towards non-personal Consciousness. These practices are entirely consistent with the spiritual principles of the twelve-step program, and hence can be seen as an important tool in the overall toolkit of recovery.

47. The Spiritual Toolkit

On page 95 of the fourth edition of the Big Book, Bill Wilson makes reference to a kit of spiritual tools to be laid out for inspection by addicts who seek recovery. This spiritual toolkit is not defined in any detail and is widely assumed to be the various actions contained in the twelve steps. The steps certainly contain the core tools but there are others that can usefully be added in order to produce a complete set that is fit for daily use.

The word *toolkit* is defined as a set of tools that are used for a particular purpose. A tradesman will make use of a toolkit that contains various different tools that are needed to complete specific tasks within an overall job. He will need to be skilled in using each of them so that he can undertake the various tasks as needed. If we apply the same approach to a spiritual toolkit for the purpose of recovery then this would mean including a range of tools that cover all aspects of the overall process.

Based on everything that we have covered so far, we ought to be able to come up with the ideal contents for such a toolkit. This is not intended to be a definitive list of the available tools, but is a suggested list of those tools that we should become skilled in using. There is no point in having a tool in the toolbox if we do not know how to use it effectively.

In keeping with the numerical theme of twelve-step recovery, this suggested toolkit contains twelve tools of recovery. Each of them is a tool in its own right, and each will become increasingly effective through regular practice.

Humility – this is the most important tool in the box. There can be no sustainable recovery until we can admit and accept our brokenness. Humility arises when denial ends. This is the basis of step one and it is foundational. Humility is not something that we recover from or something that we look back upon as a previous weakness. Humility is the ongoing acknowledgement that the personal ego self is inherently flawed. There are no exceptions. All humans suffer the same traits to varying degrees. Humility is simply the recognition of personal imperfection. The tool of humility needs to be in constant use.

HOW – this tool is three-pronged and comprises the essential attributes of honesty, open-mindedness and willingness. If any one of these is missing then the tool will not work. If this is the case then we need to pray earnestly for the missing piece. We need to use this tool to practice being honest with ourselves and others, being open to new ideas and being willing to take action against the wishes of the personal self. It is too easy to just claim that we are already honest, open-minded and willing. This would be the equivalent of having a tool and not using it. This tool will reap great benefit provided we keep it deployed.

Fellowship – addiction causes isolation and loneliness. It may seem surprising to include twelve-step fellowship as part of the spiritual toolkit but actually it is a vital constituent. We need the love, support and encouragement of each other in order to recover. Many of us have battled with dis-ease for far too long on our own. It takes courage to open ourselves up to being vulnerable, but it is tremendously reassuring to do so with fellow addicts who truly understand. We fear rejection but actually we are welcomed with open arms. Fellowship obviously incudes twelve-step meetings but there are also numerous opportunities for friendships, social events, twelve-step conventions, workshops, overseas trips and all manner of other interactions. All we have to do is show up and participate. The tool of fellowship is always available and is accessible worldwide.

Sponsor – the personal self is generally reluctant to ask for help, but brokenness and desperation do tend to force the issue. Fellowship is a vital tool for recovery, but it is just part of the toolkit. We need a sponsor to guide us through the twelve-step program and share their particular experience, strength and hope with us. A sponsor can variously provide guidance, discipline, emergency support, advice, spiritual understanding, compassion and inspiration. Potential sponsors will have different qualities and varying availability so we need to choose this particular tool carefully. The general advice is to choose a sponsor who demonstrates the spiritual characteristics that we aspire to. Having made our choice we should use this important resource as much as we can. The primary activity with a sponsor is to work through the twelve-step program.

Literature – each fellowship has its own set of approved literature. It makes sense to obtain our own set as a tool for frequent and easy reference. As well as the Big Book, or its equivalent, there is the Twelve Steps and Twelve Traditions book and also various other publications. In particular there are several different compendiums of daily quotes and meditations that can be a useful addition to a regular routine of spiritual practice.

Just for today card – this tool is analogous to a Swiss army knife. The nine different components can be used together or separately to loosen the grip of personal self-identity. We can only remain abstinent one day at a time, and we can only make spiritual progress one day at a time. If we use this tool every day then the cumulative effect will be significant.

Twelve-step prayer – a simple and vital tool is to pray in the morning for a sober day and give thanks for sobriety in the evening. As we have seen, there are also prayers associated with steps three and seven and also the St Francis of Assisi prayer referenced in step eleven in Twelve Steps and Twelve Traditions. In addition we also have the serenity prayer that can be used at any time during the day when we meet challenging circumstances. The combination of these prayers provides an essential tool to keep the process of transformation moving forwards. It is a continual affirmation of our willingness to recover. If we stop praying then we will stagnate and then start going backwards.

Self-awareness – this tool relates to step ten and includes steps four through nine. The components of this tool comprise daily inventory, disclosure, readiness to change, acting as if, preparedness to make amends and the act of reparation. With constant practice, these elements combine to produce the single tool of self-awareness, the use of which gradually becomes second nature. Another important part of inventory is gratitude. Writing a daily gratitude list helps to bring focus to the positive aspects of our lives and balances up the inventory of shortcomings. Whatever the circumstances of our lives, there are always things to be grateful for. If we let go of our expectations and demands then everything in life can be seen as a gift. Gratitude arises from humility. A constant attitude of gratitude is a powerful spiritual practice.

Self-contemplation – step eleven provides another multi-faceted tool that eventually becomes a single practice. The constituent parts are meditation, yoga, prayer and self-inquiry. Each of these can be practiced separately during the early phases of transformation but eventually they will begin to merge and become the single tool of self-contemplation. This tool is all about shifting our identity from personal ego self towards non-personal Consciousness. The more we practice the more the constituent parts will converge into one. The goal is to increasingly abide in Consciousness, as Consciousness.

Self-forgetting – step twelve is the practice of forgetting all about the personal ego self, both inside and outside of twelve-step fellowship. It takes practice precisely because our human tendency, when identified as the personal self, is to be self-centered and take life personally. Self-forgetting is a tool that has to be used as often as possible. The more we use it, the less selfish we become and hence the easier and more natural it is to be selfless. Non-personal Consciousness is not personal. If we are continuing to worry about ourselves all of the time then we still have a long way to go on the spiritual journey, regardless of how long we may have been sober.

Service – the whole point of spiritual recovery is that our liabilities turn into assets to be used for the benefit of others. Each human being is asleep to their own true nature as Consciousness, and once Consciousness awakens in one individual it naturally wants to use this instrument to awaken yet more. This implies being of service to others in any way that supports the process of transformation. Twelve-step fellowships are independent, voluntary organisations that rely upon individual participants for maintenance and growth. All twelve-step meetings have service positions such as greeter, refreshments, literature, treasurer, secretary and general service representative. There are also various service opportunities at inter-group, regional and national level. We can be of service simply by agreeing to visit other groups and share our experience, strength and hope. We can collect telephone numbers and call others to encourage and support them. We can also volunteer to go out on twelve-step visits to talk with addicts who have reached out for help. Service is not an optional extra. It is an important part of the spiritual toolkit and it should be practiced. If we are reluctant to do service then we have fundamentally missed the entire point of recovery.

Sponsorship – the final tool in the box is the specific act of sponsoring others through the twelve-step program. One addict working with another is the founding principle of twelve-step recovery. We should not underestimate how valuable an activity this can be. Once we have been taken through the steps by a sponsor, and become proficient in using the tools, then we are ideally placed to use our experience for the benefit of others. We may lack confidence but we can take advice from our own sponsor each step of the way. The experience of sponsorship is mutually beneficial because it not only helps those we sponsor, but it also strengthens our understanding of the steps and our commitment to recovery. We are now engaging in recovery in order to help others rather than ourselves. This is an act of selflessness instead of selfishness. This is a further shift from personal ego self to non-personal Consciousness. As with all of the other tools, we become more skilled in sponsorship the more we practice. If we are reluctant to sponsor others then we need to ask ourselves why. The honest answer will always be the same. We are still making decisions based on personal self rather than non-personal Consciousness.

These twelve tools are what I would consider to be the essential toolkit for recovery. Any resistance that we may have in using these tools is itself an indication that we need to be practicing the very things that we are reluctant to do. It is the personal ego self that is reluctant, and it is the personal self that is the cause of all of our suffering, including addiction.

This toolkit is readily available, free of charge and utterly priceless. If we want effective recovery then we need to use all of it. If we only use half of it then we will most likely make little progress, or no progress at all.

48. Al-Anon Family Groups

Al-Anon is a fellowship of support groups for families and friends of alcoholics. The Al-Anon fellowship also includes Alateen, which provides specific support for teenage family members and friends. The idea for Al-Anon sprung out of the early days of AA and is based on the understanding that alcoholism, and hence addiction, is a condition that impacts the whole family as well as the addict. Informal meetings started as early as 1939 but the fellowship was not officially founded until 1951. The co-founders were Anne B and Bill Wilson's wife Lois. Alateen began in 1957 as a result of teenagers seeking mutual support due to addiction within the family. Al-Anon and Alateen use the same twelve-steps and traditions used by other twelve-step fellowships.

There are also family support fellowships for other addictions. These include Co-Anon, which focuses on families and friends of cocaine addicts, Gam-Anon that offers family support for gambling addicts, Nar-Anon that focuses on families of narcotics addicts and Families Anonymous that covers general substance abuse within families. Again all of these fellowships are based on twelve-step recovery.

These family support groups are non-interventionist. One might imagine that the purpose would be to provide family members with strategies to help the addict into recovery. This is not the case. If an addict is powerless over addiction then family members certainly are as well. Instead, the support groups focus on helping family and friends cope with addiction as it impacts them in the guise of the addict.

I have had cause to attend Al-Anon meetings due to my own particular family circumstances. As well as finding them very helpful, they have also given me further insight into the transformational power of twelve-step recovery. Some people who attend these support groups admit to being addicts themselves, as in my case, but many others do not identify themselves as such. Initially they firmly believe that it is the addict that has the problem and is causing all of the family disruption. This is seemingly true to a large extent, but it quickly becomes apparent that not only is the family member powerless over the addiction but that they also might be enabling or compounding the problem through their own reactions and behavior. The sharing of experience within the group is particularly important in this respect. The group is also able to provide compassionate understanding and support, but the real solution is in twelve-step recovery for the family member. This may seem surprising, but actually it makes complete sense. This is perhaps best explained by taking an example and following it through to its conclusion. This example is hypothetical, but has relevance because it is not untypical.

Suppose for example that a married couple is committed to each other, but that one of them is in active addiction and becoming progressively worse. The non-addict spouse is suffering various consequences as a result of the addict's behavior and eventually decides to attend a twelve-step family support group. Upon attending a few meetings, there is reassurance that others have similar problems, and there is identification with their own experiences. Others in the group seem to have found a way to cope with life despite still having an active addict in the family. The suggestion is made that the non-addict spouse get a sponsor and work through the twelve-step program. This seems difficult to accept at first, but the experiences of others in the group seem to indicate that the solution works.

A sponsor is selected and the work begins. The process is identical to the one that we have covered in detail. The non-addict spouse admits that they are powerless over the addict and the addiction. They come to believe that a Higher Power can help them to cope. They make a decision to hand over the problem to some concept of the God word. They take personal inventory and then share it. They begin to see that it is their own personal ego self that is the cause of the suffering rather than the behavior of anyone else. They become willing to change and start acting as if they are no longer taking things so personally. They recognise that they themselves have caused harm to others through selfish and self-centered thinking and behavior. They make amends to those they have harmed and continue to remain self-aware. They adopt spiritual practices such as meditation, yoga, prayer and self-inquiry. They awaken spiritually and begin carrying the message of recovery both inside and outside of the fellowship. They detach from the behavior of the addict spouse and start to react and behave differently themselves. They find happiness, peace, love and unity regardless of what their addict spouse may or may not do. Sometimes this has a positive impact on the addict spouse and they may also begin to engage in twelve-step recovery. Sometimes it has no impact at all on the addict, but it does not matter. The non-addict has found a solution to life and now relies upon moment-to-moment inner guidance rather than the old patterns of thinking, feeling and behaving. The relationship may continue or it may come to an end. There is gratitude that the relationship with the addict has led the non-addict to awaken to his or her own true nature. It is seen that suffering has resulted in transformation.

Such an example may be difficult to believe, but this is generally what happens to a greater or lesser extent. In some ways, the examples of spiritual recovery within family support groups are even more compelling than the many, many recoveries that I have witnessed within AA. It is one thing for an alcoholic to admit defeat and submit to the twelve-step process. At least an addict has the gift of desperation to spur them on. It is another thing for family members to have the humility to turn the focus away from the addict and begin to look within themselves for the solution. The fact that it works at all is a very powerful endorsement of twelve-step recovery, even if the reasons are not always entirely clear to those who benefit.

If we look at this example using the model of Consciousness that I have described, and a true understanding of twelve-step recovery, then it is no surprise at all that twelve-step family support groups can work so effectively.

We have seen that addiction is multi-layered but ultimately rooted in the misidentification as a personal ego self. The twelve-step process digs down through these layers and addresses the core problem by shifting identity away from the personal ego self towards non-personal Consciousness. In respect of this core problem, addicts are no different from any other human being. Collective and individual lack of awareness and understanding of our true nature is the cause of all human problems, of which addiction is just one example. The non-addict spouse has a big problem and is unable to solve it. The suffering caused by loving and caring about an addict in active addiction is ultimately a manifestation of the same problem that causes addiction in the first place. Both the addict and the non-addict are suffering from the same core problem and hence they are eventually led to the same solution. The prodigal son may suffer in countless different ways but it does not really matter what specifically causes him to turn around and head home. The only important thing is that the journey of transformation eventually begins. Consciousness manifests uniquely in each human being, and hence each self-awakening is also unique in both timing and particular path. Whichever way it comes about, we cannot truly experience the beauty and wonder of life and creation until this happens.

The existence, growth and effectiveness of twelve-step family support fellowships provide a further compelling endorsement of the powerful healing and transformative efficacy of twelve-step recovery. It is a holistic solution to many forms of human suffering. It may not work in all cases, but this is only because the process is not sufficiently understood or practiced.

49. Why It Works

We have now seen how the twelve steps bring about a spiritual awakening. This transformation is effective, guaranteed and ongoing, provided the steps are practiced diligently. The quality of recovery will be directly related to the extent of the practice of self-awareness, self-contemplation and self-forgetting. Many addicts try to get an adequate recovery through minimum effort, and the result will always be disappointment and frustration. The ingredients needed for effective recovery are honesty, open-mindedness and willingness. If one or more of these is missing then we can always petition or pray for them. If we are not willing to pray then we have not yet reached the necessary stage of brokenness. This level of brokenness will vary from individual to individual, but if we are not yet ready to concede that we are broken then our life circumstances will inevitably get worse until we are ready. This is not theoretical scaremongering. This is what happens.

As mentioned in the introduction, twelve-step recovery works simply because it is a spiritual solution to a spiritual problem. It is often difficult for an addict to grasp that the damaging physical addictions and mental compulsions are really symptoms of an underlying dis-ease. This is why it is so important that the message of recovery is carried by those who really understand what it is like to suffer from addiction, and who also know what needs to be done in order to recover.

We have looked at aspects of addiction and have seen that it is a complex and multi-layered condition. There is the physical addiction, the mental compulsion, the deeper psychic issues and the misidentification with the personal ego self. There is also the risk that abstinence will cause vulnerability to symptoms of grief and also cross-addiction. Early recovery is often emotionally painful and very challenging. The risk of relapse is high during the first few months of abstinence and an addict needs a great deal of support to help them through this period. Abstinence is necessary for recovery, but abstinence deals only with the first layer of physical addiction. The other layers also need to be addressed otherwise there can be no sustained recovery.

The combination of twelve-step fellowship and twelve-step recovery provides a powerful solution to all of the aspects of addiction. The root of the problem is spiritual and so too is the solution. Prior to this, fellowship provides guidance and support during the early months of recovery. This help is multi-faceted and includes a safe place to spend time, companionship, identification as an addict, motivation, advice on relapse prevention, practical support, emotional support, literature, an early understanding of the steps, service opportunities, a sense of belonging and a social life. There is also the positive vibrational effect of spending time in the company of honest, humble, loving fellows.

After a period of attending twelve-step recovery meetings, it becomes apparent and obvious that it will be a struggle to sustain recovery just by relying on fellowship. It is the twelve-step program that will address the problems of mental compulsion and deeper psychic issues. It may be that additional professional help is required later to deal with underlying mental health issues but the steps will certainly be a good start. Crucially, it is also the latter part of the twelve-step program that will bring about the much-needed vital spiritual experience. There is no standard timing or stage for when this will happen, but the step nine promises indicate that something should have changed by then. Regular practice of steps ten, eleven and twelve will then continue the transformation towards letting go of the personal ego self and increasingly abiding as non-personal Consciousness. It is this self-realisation that will finally cut the root of addiction and provide the desired freedom.

A sponsor facilitates the link between twelve-step fellowship and the twelve-step program. The idea of one addict working with another is foundational to twelve-step recovery and can be seen as the third essential component in addition to fellowship and the steps. Addicts in recovery are best placed to carry the message of recovery to those seeking help, and likewise addicts who practice the twelve steps provide the best resource to guide others through the process. There is no formal training for a sponsor, although there are workshops available in some inter-groups for those wishing to obtain additional guidance. Typically a sponsor will base their approach on their own experience of being sponsored themselves. As a consequence, there is no standard approach to sponsorship. Each has their own style and preferences based on experience. Some expect strict adherence to suggestions and others are more flexible. This is ideal given that each addict is unique and will react differently to different styles. The important thing is to find a sponsor who demonstrates the kind of recovery that we aspire to, and then to trust the guidance received.

Once an addict is ready to work through the twelve-step program, the first important step is simply to ask a member of the fellowship to sponsor them. The general advice is to select someone who is experienced in practicing the steps and who has a quality of recovery that we find desirable. Sound advice is to select someone with whom there is zero risk of intimate emotional entanglement. Other than this, there is no specific guidance. If the individual that we select is not available for any reason, then we simply select another. It is important to remember that sponsorship is not a burden on the sponsor. It is part of their own practice of step twelve and most addicts in recovery will be glad for the opportunity to share their experience. If the subsequent relationship does not work well, becomes stale, or becomes logistically difficult, then it is not uncommon to change sponsors. The important thing is to keep up the momentum of working through the steps.

Although there is no standard approach or style, a sponsor will typically offer help in all aspects of recovery. There will be specific suggestions concerning service and participation in fellowship meetings. There will be emotional support and guidance for particular personal problems. Time will be spent reading through literature on each of the steps in turn. Experience and understanding of each step will be shared. Typically the sponsor will be the individual with whom we share our step five, although this does not have to be the case. There will be guidance on the making of amends and encouragement to maintain the practice of steps ten, eleven and twelve. Finally the sponsor will be able to offer guidance and support when we ourselves have the eventual opportunity to sponsor others.

The platform for recovery is therefore fellowship, sponsorship and the twelve-step program. If this platform is embraced, together with the ingredients of honesty, open-mindedness and willingness, then the result will be transformational. This transformation is the solution to addiction, and it also touches every other aspect of our lives. This new freedom is the carrot that eventually replaces the stick of suffering. We have all of the tools needed to continue the journey all the way home.

There is no doubt that twelve-step recovery works if we work it. There is also the experience of those in Al-Anon who have found tremendous benefit in twelve-step recovery, even though they are not addicts themselves. It can be seen that all human beings would benefit from working through a similar process in order to progress through to the second stage of life. This wisdom is perennial yet somehow remains hidden from the majority despite its ready availability in multiple guises.

Given that twelve-step recovery really does work, it begs the question as to why success rates are so low. For every addict that recovers, there are, on average, at least nine others who not only fail to recover but miss the opportunity to experience life as it truly can be. The solution is simple, but the reasons that we fail to grasp it are varied and complex. Each individual human being is unique, so it is not possible to offer a complete explanation, but there are some common traps and mistakes that can be usefully identified. Having now understood why twelve-step recovery works, we can now use this explanation to gain an understanding as to why it does not currently work in the majority of cases. In many respects, the next chapter is the most important of all.

50. Mind the Gap

Addiction can be a baffling condition to overcome. The root of the problem is the personal ego self, yet this personal identity is so habitual and ingrained that it takes time and practice before it begins to loosen its grip. This process takes quite some time for most of us. It will certainly take several months, and in many cases it will take several years. For others it may take even longer. Some addicts remain abstinent and struggle with recovery for decades without ever fully grasping what recovery is all about. Such is the power of being attached to the personal ego self.

This attachment to our personal thoughts and feelings creates many traps and obstacles to recovery. Until the necessary self-realisation occurs, the overall problem is that the personal ego mind makes most of the decisions, and yet it is the personal ego mind that is the core problem. We are using a selfish, self-centered mind to decide how and when we will go about trying to be less selfish and self-centered. This catch-22 type problem can easily keep us trapped in personal suffering for a long time and can often lead us back to a relapse with devastating consequences. I have witnessed many recoveries and I have also seen many relapses. These relapses never have a good outcome for the addict or their loved ones. Sometimes a relapse results in death. This is the nature of addiction. Recovery is a serious business and it is wise to be aware of the many pitfalls.

It would be unrealistic to attempt to provide a definitive list of all of these pitfalls. Unique human beings have unique problems, but nevertheless there are similarities and common mistakes. Our deeper understanding of the problem of addiction, and the solution, should enable us to identify these common mistakes and comprehend why they occur. If we can be forewarned then we can at least be forearmed.

I can only share my experience. I have made most of the mistakes listed below, and have observed the remainder in others with whom I have worked closely.

Effective and sustained recovery requires persistent, consistent effort until it becomes effortless. The purpose is to facilitate a transformation in identity from personal self to non-personal Consciousness, from mind to Mind, from human to Being, from body and mind to Spirit. All of the pitfalls fit into the category of traps and obstacles that prevent this persistent and consistent effort. All of them are the product of thoughts, opinions and beliefs of the personal ego mind. We are not only the entire problem but we also create the barriers that prevent the simple solution from being effective. Little wonder that the success rates are so low. We are literally sabotaging ourselves.

The title of this chapter sums up the potential problem. Any gap in our commitment to recovery will create difficulties. These difficulties will range from dis-ease to despair to relapse to death. If we want effective recovery then we need to mind the gap as if our lives depend upon it.

The first barriers arise before recovery even starts. Twelve-step recovery is either unheard of, or perceived to be unnecessary or not attractive. The mythical cult status may also be off-putting. Other treatment options may seem more desirable and twelve-step recovery may be seen as a last resort. We may believe that our addiction or mental health condition is different from others and that twelve-step recovery is not sufficient. We may feel that a solution that is free of charge cannot possibly be as good as those that we have to pay for. There may be shame or embarrassment at the idea of having to attend twelve-step meetings. We may have a friend or family member who has tried twelve-step recovery and not found it to their liking. The list of reasons for not even starting goes on and on. All of them are based on misunderstanding.

If we do finally attend a twelve-step meeting then we are immediately confronted with the God word. Most personal selves have preconceived ideas about what this word means. Some of these ideas are helpful but many of them are not. The fact that all fellowships clearly state that it is *God as we understood Him* is often not sufficient to overcome prejudice. There is suspicion that this is just a ruse to get us started and that eventually we will have to concede to the Christian idea of God, or some other collective concept. If we are not prepared to be open-minded from the outset then the God word can be a big barrier to recovery. The personal self thus creates a self-imposed restriction on its own potential salvation.

Another early pitfall is a lack of belief that a simple twelve-step program can be an effective solution to the complex and soul-destroying handicap of addiction. Other fellowship members tell us sincerely that it does work, but the personal mind struggles to see how it possibly can. There is skepticism and a lack of trust. We place too much faith in our own minds and reject the well-meaning help and advice of others. Our own arrogant thinking continues to thwart us, despite the positive evidence of success in others that is readily available.

Another problem is that the personal ego self considers itself to be special and different. There is a tendency to compare ourselves to others. If we feel that others are far worse than us then the personal mind will conclude that twelve-step recovery is not necessary, or that we do not need to put in as much effort as they do. If we think that we are worse than others then we may feel that twelve-step recovery is not a strong enough solution for our particular case. The personal self will find ways to maintain its uniqueness and hence rule itself out of the solution. It will resist true fellowship in favour of illusory independence.

Addicts have formed the habit of self-harm. The abuse of substances and behaviours arises from low self-esteem and a lack of self-worth. We are not used to taking care of ourselves.

Even if we do seek recovery, these tendencies towards self-harm can prevent us from engaging in the very practices that will lead to the solution. We are now so familiar with not feeling good that the idea of a more positive outlook on life seems uncomfortable. We can actually feel safe in a state of depression, resentment and self-pity. We seem to suffer from a subconscious desire to sabotage our own wellbeing. All of this is a distorted function of the personal ego mind and it prevents the qualities of Consciousness from being expressed. We have to let this go. Each of us is worthy of recovery, whatever may have happened in the past.

Human beings prefer not to look at their own shortcomings and instead deny their own brokenness. We would rather judge, criticise and blame others than admit our own faults. Even if we admit that we are addicts, there will still be a reluctance to turn the spotlight inwards and look at our shadow self. We may fear exposing deep-seated issues and prefer to let sleeping dogs lie. We maintain the mask of persona at the expense of self-honesty. The personal self protects its own self-image. We may see addiction as the problem rather than our own selves. We talk about addiction as if it is an illness that can be cured whilst leaving the rest of the personal ego self intact. We hear what we want to hear and discard the real wisdom.

We can fall victim to the mistake of cherry-picking those parts of the fellowship and the steps that seem acceptable to the personal self. We may attend meetings, read the literature and even undertake service yet still avoid recovery. We create our own tailored version of recovery based on what we think is best and ignore the rest of it. We are allowing the personal ego mind to pass judgment on perennial wisdom and then we try to fool ourselves into believing that our thinking is correct. Self-righteousness prevents us from surrendering to the specific process that has helped so many others. We shoot ourselves in the foot and then blame it on the gun.

We may fail to appreciate the seriousness of our condition. We hear that addiction is progressive but we do not believe that it can possibly get worse for us. We consider that worsening consequences are highly unlikely in our case. We ignore the wealth of evidence to the contrary and convince ourselves that our case is different. Our personal minds filter out anything that does not fit within our preconceived ideas. We are blinded by our own self-serving opinions. The personal ego mind always likes to think that it knows best. We are full of opinions and beliefs but we lack wisdom.

Most human beings do not like to feel uncomfortable, and addicts in particular are past masters at avoiding dis-ease. This is why we used substances and behaviours in the first place. Change can be uncomfortable, and hence the idea of change is not appealing. Change cannot happen within our comfort zone. We make the mistake of trying to ease our way through recovery by largely avoiding discomfort. The caterpillar tries to find an easy way through metamorphosis and hence never actually surrenders to the process. We can waste a lot of time pretending to be in recovery without actually making any progress at all. Discomfort is part of the process. This is one reason why fellowship is so important. We provide each other with support and encouragement. It is ok to feel uncomfortable, and it is also necessary.

We may confuse recovery with abstinence. This is an easy and understandable mistake to make, but nevertheless it is a big mistake. Abstinence is obviously necessary and desirable, but it is not the be all and end all. We may collect our sobriety coins and receive the applause of our fellows yet remain firmly stuck in early recovery. This can sometimes go on for years. The personal self is resisting the opportunity for transformation. We fall victim to the acronym JEST, which stands for Just Enough Sobriety To achieve our particular personal objectives. We trick ourselves into believing that abstinence is the cure to addiction, and that the longer we go the safer we will be. The truth is that we will remain vulnerable to relapse until the spiritual solution is in place. Self-sabotage lurks unseen and can surface through all manner of triggering events.

After a period of abstinence we may begin to forget how bad it really was when we first came into recovery. We may experience euphoric recall, and dwell upon the seemingly good and happy times and conveniently overlook all of the misery and harm. The idea may come that perhaps we could resume using previous substances and behaviours and this time keep it all under control. We may conclude that we are exceptions to the rule of inevitable progression. All the while that we remain identified as the personal ego self we have the capacity to think ourselves into a disastrous relapse. We are then puzzled as to why this has happened. We have failed to understand the true nature of the problem and the necessity for the solution. Sometimes this cycle is repeated many times, and it always gets worse.

We may be confused about the idea of lifestyle balance. Recovery can be seen as a part-time activity to be fitted in with other aspects of life. We may limit our commitment to recovery due to other priorities. We are told that anything that we place ahead of our recovery will eventually be lost through relapse. We hear the advice but we do not believe it. We insist that we are entitled to set our own priorities. We fail to understand that all of these other priorities are pulling us back into identity as the personal ego self and actually undermining any progress that is being made through twelve-step recovery. We are taking one step forward and two steps backwards. We obviously need to attend to our particular responsibilities but recovery needs to be the number one priority until the transformation is well underway. We need an intense period of focus on recovery. The caterpillar does not eat leaves and wander around whilst it is in the cocoon. There will be plenty of time and opportunity to engage fully in life once the spiritual awakening has begun and the tools are being used. It is a big mistake to try to achieve balance too quickly. This is yet another way in which the personal ego self tries to stay in control of the process.

If we mange to overcome all of the obstacles so far then it will become obvious that we need to get ourselves a sponsor. Addicts generally do not like being told what to do. The idea of having to follow suggestions is not appealing. We may have a clear idea of what sort of sponsor we prefer. We may choose someone who we like and with whom we feel comfortable. The personal self is thus dictating the terms of its own recovery. We may delay getting a sponsor indefinitely because we have not yet met anyone who fits our preconceived requirements. We may make a start and then part company because we do not like what is being suggested. We want recovery on our own terms. We lack humility. We are reluctant to commit. We fail to understand that the personal ego self that is making these decisions is the source of the problem.

We can misunderstand the meaning of the word *suggestions*. The twelve step program works, and is a suggested means of recovery. If we want recovery then we need to follow the whole process and use all of the tools. The individual components of the program are not suggestions. It is a mistake to assume that certain elements of the process are not necessary. If we view them as suggestions then we are likely to avoid the ones that seem unpalatable. We thereby avoid recovery. Twelve-step recovery is obviously optional, but if we want recovery then the whole program is compulsory. It is a potentially fatal mistake to be fooled by the idea of suggestions.

Working with a sponsor can be a struggle if we insist on remaining closed-minded. We all have preconceived ideas and beliefs but we need to let these go. If we have a misplaced faith in our own personal intelligence then we can create big problems for ourselves. We can end up with paralysis through analysis. We can get stuck at any stage by insisting that we have to fully understand and believe in the process before progressing. Understanding comes through wisdom, and wisdom has nothing to do with personal intelligence. Wisdom is revealed by Consciousness later as the transformation proceeds. If we want recovery then we have to trust the process. Those already in

313

recovery are telling the truth. There is no reason not to trust them, yet the personal ego mind trusts only itself. There is no recovery without surrender.

We may remain convinced that addiction is a specific problem rather than a feature of the holistic human condition. If addiction is perceived to be a faulty part of an otherwise perfect ego mind then we are in for a long struggle. We may blame all of our shortcomings on addiction rather than seeing addiction as a manifestation of our human nature. Addiction is not an isolated aspect of the personal self. Addiction is a malfunctioning of the entire personal ego, based on over-identification as only a personal self. Twelve-step recovery is a holistic solution to a holistic problem. If we focus only on sobriety then we will continue to suffer the consequences from living life only on the basis of being a person. This is often so clearly obvious from our continuing struggles, yet somehow we manage to miss the fundamental point of recovery.

Steps four and five can be a big stumbling block in recovery. It is not unusual to get stuck at this stage, and sometimes it can result in relapse. We fear looking at our shadow selves and we fear exposing ourselves to someone else. This self-centered fear is an aspect of the personal self, and it keeps us trapped in the personal self. Despite praying to be relieved of the bondage of self in step three, we do not really understand what this means. We know that we need to move forwards, but we come up with all manner of excuses to delay. The personal self is protecting itself, and self-centered fear is the primary shield. We come into recovery initially because the fear of relapse outweighs the fear of engaging in twelve-step fellowship. If we wait too long, and experience a period of sobriety, then the fear of relapse recedes and the fear of looking at ourselves regains the upper hand. What happens next is inevitable. Either we will relapse, or we will suffer the consequences of holding onto personal self in sobriety. If this is understood then we will push through the fear of steps four and five.

We may find the process of recovery emotionally challenging and uncomfortable. We have spent our lives suppressing and avoiding intense emotions and we have medicated these feelings with substances and behaviours. We are now having to go through a potential roller-coaster of emotions without our usual coping mechanisms. We assume that we are struggling more than others. We may feel that the process is not working. If we are not cocooned sufficiently in fellowship then these feelings may lead us to a relapse. If it all gets too uncomfortable then we may even decide that sobriety is not worth the effort and hence deliberately relapse in order to stop the process. Until the personal self loses its grip, we remain vulnerable to a moment of insane self-sabotage. We need to be honest about these doubts and fears and share our thoughts and feelings with our sponsor and fellows. We may be unique individuals but there are many who have travelled this path before us and have experienced similar issues. We fear judgment, but there will be none. The personal self will be tempted to hide these feelings and pretend that all is well. It is far better to be honest. This is one of the reasons why honesty is so important in recovery.

Once we have finally worked through the twelve steps and gained a period of sobriety, then we are faced with a new set of obstacles that need to be navigated. The first of these is the belief that we are now cured and can resume our lives without any further involvement in twelve-step recovery. The crisis is over and fellowship is no longer required. Not only is this selfish, ungrateful and inconsiderate, but it completely misses the whole point of recovery. We have been taken to the edge of our existence, been freely offered the golden opportunity of transformation and have turned our back on the invitation. We have returned to living as a caterpillar and selfishly acted against the will of life itself. There can only be one outcome. Sooner or later, Consciousness will issue another invitation, and this time it will be more forceful. We all have freewill, but freewill of this kind will come at a very heavy price.

If we do engage effectively in recovery, then life will very likely become busy again. Relationships will be repaired and renewed, careers may take off, new opportunities will arise and we will be keen to make up for lost time. All of this activity will place pressure on our priorities. The longer we are in recovery, the more these pressures are likely to build. It will be tempting to push recovery down the priority list. Other previously mentioned factors will also be influential. Gradually we drift away from twelve-step fellowship, and gradually we phase out our daily practices. Slowly but surely the personal ego self regains control. We start moving backwards on the spectrum of balance between human and Being. If we do not keep spinning the plate of recovery then eventually it will wobble and crash to the ground. The length of sobriety previously enjoyed will be irrelevant. We will be back in the hell of addiction.

The next trap is similar, but relates specifically to over-confidence and complacency. We know that we are not cured, but there is a feeling that we no longer need to put in so much effort. We give ourselves permission to ease off, safe in the knowledge can we can always ramp it back up again if things get tricky. There is an assumption that we can control the wild horse of personal ego and live dangerously. We still think that life is all about the personal self. This attitude always leads to suffering, with or without a relapse. We are making the same mistake as previously, but this time the motives are more subtle. The further we go in recovery, the more subtle the machinations of the personal ego become.

We may become bored with twelve-step fellowship. Going to the same meetings every week and hearing the same old shares can become tiresome. We have heard it all before and are no longer learning anything new. We can become irritable and judgmental. All we hear are people moaning about their personal lives. Either that, or evangelical sharing which tends to create rejection rather than attraction. We can come away from meetings feeling worse than before we went. Our initial enthusiasm is long forgotten and it all becomes a bit stale. Now we are vulnerable to the familiar thoughts that we do not really need to bother anymore with recovery. All of this is in the realm of the personal ego mind. We are supposed to be participating in fellowship in order to help others. We are supposed to be selfless rather than selfish and self-centered. If we are bored, then we are being selfish and going backwards.

Twelve-step fellowships are comprised of all sorts of people and personalities at different stages of recovery. There may be many that we like but some that we do not. We may get involved in service at group or inter-group level and get tangled up in the politics of ego. There may be people who disrupt meetings or others that share in ways that we consider inappropriate. The general tone may be one of unconditional love but we can still find ourselves getting irritated or resentful. We might even clash with others and find ourselves reluctant to attend a particular meeting for fear of conflict. Twelve-step fellowship can be a battleground for personal egos just as much as life outside. All of this is a reflection of our attachment to the personal ego self. We learned in step four to take our own inventory rather than focusing on the behavior of others. All interactions are an opportunity for self-awareness and the further practice of step ten. It would be a mistake to allow challenging personal relationships to push us away from fellowship. Our purpose is to let go of taking things personally and focus instead on being of service to others.

Any fellowship of men and women is bound to produce romantic relationships. Mutual vulnerability can be powerfully attractive. The issue here is not one of taboo but of practicalities. Personal relationships are by definition personal. Our purpose in recovery is to move away from the personal self. Intimate relationships can be a trigger for the whole range of negative human attributes and hence restrict recovery. If we are single, then it is suggested that we remain so until we are fully established in recovery. If we are married, or already in a relationship, then again the suggestion is to maintain the status quo until we are in a position to be guided by Consciousness rather than the ego mind. These suggestions make sense in the context of the overall objective of recovery. We are, of course, at liberty to ignore these suggestions, but it would be wise to at least understand our motives. Romantic relationships can be another subtle trap that frustrates recovery. In some cases it can lead to relapse.

The spiritual toolkit is comprehensive and necessary. We are bound to individually favour some practices over others. It will be tempting to practice those tools that we like and enjoy and to avoid those that we do not. This is the personal self trying to muscle in on spiritual practice. This is a very subtle form of self-sabotage that perpetuates the personal self-identity. We will tend to dislike the tools that feel personally uncomfortable. We need the courage and wisdom from the serenity prayer to see this trap. It is the tools that we personally dislike that offer us the most potential for change. The very fact that we do not like them is the best reason possible for practicing them. We are acting against the preferences of the personal self and thereby working to shift the balance of identity. We can fool ourselves that we are doing well in recovery by practicing with only part of the toolkit. It is far more worthwhile to practice the tools that we resist. Wisdom arises from non-personal Mind rather than personal preferences.

If we come into recovery having already been strongly indoctrinated into a particular faith then we may find difficulty in reconciling these pre-existing beliefs with the principles of twelve-step recovery. We have explored how all faiths and spiritual traditions are actually underpinned by the same perennial wisdom but this is not always obvious to those who believe that their faith is exclusively correct. There can also be an immature understanding of what any particular faith truly means. We may have faith, but this is of little use if the identity of the personal self remains unchallenged. If parts of the spiritual toolkit do not fit into our current faith-based understanding or practice it may seem to make sense to ignore them. We need to remain open-minded. There is tremendous wisdom in twelve-

318

step fellowship. The great thing about the twelve step program is that it is a process intended to bring about individual transformation and revelation. Whatever our conditioned faith may have been, it has previously been insufficient to overcome addiction. Twelve-step fellowship will allow access to wisdom that reveals and heals the core problem. It can also provide a deeper understanding of any pre-existing faith.

We may find it relatively easy to follow spiritual principles within twelve-step fellowship but might still be tempted to think and behave selfishly or dishonestly in other areas of our lives. This is another example of where we can make progress in recovery on the one hand and then undo all of the good work by continuing with behaviours that pull in the opposite direction. Selfishness and dishonestly are aspects of the personal ego self. It will often be tempting to act selfishly but this is more destructive than we may realise. If we want good recovery then we need to be practicing these principles in all of our affairs. There are no exceptions. Even small acts of selfishness are counterproductive. We need to remain self-aware and watch out for the many subtle ways in which the personal self continues to hold on.

It is difficult enough for us to understand twelve-step recovery, let alone our family and friends. It may be that they do not support our involvement. They may even feel that our loyalties have been diverted elsewhere and that we now give them insufficient attention. They may complain or make it difficult for us to give priority to recovery. They can be so familiar with our old personal selves that they do not like how we are changing as we recover. We may find family and friends pulling us away from twelve-step recovery at the very time that we need it. We cannot expect them to understand but we do need their encouragement and support. If this is not forthcoming then we will need the support of the fellowship even more. It is sometimes difficult to trust strangers above our own family and friends but, in truth, we have little choice. Our loved ones will reap the benefits once we become established in recovery.

We can become proud of our period of sobriety, proud of our recovery, proud of our own story, proud of the service that we do, proud of our ability to help others, proud of our track record as a sponsor, proud of our achievements outside of fellowship, proud of our spiritual qualities and wisdom and basically proud of anything that the personal self can find to take pride in. We can even be proud of being humble. This pride is so very subtle, yet pride is the biggest hurdle to overcome. We are seeking freedom from the bondage of personal self, and pride is obviously personal. Consciousness has nothing to be proud of. It just is itself and it is non-personal. Honest self-awareness is again the answer to this trap. Pride will sneak in from all directions but we have the power to see it and discard it.

The final trap in this list may perhaps seem to be a bit of a surprise. When we attend twelve-step meetings it is traditional to identify ourselves as addicts. Typically we state our name and our addictions. This identification as an addict is repetitive and powerful. We are restating our personal identity time and time again at each meeting that we attend. The purpose of recovery is to let go of the personal self yet we habitually remain attached to it. The personal self is the addict. Our true identity as Consciousness is not an addict. Recovery is all about this change in identity. The personal self is powerless. Consciousness is powerful. We need to submit to a process that brings about a transformation in this identity. Anything that we do to undermine this process is not helpful. It is not for me to suggest a change in tradition, but we do need to be mindful of how we identify ourselves. We are far more than we think we are. Personal identity is just a thought, and it is our belief in this thought that convinces us that we are only a personal ego self. This common belief is a misunderstanding and it is the ultimate block to the transformational freedom that we all seeking.

This list of thirty potential pitfalls in recovery is fairly comprehensive but is highly unlikely to be complete. The personal ego mind ranges from gross to subtle, and hence there must be many more ways in which we can trip up. I have made nearly all of these mistakes during my eight years in twelve-step fellowship and I dare say that I will make many more yet. All thirty of these pitfalls, and many more besides, have one factor in common. They are all ways in which we hold onto identity as the personal ego self. We make a decision in step three to hand over our will and our lives but somehow we never actually go through with it. This is why recovery is progressive rather than definitive. We need to keep using the tools in order to continue to make progress.

Given that effective recovery hinges on the extent to which we remain over-identified as a personal self, it can be seen that perhaps the most incisive and helpful tool in the box is the tool of self-inquiry. Whichever hurdle we may be facing at any given time, we can always ask ourselves who it is that thinks there is a problem. The answer is always the same. It is the personal ego self. This simple tool disempowers the personal identity every single time that it is used. By asking the question and observing the personal ego mind, we automatically drop back in Consciousness to the position of witness. If self-inquiry is practiced on a daily basis then we become increasingly aware that there is more to life than we had previously understood. We cannot be the personal ego self because we are always present to witness it. It follows therefore that our true nature must be that of a deeper Consciousness. We may struggle to believe it, but the truth is present every time that we take the trouble to look.

The best way to mind the gap is to remain self-aware and practice self-inquiry. This simple tool will immediately highlight the problem, and we can then get on with using the rest of the toolkit to continue the journey home. The result will be happiness, peace, love and unity. The kingdom of heaven is indeed within.

51. Before, I am

Before suffering from addiction, I am
Before the personal ego mind, I am
Before any word or language, I am
Before breathing in and out, I am
Before becoming a human, I am
Before emergence of life, I am
Before the unified field, I am
Before all movement, I am
Before all vibration, I am
Before existence, I am
Before knowing, I am
Before thinking, I am
Before sensing, I am
Before sound, I am
Before peace, I am
Before unity, I am
Before space, I am
Before time, I am
Before love, I am
Before I, I am
Before I, I
I, I
I

The triangular paragraph above is my attempt to represent and summarise all that we have covered in the preceding fifty chapters. The triangle can be interpreted from the bottom up and from the top down. Both directions encapsulate perennial wisdom and provide an image of the journey of discovery that is available to all of us.

Working from the bottom up, the space around the words, and in between the words, represents the infinite and eternal Source from which the whole of creation arises. The Source is aware of itself as 'I'. This is Pure Awareness. There is nothing to be aware of other than this. The first arising out of this 'I' is the concept of 'I'. This is non-physical Consciousness, Awareness, Knowingness, Mind, Spirit or Being. It is also infinite and eternal. The Source 'I' is aware of the 'I' of Consciousness, and it is aware that it is prior to Consciousness. The Source 'I' exists before the concept of 'I' and knows of its existence through the sense 'I Am'. Consciousness also senses its own existence, and its essential nature is happiness, peace, love and unity. Out of this non personal Consciousness arises the concepts of time and space. This level of Consciousness is now limited by its own conceptual boundaries.

The levels of Consciousness give rise to the next level, and the limitations gradually increase. Sensing, thinking, vibration and movement are all levels of Consciousness in motion and these combine to form what is known scientifically as the unified field. This field of Consciousness gives rise to all forces, waves and particles out of which the manifest world flashes in and out of existence. The system is self-aware and self-knowing and it evolves through its own experience. Gradually the configuration of the unified field produces multitudinous forms of life. The sense of 'I am' exists in all of these life forms, but there are also mechanisms based on self-centered fear to ensure survival.

One particular expression of all of this complexity is the genus homo sapiens. Human beings live and breathe. They develop language in order to communicate. They each believe themselves to be the individual body and mind and develop a sense of personal identity. Consciousness is processed through the brain, but the personal self claims these thoughts for itself. Thoughts, feelings and behavior become dominated by self-centered fear and cause personal suffering. The original sense of 'I am' is secondary to the localised ego version and is gradually lost. The personal ego self is now seemingly estranged from its Source and seeks ways to satisfy the inherent dis-ease. Substances and behaviours seem to bring satisfaction but the relief is temporary. Repeated use of these coping strategies leads to addiction and to even more suffering. The personal ego self has created its own individual and collective version of hell.

The suffering exists at the surface level of Consciousness in the form of the personal ego self. However, the deeper levels of Consciousness are non-personal and hence do not suffer. All experience is a vibration and movement of Consciousness and is known by Consciousness. There is nothing but Consciousness and hence there is no concept of good or bad experience. It is all just an incredible and wondrous expression of its own creativity. It all arises from the Source 'I' and it is all an expression of the Source 'I'. The entire universe is created in the Mind of 'I' so that the 'I' can love and experience itself. This is the purpose of creation.

You may not believe these words, but words and belief only exist in the realm of the personal ego mind. Consciousness has no need for belief. It Knows. Consciousness simply knows that 'I Am'. The Sanskrit words for this state of Being are *Sat, Chit, Ananda.* These translate as Existence, Consciousness, and Bliss. Human beings knew all about Consciousness over 5,000 years ago. We have made tremendous material progress since then but this has simply pushed us further up the triangle and away from the underlying reality of existence.

If we now start at the top of the triangle and work our way down then we can immediately see the direction of all spiritual journeys. This will be the same journey whatever religion or spiritual tradition we may subscribe to. Twelve-step recovery is just one of these traditions, and it is a process and fellowship designed to help addicts escape from the surface suffering and return to their own true nature. It is therefore far more important than just achieving sobriety, although this will be one of the many beneficial outcomes.

The journey starts with suffering. Without suffering there is little reason for human beings to look deeply within themselves for a solution. There are some who undertake the journey simply

324

through curiosity but for most of us we need a reason. Often this reason needs to be compelling. The suffering of addiction provides this reason, and it will progress until we feel compelled to change.

Once we engage in recovery, we firstly come to understand that the body is addicted but that it is the personal, fear-based ego mind that is ultimately giving rise to the addiction. We are told that the solution needs to be spiritual and we begin to use the spiritual toolkit. As we practice self-awareness, self-contemplation and self-forgetting we gradually step back in awareness. We come to understand that there is more to our Consciousness that we had previously realised. We find that there is a non-physical aspect to ourselves that is able to witness all activity of the personal ego mind. The journey now begins in earnest.

The more we practice, the deeper we go. We begin to find that there is awareness of a non-personal Consciousness that is observing the personal non-physical witness. As this awareness deepens, the deeper positions provide a broader perspective that is increasingly less personal. This Consciousness has the qualities of happiness, peace, love and unity. We experience these qualities in our lives. We finally start to see that there is an 'I' that exists prior to all manifestation, and that we must be this 'I' because we are the one who is here to perceive everything in front of us. We continue to practice with the toolkit and the experience continues to deepen. Old patterns of thinking, feeling and behaving fall away in the light of this new understanding. Wisdom emerges and the true nature of reality begins to be revealed. The journey never ends but the personal ego self gradually melts away and becomes increasingly less significant.

Abiding as non-personal Consciousness, we find that we already are the very things that we have been seeking our whole lives. The entire world is seen in a different light. There is nothing more to do other than be present in each moment and move in accordance with the will of Consciousness, which is now our will. Consciousness is infinite and eternal. These are the ultimate prizes. We have escaped from hell and found heaven whilst still here on earth. We look around and see that so many others are suffering. We cannot preach to them because they will not hear what we are saying. All we can do is be our true selves and lead by example.

Twelve-step recovery is a spiritual solution to *the* spiritual problem of human existence. The prodigal son travels far away and then returns home. The Being becomes human and then returns to Being. This is the natural flow of Consciousness. This is the intended purpose of life.

There is no substitute for the individual spiritual journey. Each transformation is intentionally unique. We can read as many books as we like, but nothing will happen unless we engage fully in the process of change. It does not matter which path we choose, provided that the path leads all the way to the beginning. There are many paths that stop short of revelation. We can spend our whole lives travelling these paths yet never find what we are looking for. The great irony of spirituality, in all of its guises, is that we are already here and always have been. We are looking for our True Self. The end of the road is the beginning.

I can only speak from my own experience but, based on all that we have covered so, far I can confidently make the following six statements. They are all true but they each become progressively closer to the Truth.

My given name is Michael
Michael is an addict
I am not Michael
I am Being
I Am
I

This is the solution to addiction. Michael is an addict but I am far more than that.

This is true for all of us.

52. Keep Coming Back

This simple slogan has probably saved more lives in twelve-step fellowship than any other. There is no requirement for attending a twelve-step meeting other than the desire to escape from addiction. All are welcomed, no matter what they may have done or how many times they may have relapsed. The kindness, compassion and love shown within twelve-step fellowship is unconditional. Each time a story of relapse is told it reinforces the commitment to recovery in all of those present. We need to be reminded of what is was like, lest we forget.

It often takes time and repeated exposure to spiritual concepts before such ideas penetrate the self-sabotaging defenses of the personal ego mind. Some of us may grasp the relevance of recovery through spiritual principles fairly quickly, but for most of us it will take time and repetition. Even if we are honest, open-minded and willing we will still need to keep coming back in order to absorb what is being shared in the meetings. It may be tempting to read the literature and work on the steps in isolation but this would be a big mistake. We need the energy and wisdom of fellowship in order to make meaningful progress. We obviously cannot be part of twelve-step fellowship unless we keep coming back to meetings.

It is also essential to keep coming back regardless of how long we may have been in recovery. As well as being reminded of the importance of step one, it is also part of our spiritual practice. Twelve-step meetings are where we can be useful. We can carry the message of recovery to those who are lost and lonely. We can share our experience, strength and hope so that it may be of help to others. We can be of service in helping to keep the meetings running smoothly. We can be a demonstration of spiritual principles in action. We can raise the collective vibration of Consciousness through our presence. We can be available to accept requests for sponsorship. We are the fellowship. We are responsible. We need to be attending meetings. We need to keep coming back. I have listed thirty reasons why we may drift away from twelve-step fellowship but none of them are valid excuses. We have a responsibility to give back what has freely been given to us. Any hesitation can only be a residual aspect of the personal ego self. If we are practicing self-awareness, self-contemplation and self-forgetting then we will keep coming back. There is always further to go and more to be revealed.

I mentioned at the outset that current success rates in twelve-step recovery are only in the range 5% to 10%, with success defined as sober after twelve months and still actively engaged in recovery. These figures clearly indicate that the majority of those who initially reach out for help do not keep coming back. They fall victim to one of the many self-centered reasons why they should stay away, and they inevitably struggle and often relapse. This is not a failure of the twelve-step program of recovery. This is either a failure to understand the severity of the problem or an over-reliance on the personal ego mind to make decisions about how to recover. This attachment to the personal ego mind is of course the cause of all forms of addiction. It is not only the core problem but also the reason why so many addicts prevent themselves from engaging in effective recovery.

My own experience of sponsoring others has resulted in a success rate nearer 90%. The sample size is obviously of no statistical significance but it does at least show that much higher rates are achievable. This does not make me a good sponsor but it does demonstrate that recovery is highly probable given an effective understanding and practice of the program. A good understanding of the program does not produce recovery in itself but it does increase the motivation and commitment to use the spiritual toolkit on a regular basis. It really does work. It would be a selfish and self-centered act of self-sabotage not to engage in a simple process that will transform our own lives for the better, and the lives of others.

The Dalai Lama is credited with saying that if we were to teach meditation to all children in the world then we would eliminate violence within a single generation. In a similar vein, it can be seen that all adults would benefit enormously from working through the twelve step program at an appropriate time in their lives. Most humans will not feel the need to undertake such a process. For those of us who suffer with addiction in our lives, we can consider ourselves very fortunate to have been given this opportunity. I have been blessed to live a full and varied life so far, but I can say with absolute conviction that engaging in twelve step recovery has been by far the best and most worthwhile undertaking. In this respect, I am extremely grateful for my brokenness.

I have written this book because I sincerely believe that a deeper understanding of twelve-step recovery can lead to improved success rates. This is my motivation and my deepest wish. If you have found this book helpful then please share it with others. We each have the ability to share the light of understanding and to help our fellows in their recovery.

Twelve-step recovery works if we work it, and continue to work it. I wish you all the best in your own recovery. Our paths may never cross but our common humanity means that we are already together in the fellowship of the broken.

Keep coming back.

Appendix – List of Twelve-Step Fellowships

Name of Fellowship

Primary Focus

Name of Fellowship	Primary Focus
Al-Anon / Alateen	Friends and families of alcoholics
Alcoholics Anonymous	Alcohol addiction
Adult Children of Alcoholics	Adults effected by parental alcoholism
Adult Survivors of Child Abuse Anon	Childhood abuse and trauma
Anorexics and Bulimics Anonymous	Anorexia and bulimia
Chemically Dependent Anonymous	Substance addiction
Chrystal Meth Anonymous	Chrystal Meth addiction
Clutterers Anonymous	Physical and emotional clutter addicts
Co-Anon	Friends and families of cocaine addicts
Cocaine Anonymous	Cocaine addiction
Co-Dependents Anonymous	Functional and healthy relationships
Compulsive Eaters Anonymous	Compulsive eating
COSA	Friends and families of sex addicts
COSLAA	Friends and families of sex and love addicts
Debtors Anonymous	Compulsive debtors
Dual Recovery Anonymous	Addiction and mental illness
Eating Addictions Anonymous	Eating addictions
Eating Disorders Anonymous	Eating disorders
Emotions Anonymous	Mental and emotional illness
Families Anonymous	Friends and families of addicts
Food Addicts Anonymous	Food addiction
Food Addicts in Recovery Anonymous	Obesity and bulimia
Gam-Anon / Gam-A-Teen	Friends and families of gambling addicts
Gamblers Anonymous	Gambling addiction
Heroin Anonymous	Heroin addiction
Marijuana Anonymous	Marijuana addiction
Nar-Anon	Friends and families of drug addicts
Narcotics Anonymous	Drug addiction
Neurotics Anonymous	Mental and emotional illness
Nicotine Anonymous	Nicotine addiction
Online Gamers Anonymous	Video game addiction
Overeaters Anonymous	Compulsive eating disorders
Pan Fellowship	Emotional Sobriety
Parents Anonymous	Parenting
Pills Anonymous	Prescription pill addiction
Recoveries Anonymous	Recovery from behaviours and problems
Recovering Couples Anonymous	Relationship issues
Self Mutilators Anonymous	Physical self mutilation
Sex Addicts Anonymous	Sex addiction
Sex and Love Addicts Anonymous	Sex and love addiction
Sexaholics Anonymous	Compulsive sexual acting-out
Sexual Assault Survivors Anonymous	Sexual assault
Sexual Compulsives Anonymous	Compulsive sex
Sexual Recovery Anonymous	Sex addiction
Spenders Anonymous	Overspending
Survivors of Incest Anonymous	Childhood sexual abuse
Underearners Anonymous	Under earning
Workaholics Anonymous	Work addiction and work aversion

Printed in Great Britain
by Amazon